INVERTING THE NORM

RACIALLY-MIXED CONGREGATIONS

IN A SEGREGATIONIST STATE

INVERTING THE NORM

RACIALLY-MIXED CONGREGATIONS

IN A SEGREGATIONIST STATE

DAWID VENTER

PH.D. (RELIGION), PH.D. (SOCIOLOGY)

GALJOEN ACADEMIC

For Chuck Foster,
Jack Carroll,
and Hendrikus Boers
for hospitality and insights.

Copyright © Dawid Venter 2007

All rights reserved. No portion of this book may be
reproduced by any process or technique
without permission in writing from the author.

Library of Congress Control Number: 2007908613

ISBN: 978-0-6151-7223-1

First published in 2007.

Galjoen Academic,
An imprint of Galjoen Press.
Website: galjoenpress.com
E-mail: info.galjoen@gmail.com

Copyright acknowledgements
The author and publisher gratefully acknowledge permission for adaptation and expansion of sections of the author's material that originally appeared as:

"Mending the multi-coloured coat of a rainbow nation: cultural accommodation in ethnically mixed urban congregations". *Missionalia* 23 (3) 1995: 312-338. Permission granted by the editor of *Missionalia*.

"The inverted norm: the formation and functioning of racially mixed congregations in South Africa." In *Religion in a Changing World: Comparative Studies in Sociology*, edited by Madeleine Cousineau, 69-78. Copyright © 1998 by Madeleine Cousineau. Permission granted by Greenwood Publishing Group Inc., Westport, CT.

Cover image courtesy of Sylvain Margaine, www.forbidden-places.net.

Contents

Figures and Tables … vii

Foreword … ix

Introduction:
Inventing Alternatives in a Segregationist State

Comparison with Other Studies … 3
Defining 'Racially-Mixed' … 5
Race, Agency and Norms of Social Interaction … 6
Presuppositions … 9
The Structure of this Book … 13

1. Establishing the Norm in Colonial and Apartheid Churches

Introduction … 17
Racial Mixing and Racial Segregation as Historical Ideals … 23
    The Colonial Norm of Limited Institutional Integration … 24
    The Union Norm of Limited Institutional Segregation … 43
    The Apartheid Norm of Complete Segregation … 48
    The Post-Apartheid Norm of Institutional Integration … 63
An Explanation for Racial Integration and Segregation … 68

2. Resisting the Apartheid City:
Central Methodist Mission Johannesburg

Introduction	71
Methodism and Race in the Old Transvaal	72
From Mining Camp to Colonial City (1886–1909)	75
Growing in Stature During the Union Period (1910–48)	79
From Awareness of Apartheid to Opposition (1949-90)	84
Towards a Post-Apartheid Congregation (1990-94)	101
Explaining Central's Racially-Mixed Composition	104

3. Integrating the Segregated Suburb:
Saint Francis Xavier Catholic Church, Martindale

Introduction	111
Catholicism and Race in the Old Transvaal	113
From Farm to Freehold (1897-1909)	116
From Mission to Some to Parish for All (1910–48)	116
From Forced Segregation to Voluntary Integration (1949-90)	119
Towards a Post-Apartheid Congregation (1990-94)	124
Explaining Saint Francis' Racially-Mixed Composition	127

4. Erasing Boundaries of the Black City:
Johweto Family Vineyard

Introduction	135
The Independent Charismatic Movement and Race Relations	136
A Brief History of Soweto	139
From Challenge to Commitment (1985–89)	142
Towards a Post-Apartheid Congregation (1990-94)	154
Explaining Johweto's Racially-Mixed Composition	164

5. Inverting Segregationist Norms

Introduction	173
Mixed Congregations as Inversions of Segregationist Norms	174
Redux: Segregated Institutions and Contested National Norms	177
Contesting Segregation and Integration	188
Relating National Norms to Global Institutions and Ideologies	192
Inverting the Racialised Organisation of Neighbourhoods	202
Inverting Race Relations within Congregational Structure	216
Inverting Racialised Norms of Social Interaction	217
Theorising Racially-Mixed Congregations under Apartheid	219

List of Works Cited   227

Index   245

Figures and Tables

Figure 1: Congregations in Relation to Historic Locations   2

Figure 2: Segregation-Integration by Congregation and Denomination (ca. 1994)   64

Figure 3: Growth of Early Soweto in Relation to Johweto Meetings   140

Figure 4: Alternating National Norms (ca. 1665-1994)   176

Figure 5: An Open-Ended Typology of Racially-Mixed Congregations   212

Table 1: Stages of Congregational Transition by Levels of Racial Integration   207

Table 2: A Typology of Racially-Mixed Congregations   210

Foreword

When Dawid Venter arrived at Johannesburg's Central Methodist Mission (CMM) to research how we had transformed from an all-white congregation into a multi-racial one, we were unsure what to make of him. At that time, CMM was a 'site of struggle,' not only because we had integrated our congregation, but because our sanctuary was Johannesburg's main venue for anti-apartheid protest gatherings. Bomb threats and the scent of tear gas were common. On one occasion, because of our defiance of apartheid, we were invaded by armed troops.

At the height of our struggle against that system of enforced segregation, Venter, a white Afrikaner from the culture that coined the word 'apartheid,' came to a largely English-speaking church community, asking to dissect us! Who did he represent? What was the motive? Fortunately, we decided to take him at face value. He came among us quietly, sharing in the life of our multi-hued congregation, winning the confidence of a very diverse group of persons with his genuineness and obvious fascination with our journey toward integration. He also challenged us with probing questions that helped us see ourselves more clearly. The result of that stay with us and with other integrated church communities, and years of research since, is a book that I hope will help us all understand more deeply the struggle of Christians everywhere to live the Jesus prayer, 'that we may be one.'

It remains a source of deep satisfaction that the corrosive power of apartheid South Africa's inhuman and pervasive racism was resisted in some crucial places in the church. One of my most precious possessions is a photograph of the people of Central Methodist Mission, Johannesburg—the usual morning congregation of those days. The picture shows a special joy in all of them, young and old, black, white and brown: they knew what that picture would declare to a divided nation. At a time when apartheid's addiction to division seemed paramount, there were worshipping communities who fashioned prototypes of a different South Africa into being. Imperfect and few they may have been, but their very existence gave the lie to apartheid's basic premise that black and white South Africans could not share the same space peacefully and joyfully. This book tells some of the story of how such congregations happened.

This is a scholarly work. While its existence is a worthy celebration of Christian efforts to break out of racial and cultural imprisonment, there is nothing sentimental about it and it also uncovers our nakedness, not unkindly, but with a necessary honesty. Looking back, it would be easy for me to gloss those years with romantic hindsight, but the truth is that our struggle—and those of other groups—to become truly inclusive congregations was stumbling and incomplete. Certainly, we could have done more, risked more, been more intentional and explored our multi-culturalism more deeply.

However, the fact that it happened at all, perhaps with even more determination under apartheid's iron fist than in today's free South Africa, is one of the mysteries Dawid Venter explores. He and I have a smiling divergence around this mystery: he delves into all the determinative influences that sociologist/historians ought to uncover, and I quote the Gospels and the Acts of the Apostles...and my guess is that if we are to understand how such profoundly counter-cultural communities came about, we need both.

Peter Storey

Williams Distinguished Professor of the Practice of Christian Ministry,
Emeritus, Duke University Divinity School, Durham, N.C.

Former Bishop, Central District, Methodist Church of Southern Africa

Former Superintendent Minister, Central Methodist Mission, Johannesburg

Introduction:

Inventing Alternatives in a Segregationist State

The emergence of racially-mixed congregations in South Africa under successive political regimes bent on forging an increasingly racially segregated state is remarkable. The racially-mixed composition of such congregations contrasted starkly with their racially segregated urban and national contexts. Rare during apartheid, racially-mixed congregations continued to be scarce in South Africa after the first democratic elections in 1994. Their rareness, contrast with their segregated urban contexts, and the absence of academic literature on contemporary examples prompted this sociological study of racially-mixed congregations. Even more notable are the few congregations that maintained a continuous history of racial integration under conditions of segregation imposed by the state.

This book highlights case studies of three congregations from three different denominations in Johannesburg, South Africa. Each congregation was located in a site that reflected the development and spatial organisation of Johannesburg from a colonial to a post-apartheid city (see Figure 1, next page). Central Methodist Mission was located in the inner city which, at the time, was becoming a black residential area. Saint Francis Xavier Catholic Church lay in the white suburb of Martindale (today part of Sophiatown), which was transitioning to a mixed residential neighbourhood. Johweto Family Vineyard was situated in the black ghetto of Soweto.

The case studies emerged from qualitative empirical investigations of racially-mixed congregations that I undertook in South Africa between 1992 and 1999. My research divided into two parts. On the first leg, I studied how such congregations emerged under the apartheid regime. For comparison's sake, I surveyed racially-mixed congregations in the United States during the same period, travelling to Hartford (Connecti

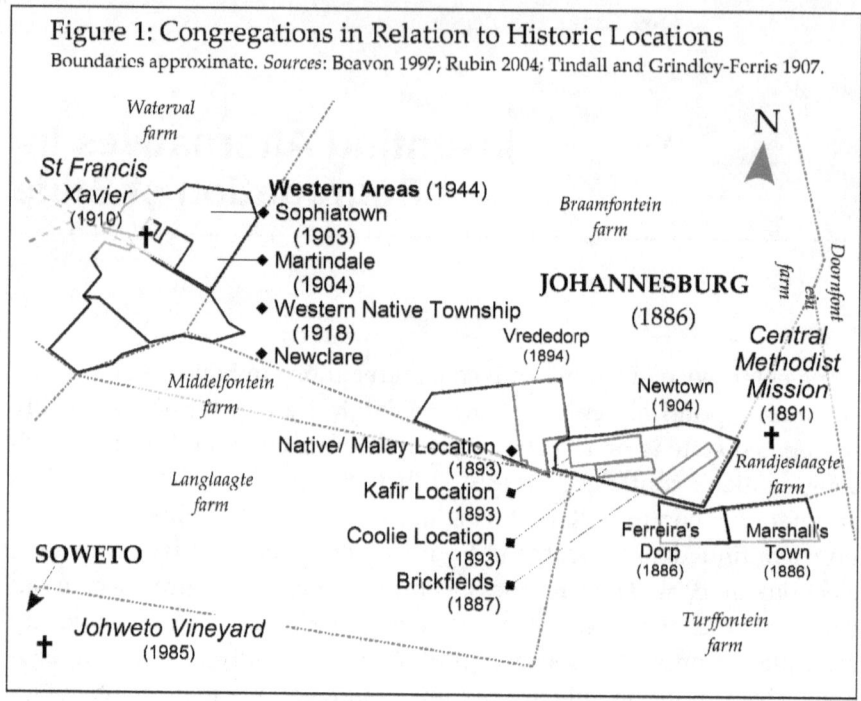

Figure 1: Congregations in Relation to Historic Locations
Boundaries approximate. *Sources*: Beavon 1997; Rubin 2004; Tindall and Grindley-Ferris 1907.

cut), Atlanta (Georgia), Providence (Rhode Island) and New York City. A second project examined the linguistic configurations of racially-mixed congregations in four denominations in relation to the post-apartheid state—see the companion volume, Assimilating the Norm.

My purpose in this book is to offer a general sociological explanation for the emergence of racially-mixed congregations. To do so, I analyse the social, political, and economic forces that prompted their formation and affected their functioning, using the sociological notions of agency and structure. I regard racially-mixed congregations as voluntary social institutions that pursued racial integration in a context marked by legalised racism and state-enforced involuntary segregation.

My intention is to advance our knowledge about congregations under apartheid and beyond, rather than to supply new insights into studies of South Africa's cities, politics, or even of "race" itself. While I stress the interaction between congregation, urban setting, and political dispensation, my primary focus remains on the congregations themselves. I combine existing analyses of South Africa's cities and politics with previously unexplored data about racially-mixed congregations. I emphasise how the congregations reflect changes in their contexts as prisms that refract their ideological and spatial contexts.

Obviously, South Africa's urban areas exhibit enough historical similarities that a general periodisation of segregation can be constructed, although differences exist as well. Urban areas historically displayed common patterns that range from limited segregation under colonialism, to pragmatic segregation in the union period, to the rigid pattern of apartheid, to limited integration in the post-apartheid period. Yet within these similarities, South Africa's urban areas differ in historical development and other relevant features, such as size, demographics, and geography. The spatial organisation of Cape Town and East London, for example, historically developed in diametrically opposed directions. Cape Town grew from a wooden fort and some huts in 1652 to a settlement which incorporated all races. While barracks were built for black dock workers in 1881, Cape Town's first black township, Ndabeni, was created only in 1901. By comparison, East London in the Eastern Cape started as three separate villages in 1847, and continued along this segregated trajectory.

COMPARISON WITH OTHER STUDIES

When I initiated my research, my approach differed from other studies at the time of South African churches under apartheid in respect of unit of analysis, subject matter, methodology, and theoretical approach.

Scholarly work on South African churches under apartheid tended towards broad discussions of the interaction between national policies and denominational structures (De Gruchy 1979, Cochrane 1987, Kinghorn 1986, Villa-Vicencio 1988). As such texts originated in academic departments of theology or religious studies, they contained a mixture of social-historical analysis and theological argument. Published works usually focused on the general degree to which various denominations supported the ideology of apartheid. Scholars were especially drawn to critical examinations of the positions of so-called Afrikaans-speaking or "English-speaking" denominations in relation to apartheid. The relative political support of the Dutch Reformed Church for apartheid were, for example, weighed against those of the Church of the Province in South Africa (e.g. De Gruchy 1979).

In the relevant literature, a two-part consensus congealed around the complicity of most denominations with apartheid, and around the segregated nature of congregations.

The first part of the consensus was that South African denominations tended towards pragmatic compliance with apartheid—with few exceptions, and despite vocal opposition by individual clergy and officials of denominations or ecumenical bodies.

Arguments about complicity can be classified along a theoretical continuum that ranges from functionalism to historical materialism. Accordingly, from a functionalist perspective white church members can be described as obviously having provided political support for the apartheid status quo (compare Villa-Vicencio 1988). A materialist approach would conclude from documentary analysis that class interests of white churchgoers coincided with the economic rationale behind apartheid (compare Cochrane 1987). A Weberian view, drawing on empirical research, could lambaste Pentecostal theologies for their dampening effect on political consciousness (compare Morran and Schlemmer 1984). Similar conclusions had been advanced for the perceived lack of political involvement by pentecostal denominations such as the Assemblies of God, or by the vast collection of African Independent Churches.

The second part of the consensus—as true in 1964 as in 1993—was that different races did "not normally worship together in the same church" (Cawood 1964:58,61,52,76,92). Racially-integrated South African congregations were perceived as the "marked exception" (Villa-Vicencio 1988:79), and segregated worship seen as remaining entrenched (Massie 1993:20).

The dominant focus in the prevailing literature on denominations precluded examination of lower level units of analysis, such as congregations or individual churchgoers. Unpublished empirical studies of racially-homogeneous individual congregations by graduate students of theology remained the only exceptions. Published literature on South African churches typically mentioned racially-mixed South African congregations only in passing, with examples drawn from larger metropoles (compare Hope and Young 1981). More extensive academic discussions of contemporary racially-mixed South African congregations were limited to contributions by Massie (1993) and my own studies (D. Venter 1994, 1995, 1998, 1999, 2000). Since, popular histories of two racially-mixed congregations has been self-published by their former minister (Robertson 1997). In addition, Dan Sheffield discussed Ubunye Free Methodist Church, which he had initiated in Pietermaritzburg, KwaZulu-Natal (Sheffield and Sheffield 1998). I provide a more detailed discussion of extant literature in Chapter One.

By contrast to the prevailing trends, then, I selected congregations as unit of analysis, and emphasised the few that eschewed the pragmatic conformity of their denominations to the racial dictates of state policies. While I was also interested in the relation of churches to apartheid, I employed empirical methods and applied sociological theories to generate my conclusions. My methods included participant observation, interviews, and documentary analysis. I wanted to understand why individuals would decide to attend mixed congregations in a context that violently militated against racial integration. Accepting the sociological predilection for embedding individual agency within social structure, I intended to uncover the possible social sources on which participants could draw to support their rationale in attending a mixed congregation.

DEFINING 'RACIALLY-MIXED'

My decision to examine racially-mixed congregations was confronted by several conceptual and operational difficulties, not least with the notions of 'race' and of racial interaction, but also about what constituted 'racially-mixed.'

Racial studies is haunted by the charge that by referring to 'race,' scholars continue to entrench the concept even while arguing that it has no scientific content. But while race clearly lacks scientific content, it equally obviously continues to have social significance. In public discourse, race tends to refer to visible differences in physical appearance, regarded as indicative of further differences in culture, history, and language. I chose to attend to race because I accept that the notion that race exists does affect social interaction. The contents of who belongs to what 'race' is shaped by political structures and attendant socio-economic forces. These affect how people construct culture as a way of thinking, relating, and dealing with others.

I chose to emphasise the effects of race as social construct, without accepting the accuracy or validity of its constituent elements. I understand race to refer to a social (relational) concept that indicates the boundaries of group membership, which individuals can claim, or to which they can be assigned. The term 'race' remains an operational social construct in South Africa as in other contexts. Despite the demise of racism as a legal system in South Africa, racial classification (e.g. in census categories) and segregation persists, as it does elsewhere.

The persistence of 'race' encourages the theoretical debate about race to continue among scholars. While I did, by implication, focus on racial interaction, I emphasised the resultant institution that is produced and its effect on the organisation of diversity within congregations.

In general terms I used 'racially-mixed' to refer to a congregation composed of more than one group that can be assigned to a particular racial category. Much of the historical discussion in Chapter One is made possible by this strategy. More specifically, the case studies of Chapters Two to Four were defined as comprising at least one putative racial group of 20% or larger than that congregation's total population. A 'congregation' referred to the average number of people (i.e. 'congregants'), no longer of school going age, who attended meetings on Sundays for the purpose of participating in Christian worship. I used 'integration' primarily in a general sense to mean racially and ethnically mixed. Though not used in this book, a more specific meaning of 'integrated' is possible that refers to a type of racially-mixed congregation that has a (relatively) stable racial/ethnic mix. In such a case, the diversity of members would be represented at all levels of decision-making, and allowed to affect the content and structure of the service. In this restricted sense, integration proceeds from "a recognition of a racially and culturally pluralistic society...in which cultures, languages, and races interrelate so as to bring strength, depth, and diversity to the whole. Integration should not mean, or require, the giving up of one's accent, songs, or life-style, but it can be the framework in which diversity is shared and appreciated by all" (Davis and White 1980:100).

RACE, AGENCY AND NORMS OF SOCIAL INTERACTION

A central paradox marks many racially-mixed churches in South Africa, and no doubt affects others elsewhere as well. On the one hand, congregants generally expressed the ideal of racial integration as rationale for why they belonged to racially-mixed congregations. Yet the very segregationist ideological and spatial contexts that they rejected seemed to continue to affect their congregations' structures and, judging by their comments, the thinking of some white congregants. How does one reconcile this state of affairs with the reserves of courage and ingenuity that was required to deliberately swim against a repressive tide? Similarly, how could one explain why black Africans in mixed congregations often seemed reluctant to indigenise the worship services in which they participated? This seemed particularly odd in congregations where both clergy and white congregants supported such acculturation.

In an attempt to solve the paradox, I will utilise an institutional approach in which agency and structure interact mutually to contribute to the construction, maintenance, and alteration of norms that promote or oppose integration. Integrative or segregative norms gradually accumulate within various social units (ranging from individuals to organisations) until they eventually become institutionalised within a society. By the same mechanisms, norms are transmitted across societies until they became globally institutionalised; for instance, in transnational organisations and the global agreements often associated with them. Obviously the reverse can also be true; global institutions not only act as repositories of global norms, but also function to diffuse them across societies. Note that I am arguing for a dialectical cycle operating between individual, organisational, state, and transnational actors, similar to Anthony Giddens' idea of structuration (Giddens 1984).

To facilitate discussion of how segregation and integration was instituted in South Africa as contested norms, I will briefly explain what I mean by these terms. A norm is a shared understanding of standards of behaviour that evolve from the interaction between actors. Norms define actors and motivate their actions by rationalising self-interest, self-affirmation, and group interests (Klotz 1995:13,17). Definitions may shift over time as the norms themselves are changed by actors who strengthen or weaken their significance, for example. The variability of norms is the reason why researchers should pay attention to historical context when they engage in any normative analysis. Different social agents can generate competing norms that vie for their allegiance and define their interests (Klotz 1995:19). Actors can combine regulative and procedural norms into regimes that structure how they behave (Klotz 1995:14). An indicator that a norm has become reified as an institution or regime is that contestation about it diminishes (Klotz 1995:24). Yet lack of contestation does not necessarily imply a consensual reification. The decline of opposition to segregation in South Africa during the 1960s, for instance, was more a function of coercive state power than of social convergence around a norm. Yet it would be true to argue that between the 1960s and 1970s segregation became reified among most white South Africans and some co-opted elites from other racially defined groups.

A 'national norm' in an objective sense refers to an ideology imposed by a state within the boundaries of its territory. The diffusion of a national norm can be measured by the extent to which associated policies permeate the institutions of state and of society—that is, become institutionalised. A national norm could strictly speaking only exist in South Africa once its four colonies were unified into a single state in 1910.[1] How does this apply to our discussion of norms of racial segregation? The Natives Land Act (1913) stands out as the first statutory implementation of the spatial segregation of races at the national scale of organisation. This did not prevent colonial administrators from formally attempting to segregate indigenes from settlers several times, long before Union. And as far back as 1786 the colonial administration tried to separate trekboere (Afrikaans, 'migrant farmers') from amaXhosa in the Graaff-Reinet district. Similarly, the implementation in 1849 of the Warden Line in the Orange Free State Sovereignty separated white from baSotho communities.

But a 'national' norm also exists subjectively during a particular period when there is widespread acceptance of a particular set of ideas for organising and regulating collective behaviour among people that inhabit a bounded region. In this sense, integrative and segregative institutional processes were promoted as much by religious leaders, colonists, and indigenes during South Africa's history as by their secular officials. Yet the adoption of either segregation or integration as a means to racially organise space, movement, and interaction, was an uneven process. Some congregations, urban settlements, and social institutions were segregated, while others were not. In the secular realm, integration and segregation emerged as opposing solutions to the general problem of how successive colonial administrations should deal with colonised peoples. For church agencies the issue was how to incorporate indigenous converts alongside European settlers. The secular and religious realms overlapped to the extent that conversion symbolised a transition point from the 'uncivilised' and 'heathen' statuses that initially marked the boundaries between Dutch and British colonists and the colonised indigenes. Eventually, as South Africa's history

---

1. A proto-unified state existed between 1902 and 1906, when the Transvaal and Orange River territories were crown colonies, and the foreign and economic affairs of the Cape and Natal colonies were under British administration.

unfolded, the racial connotations underpinning these designations became increasingly important and woven into the social fabric.

'Institutionalisation' in a general sense refers to the process by which the norm of segregation, for example, became part of the political and social fabric of South African society. An institution is a set of behaviours shared among actors who accept not only that the pattern exists independently of themselves, but that it should regulate their social interaction. An institution defines who its actors are, what roles they may play, and which rules of behaviour they can regard as appropriate. While institutions emerge in order to fulfil certain general purposes within a society, they may also have more specific functions in and of themselves.

As I have indicated with reference to national norms, institutionalisation has both an objective (formal) and subjective (informal) aspect. Segregation has been institutionalised not only when legal mechanisms have been created, but when individuals perceive the separation of races as a historical structure with associated ideas and practices that must affect the organisation of groups. Yet the ideological hegemony that characterises complete institutionalisation does not require the total obliteration of opposing ideas, nor of the collectivities or of the individuals that express them. Integrated congregations under apartheid in effect prevented the total segregation of South African society. The continued existence of segregated congregations today has the opposite effect.

PRESUPPOSITIONS

My basic presupposition is that a successive history of alternation between integrationism and segregationism as national norms can be discerned in South Africa. This oscillation reflects tectonic shifts in global paradigms that had earlier become evident in the resistance to slavery (19th century), to colonialism (first half, 20th century), and to social and political exclusion elsewhere (mid-20th century). From a global perspective, such ideological shifts peak at different times at various places across the globe, as was particularly notable in the staggered emancipation of former colonies. Note that while I root my argument in ideological shifts and institutional analyses, I do not intend to offer a purely idealist explanation. Instead, I assume that ideology is also a social construct whose contents and maintenance requires human effort and which is closely linked to particular historical material and political interests. For this reason I pay attention as much to the historical effects of economic change on racial segregation as on the spatial organisation of urban settlements and on religious organisation.

I use integrationism and segregationism as broad terms to capture the essence of various larger and opposing global racial ideologies that influence local contexts. Racism may be an equally valid term for segregationism, although racism is more properly the ideology that informs segregationism as a political strategy for organising space according to racial ideas. In the South African context, segregation as a term was probably first used during the opening of the parliament of the Cape Colony in 1902 by Sir Walter Hely-Hutchinson, Governor of the Cape (Bickford-Smith 1995:7). By the same token, integrationism is similar but not completely reducible to the South African notion of non-racialism. As a set of ideas that discounts race as social identifier, non-racialism was only coined towards the middle of the 20th century, and so is less useful for the 300-year time span to which I want to apply my terms. Both racism and non-racialism seem to be more specific than what I intend.

By integrationism I mean an ideology that encompasses a set of ideas that favours racial integration and is distributed as a norm across various units, such as institutions, their attendant organisations (workplaces, schools), and residential areas. Integrationism also includes the policies and practices that adherents believe would achieve positive racial interaction. As a broader notion, integrationism encompasses non-racialism as one possible strategy for dealing with racialised categories. While an unbroken string of integrated institutions can be located throughout South African history, integrationism only won broad acceptance by the majority of the population by the 1990s. The promotion since 1994 by the state of supportive policies currently elevates racial integration into the primary norm for social interaction in South Africa.

By definition, segregationism is the opposite of integrationism. One can periodise the trajectory of segregationism by contrasting the political pronouncements, urban planning policies, legal frameworks, and political organising that supported it with the ebb and flow of integrationism across various social institutions, including congregations. The promotion by successive South African regimes of policies that encouraged segregationism, alongside its broad acceptance by the politically dominant white minority, gradually established racial segregation as the primary norm between the 1880s and 1980s.

The historical and material dimensions of my presuppositions draw attention to how norms vary in terms of level of analysis, space, and time. By implication, not only can the same norm be differentially institutionalised across units, but opposing norms can co-exist within the same unit. As much as integrated institutions oppose segregated ones within the same society, opposing norms can also occur within the same institution.

Despite the overall triumph of integrationism over segregationism in South Africa, segregationism persists, as do its constitutive elements— including racial categories and racism. While parliamentarians have formally eliminated racist legislation from South African society as unit of analysis, the picture changes in sub-national units such as cities, institutions, organisations, groups, or individuals. Despite the elimination of racist legislation, state census data continue to use racial classification systems inherited from the apartheid government. Racial categories are used by the state to enforce legislation that mandates the formal racial integration of state departments and of larger private organisations, such as businesses. Race remains a rhetorical weapon for some political actors. And racism not only persists among some individuals, for instance, but varies in spatial distribution. Media reports reflected more racist incidents in certain parts of South Africa than in others.

Racial segregation continues within institutions that are now formally integrated, while a few even remain segregated. Most congregations remain informally segregated within denominations that are formally integrated (e.g. the Methodist Church of Southern Africa). Other church groupings remain racially-homogeneous without formally intending to be so (e.g. African Independent Churches). Formally segregated denominations such as the white Afrikaanse Protestantse Kerk (Afrikaans Protestant Church) continue to exist. Many urban areas remain informally racially segregated (e.g. Soweto), while the white settlement of Orania remains formally segregated.

Such examples imply that state power varies according to the degree that the state is able to directly bring its policies to bear. Other variables that moderate state power include the extent to which individuals (e.g. state officials) can choose to accept or resist policies, which in turn affects the time lag between policy formulation, promulgation, and implementation.

The contestation between integrationism and segregationism as societal norms can be tracked against the uneven historical trajectory of attempts to implement racial integration in South African religious institutions. Some argue that developments in religious institutions anticipated and spurred on the gradual dominance of segregation in other social institutions (Saayman 1990). All Christians could in principle attend the denominations that were formally established at the Cape of Good Hope from 1665 on. But the ideal of racially-mixed churches had since about the mid-18th century waned alongside the fortunes of its supporting integrationist norm. Churches were increasingly racially homogenised during the subsequent colonial and union periods. The most remarkable aspect about racially-mixed churches in South Africa is not that some emerged in the Dutch and early British colonial settlements, but that others continued to do so under apartheid. South Africa's first democratic elections in 1994 and the creation of the 1996 Constitution signalled the dominance of racial integrationism as national norm over the apartheid norm of racist segregationism. Yet, paradoxically, the racial composition of congregations did not subsequently improve much. By 1997 a national survey that I conducted found an estimated 3% of all Anglican, Methodist, and Catholic churches in South Africa was "significantly racially integrated and culturally diverse." This translated to 255 out of a possible 7,650 churches in the Anglican and Methodist churches alone.

Careful readers would note that two implicit hypotheses have emerged that inform my analyses. The first hypothesis is that congregations refract the racial interaction of the society in which they are embedded, as they are institutions affected by social, cultural, economic, and political forces. The second hypothesis is that racial interaction in general oscillates historically between poles defined by overt or covert racism and anti-racism. These hypotheses suggest that a focus on race in congregations will expose a range of patterns of behaviour that permeate an entire society. When a general trend towards or away from racism dominates a particular society at a given time, opposing forces emerge to the extent that dominance depends on coercion. Researchers should confirm the particular bias of each social institution (towards racism, against racism, or some combination) case by case. Similarly, the direction and extent of mutual influences between social institutions should also be determined. A congregation may individually (or cumulatively, with others) influence other societal institutions, or chose to defy societal forces. Other institutions may influence religious organisation, or mutual influences may occur that vary in strength and direction.

THE STRUCTURE OF THIS BOOK

My solution for the paradox, that racially-mixed congregations contain elements of the very ideologies that they oppose, is worked out in the rest of this book. I assume throughout that racially-mixed congregations are microcosms which reflect patterns of racial interaction that are also found in other social institutions with which they overlap. As social institutions, religious organisations act as carriers of the social, cultural, economic, and political forces in society. And so a focus on race in congregations may expose overt and covert racist behaviours which may occur in society at large, or within particular institutions. Such patterns reflect the ongoing contestation between opposing norms represented by individuals and groups in congregations, as in society as a whole. The relative rareness of racially-mixed congregations elsewhere—in the United States or the United Kingdom, for example—even suggests a universality caused by global systemic forces. Studies that wish to go beyond the scope of this volume should pay attention to similarities and differences in national demographics, historical developments, and political systems. The legal sanction of segregation in South Africa and the United States as former British colonies was—and is—more obvious than the covert forms of racism at work in the United Kingdom; but the effect on religious institutions remains strikingly similar.

The extended case studies in Chapters Two to Four mirror the interdependence between religious, economic, racial, and religious forces during particular periods that affected the spatial organisation of Johannesburg. The histories of Central Methodist Mission, Saint Francis Xavier Catholic Church, and Johweto Family Vineyard relates to the transition of Johannesburg from gold mine frontier camp to industrial heartland. The historical shift from colonial patterns of urban organisation to those that mark the post-apartheid city is, for this reason, salient.

The case studies demonstrate a close interaction between political and urban contexts that prompted these congregations to move from involuntary segregation to voluntary reintegration of participants. All three cases were affected by the spatial development of Johannesburg and the subsequent distribution of residents into segregated residential neighbourhoods. Johannesburg represents an example of how the segregation of urban areas was implemented. First came a general discouragement of racial integration by town councils during the colonial periods, followed by the construction of segregated urban areas in the union period. Finally, the state enforced segregation under apartheid. Central Methodist Mission and Saint Francis Xavier Catholic Church represent attempts by church leaders to overcome the consequences of political policies that increasingly institutionalised inner city and suburban segregation. The freehold areas of Sophiatown and Martindale that fed Saint Francis' early racial mix were whitened by the forcible implementation of the Group Areas Act of 1950. Johweto's founders strove to overcome the ultimate segregated outcomes of that Act, white Johannesburg and black Soweto. Members of these congregations who ideologically opposed apartheid could engage in acts of symbolic defiance by participating in religious rituals in a transracial context.

While most of the detail for each case study concerns the apartheid era, cases are also situated within the historical continuities and discontinuities of their spatial and political environments in the colonial and the post-apartheid periods. A more rounded picture thus emerges of just how the imagined alternatives to segregation relate to the past and the future versions of the congregation.

Racial integration persists as a global issue that continues to challenge social institutions in most societies—for instance, in the United States. Why integration poses such social problems—despite the elimination of formal racism and punitive legal measures to ensure integration—is among the questions that I attempt to answer in Chapters 1 and 5. In Chapter 1 I suggest a working hypothesis: that competing global ideologies of racial segregation and integration have developed historically as the bases on which social actors established the norms for racial interaction that became institutionalised differentially over time (e.g. the 1850s versus the 1960s) and space (e.g. Africa versus North America). If this hypothesis is true, racial interaction within social institutions in general should show patterns of segregation that alternate with those of integration over time. By implication, different social institutions should also display varying degrees of integration relative to one another as they attempt to integrate these norms. The exceptions would be institutions that specifically prohibit racial interaction. As ground-level manifestations of religious institutions, congregations provide excellent micro-mirrors for the society within which they exist. As voluntary forms of organisation, they provide a more accurate reflection of how people choose to interact in social spaces that remain outside the direct influence of the state. As such they often contradict pronouncements at higher levels of authority within the same religious institution.

The formal repeal of apartheid in South Africa and the subsequent promotion of a vision of a unified state and an integrated society have not, as yet, managed to completely reverse apartheid's effects. The successful integration of South African society requires the voluntary transformation of social institutions by informed citizens. In this regard, members of racially-mixed churches have a vital role to play in South Africa, as in other pluralist countries, in the construction of a civil society in which racial interaction and integration is normative rather than exceptional.

1

Establishing the Norm
in Colonial and Apartheid Churches

INTRODUCTION

In order to facilitate the discussion of racially-mixed congregations under apartheid, this chapter relates the history of race in South African churches to the political, economic, and social forces that affected social interaction in urban areas under successive political regimes from 1806 to 1994. I use this familiar history to reflect on the less explored waning and waxing of race as organising principle in congregations. The resulting description demonstrates how congregations' organisational principles generally switched from racially integrated to segregated, in lockstep with changes in social norms. By contrast, a small number of racially-mixed congregations inverted the segregationist norm that gradually came to dominate South African society.

The 'norm' of the title refers to the dominant attitudes and racial praxis of South African churches in relation to those operating in society. I drew evidence for what passes for normative in colonial churches from contemporary writings and from later analyses of each period. Church documents—such as baptismal and marriage registers—presented additional corroboration. Interviews and participant observation supplied further data with which to triangulate the evidence. Substantiation for the dominant attitudes towards racial integration in South African society derives from the political doctrines and social praxes of successive periods.

My basic argument in what follows is that the dominant congregational norms intertwined helix-like with prevailing social and political norms, sometimes converging and sometimes diverting from them. In churches established by settlers during the 17th and 18th centuries, for instance, a nascent inclusive racial norm was institutionalised during the Dutch and early British periods—albeit weakly. The mercantile economy allowed for the incorporation of a small number of indigenous elites into urban colonial institutions, while the rest of the population was to be accommodated in rural reserves (Saayman 1997). Schools at first offered access to the accoutrements of British civilisation. Later the goal was artisanship, via "industrial education" which prepared students for blacksmithing, shoemaking, and other forms of skilled labour (*Sechaba* 1982). The colonial political strategy of co-opting the indigenous elite was accompanied by the educational ideal of integrated schools where black and white would receive a similar education (Saayman 1997).

Initially, adherents who held common religious beliefs tended to participate together in public worship. Slaves and indigenous people who converted to Christianity met the primary requirement for inclusion in congregations. Yet while a common belief system tended to sublimate racial attitudes, prejudice was not completely supplanted. While some congregations included those perceived as racially different, they tended to be stratified by status and class, which coincided with race. As a result, segregated seating for slaves and for the poor differentiated congregations horisontally. Material means remained the basis for who was allowed to participate in decision-making structures in churches, as well as outside them. During the British colonial period, for instance, property ownership determined whether one could participate in church councils as well as whether one could be on the common voters' roll. The contradictory notions of racism and "civilising" mission that drove colonialism also shaped later South African society. The prevailing norm of limited racial integration was tempered by the dependence of settlers on unfree labour (slaves, Khoikhoi, captured combatants) for agricultural production, contributing to racist attitudes (e.g. towards the San).

By the late 19th and early 20th centuries, a contrary institutionalisation of racial exclusion had replaced racial inclusivity as dominant societal and ecclesial norm. Pressure to replace the integrative norm came from both inside and outside the churches, as I discuss later on. The integrationist norm did not disappear completely from the churches, nor from society, but was relegated to a secondary social impulse. Integrationism was challenged by whites who felt that successful black artisans and the educated elite threatened their interests. Economic shifts prompted by the discovery of precious minerals, the promotion of a free market economy, and incipient industrialisation affected colonial policies toward the indigenous population. Instead of skilled or semi-skilled labour, mining companies and later factories had need of unskilled workers, housed relatively closely to their operations. Both government and mission schools adjusted their goals accordingly. Cities began to devise segregated residential areas for black workers, and the Union government began to segregate black African rural areas from white areas.

Only from the mid-1960s did integrationism slowly regain the prominence that would eventually mark the post-apartheid period, when integration became a primary feature of ecclesial and state policy. In other words, attitudes towards racial integration in secular and religious institutions converged during the early colonial and post-apartheid eras. By contrast, from the late colonial through the Union and apartheid periods (1872-1989) only a very small number of congregations adhered to integrationism.

Ideological and racial convergence among whites meant that white church affiliates would generally support apartheid from the mid-20th century on. Their black counterparts in the same denomination opposed apartheid, or at least, suffered under it. Ironically, during the first decades of the 20th century, blacks in South Africa also advocated the notion of separate institutional development, which white governments would impose in extreme forms from 1948 on. Progressive political movements (e.g. the South African Native National Congress) and initially also adopted a segregationist approach, both in relation to political organisation and with regards to land; as did Clements Kadalie of the Industrial and Commercial Union in 1924 (Dubow 1989:155). Segregated political organisation continued into the 1950s, with the Congress Alliance comprising separate parties for different race groups. Throughout the Southern Africa region, segregation was promoted by almost all governments "and by most whites regardless of political persuasion" by 1945 (*Encyclopædia Britannica Online* n.d.d). The widespread acceptance of segregation during the first decades of the 20th century depended on the ambiguous promises that it held for all sectors of the South African population. Dubow (1989:9) pointed out that for black Africans segregation held out the hope of a more equitable redistribution of land, rural development, and maintenance of traditional authorities. Some whites expected an uninterrupted labour supply and job protection. Liberals wanted to preserve black interests without necessarily undoing the racial structure of society.

The discussion so far repeats a theme already touched on, namely that politics influenced the racial composition of South African congregations. Obversely, the general trend of the ecclesial organisation of race during the colonial and union periods also influenced contemporary and later racial politics. Willem Saayman, for example, has argued that the decision to establish separate missions for black and coloured Africans later influenced segregationist politics. Similarly, Hermann Giliomee concluded that missions policy would remain "intertwined with racial policy and the Afrikaners' quest for political survival" (Gilliomee n.d.:9). Obviously, I am not suggesting that the churches alone determined South Africa's racial mores—merely that there was a mutual influence during specific times. The tendency of colonial authorities to spatially segregate particular settlements demonstrates that racial separation as potential organisational strategy operated both inside and outside the churches.

Clearly, congregations are interdependent and interactive with their surrounding ideological and geographic spaces. Yet, as the emergence of racially-mixed congregations under apartheid shows, interdependence does not completely preclude independent action by congregational actors. Alternative actions remain possible, if limited, even where social agents were constrained by repressive state power and by dominant social norms. Still, South African congregations remained linked to policies that racialised spatial urban patterns across the country.

My analytical strategy requires elaboration of how the 'periods' and 'urban patterns' are constructed. As a direct relationship existed in South Africa between urban spatial organisation and the broader policies pursued by a particular political regime, we can combine urban patterns and periods into an analytical device. At the start of the subsections that follow, I provide more detailed description of each period with its associated urban pattern. I attend to the successive waves of segregation, desegregation, and resegregation of cities and towns, while accounting for similarities and differences between various periods and locations.

Relevant literature has summarised the segregationist *pattern* of urban spatial organisation by descriptive titles such as 'colonial city,' 'segregation city,' 'apartheid city.' By contrast, 'apartheid-city-in-transition' and 'post-apartheid city' refers to patterns of integration. All these terms overlap significantly with the widely accepted historical periods that I use to order the discussion in this chapter, namely the colonial, union, apartheid, and post-apartheid eras. The extent to which authorities spatially segregated designated race groups defines each historical urban pattern (e.g. 'segregation city').

Each historical *period* is defined by the dates at which different regimes assumed power, as well as by policies in relation to social and spatial segregation. As polices were neither implemented immediately nor enforced equally, urban patterns do not completely line up with historical periods. Neither are historical periods completely distinct from one another, overlapping where later policies built on the foundation of earlier ones. In addition, we could subdivide each historical period further. Yet every period does contain sufficient differences for effective use as heuristic tools.

The historical overview in this chapter will reveal how 'the norm' regulating racial interaction cycled from an ideal of limited institutional integration in the colonial period back to an ideal of full institutional integration in the post-Apartheid period.

Chapter One is structured around the central question of how we can understand the formation of racially-mixed congregations in relation to the South African political economy. This wider approach sets the stage for the narrower focus of Chapters Two to Four, which is again expanded in Chapter Five into a generalised explanation that encompasses both societal and congregational dimensions. The goal of Chapter One is to highlight how a certain type of social change (racial integration) within a particular (religious) institution was affected by a context within which political actions, policies, and legislation interacted with successive economic systems. My assumption that a tight knit existed in South Africa between most religious institutions and political and economic structures is easy to substantiate. In relation to economic issues, for example, early 20th century denominations with "English-speaking" members largely supported the interests of mine owners against labourers on the Rand (Cochrane 1987).

Regarding linkages between religious and political institutions, critics characterised the (white) Dutch Reformed Church as nothing less than "the National Party at prayer." The white Dutch Reformed Church's support for apartheid caused considerable discomfort to affiliates of its black, coloured and Indian sub-denominations. Consequently, in 1974 the Belydende Kring (Afrikaans, Confessing Ring) was formed as a critical, interracial body that countered the popular perception of the white

D.R.C.'s apartheid position as representative of all Dutch Reformed branches (Belydende Kring 1999).

Similarly, members of African Independent Churches tended to support the African National Congress (Zaaiman 1994; Anderson 1992:105). Political differences about apartheid led to the general collapse of ecumenical contact between denominations with Afrikaans- and "English-speaking" members in 1960. With the sole exception of the South African Christian Leadership Assembly in 1979, Afrikaans- and "English-speaking" denominations would not resume formal relations until 1990. Within the same denominations the life experiences of white and black affiliates created differences in attitudes towards the apartheid status quo, as vast as those between English-speaking clergy and laity on the same issue. Black clergy and lay theologians such as Albert Lutuli (1898-1967) played an important role in establishing and sustaining liberation movements.

White Reformed churches generally underwrote apartheid. Rev. J.D. du Toit, a professor of theology at the Potchefstroom University for Christian Higher Education (now North-West University), published what may have been the first theological defence of apartheid. The university was then a Gereformeerde Kerke in Suid-Afrika institution. Du Toit argued that there could be no social equality between those whom God had separated (Gilliomee n.d.:6). A remarkable parallel tradition in the Apostolic Faith Mission Church credits American missionary John G. Lake's address to the Union parliament with influencing Louis Botha's government towards segregationism, although Lake insisted on holding integrated church services (Horn 1991). Racial segregation as solution to the negative effects on 'coloured people' of commingling with whites—'contamination' and 'annihilation'—was not a new idea. Anglican Bishop Robert Gray, for example, raised the issue in South Africa in 1850 (Gray 1853). The Report of the 1835-36 House of Commons Select Committee on Aborigines noted similar concerns regarding racial interaction (Elbourne 2003).

I address the central question of Chapter One in the first section, via a brief social history that highlights both integrative and segregative dynamics in racially-mixed South African congregations. Factors that contributed to the subsequent deviations towards segregation are recounted, showing how churches in their attitudes to race mimicked— and occasionally shaped—their socio-political contexts. While integration was an ideal for the churches up to the mid-19th century, from that point on segregation was ascendant. Churches offered various justifications for the eventual racial separation of 'settler' from 'mission' congregations. Catholic leadership pointed to 'insurmountable' language differences (Hinchliff 1968:250, see Cochrane 1987). Reformed leaders lamented that the "weakness of some" prevented joint communion with their darker fellow-congregants (Loff 1983). The helix-like and paradoxical dynamics of integration-segregation are fleshed out in the detailed case studies of Chapters Two to Four, demonstrating the political and economic dynamics that affected each featured congregation.

In the second section of this chapter I highlight the importance of certain integrative-segregative dynamics in the formation of racially-mixed churches. Class formation, state legislation, and historical contestations within the ideological superstructure are noted. The section illustrates the waxing and waning of race as organising principle in congregations. Over time, a demonstrable switch from racially integrated to primarily segregated congregations clearly emerges. Chapter Five relates this integrative-segregative pattern to the dynamics of the world system.

RACIAL MIXING AND RACIAL SEGREGATION AS HISTORICAL IDEALS

A brief overview follows of the major secular trends of integration and segregation in South Africa is in order, before moving to detailed descriptions of the racial organisation of congregations. I provide broad descriptions of policies and practices at national and urban levels to demonstrate the degree to which segregation or integration, or both, were dominant during a given historical period. The dominance of one trend over another can be established by the extent to which it is distributed across several institutions. The integration of Christian churches receives particular attention in the discussion, as the major expression of formal religion during all periods. More detailed descriptions in the following three chapters tie the secular trends discussed here to the organisation of race in particular congregations.

While segregationism across all institutions was already discernible by the end of the 19th century, an earlier and alternative strand of subordinated integrationism demonstrably continued on, as this chapter reveals. Some mixed congregations founded during the colonial period remained integrated while others were integrated even during South Africa's regression into apartheid.

The Colonial Norm of Limited Institutional Integration, 1652-1909

The Dutch Colonial Period (1652-1795, 1795-1806)

The General United Chartered East India Company *[Generaale Vereenigde Goctroijeeerde Oostindische Compagnie]* was founded in 1602. By mid-16th century, it was the world's largest trading corporation, controlling an estimated 6,000 ships and 48,000 sailors (Thompson 1990:33).

The Dutch East India Company, as it is commonly referred to, established a foothold at the southernmost tip of Africa in 1652 that was gradually transformed under the Dutch into the Colony of the Cape of Good Hope. The Company initiated a refreshment post to supply fresh food and water for Company ships en route to the East. A wooden fort that was later replaced by a stone building guarded company interests. From the onset of the Dutch colonial period (1652-1795, 1795-1806), employees pushed the reluctant Dutch East India Company for permission to settle beyond the limits of the military fort. Nine employees were allowed to settle in Rondebosch in 1657 on condition that they supply provisions to the Company at fixed prices (Thompson 1990:34-35).

Gradually, the Dutch established farming settlements—such as Stellenbosch (1686)— north- and eastwards after 1679. By 1707 there were 700 Company employees and 2,000 settlers in the colony, including men, women and children. Magistracies were set up at Swellendam (founded 1745) and Graaff-Reinet (1786). By 1779 settlements stretched throughout the southeastern Cape, including Drakenstein, Roodezand, and Zwartland. The number of settlers of Dutch descent was swelled by the gradual arrival of French Huguenots to 13,830 by 1793, excluding 14,747 slaves from Angola, Mozambique, Madagascar, Indonesia, India, and Ceylon (Thompson 1990:35-36,41,46). Dutch settlers supplemented the colony's labour requirements from 1730 on by forcing captured Khoikhoi, defeated in ongoing conflicts, to work as domestic servants or farm labourers (South African History Online n.d. m).

The services of the Dutch Reformed Church (D.R.C.), the only denomination permitted at the Cape during the 17th century, was open to indigenous Khoikhoi converts and baptised slaves from the start

(Kritzinger 1994:180; Cawood 1964; Brown 1960:198). Between 1665 and 1731 an estimated 1,121 slaves had been baptised into the D.R.C., although few were manumitted (Oosthuizen 1968:2; Thompson 1990:37).[2]

The D.R.C. essentially functioned as "a branch of the civil service" of the Dutch East India Company (Cawood 1964:17). The Company paid the ministers, and the governor nominated the church councils. Elementary schools were attached to churches at Stellenbosch—as at Drakenstein, Roodezand, and Zwartland—so that the religious institution also fulfilled educational functions (Thompson 1990:41). Company slave children were educated at a Company school started in 1685 (Thompson 1990:44). The roots of integrationism in the Dutch period stems from a Company policy which meant that it was possible in principle "for members of inferior status groups to be put on an equal footing with their superiors" (Gilliomee n.d.:5).

The British Colonial Period (1795-1803, 1806-1909)

During the British possession of the Cape Colony, English-speaking settlers added to the number of towns founded by Dutch descendants. Cape Town by 1795 comprised the fort, a hospital, the Company slave lodge, and a church building. Five thousand settlers and 10,000 slaves inhabited 1,145 houses. By contrast Stellenbosch at the time had 70 houses, Swellendam 30, and Graaff-Reinet about 12 (Thompson 1990:51). The Cape District contained 4,155 colonists by 1793. Freed slaves formed between 16% and 13% of the overall population between 1750 and 1770. They could presumably speak Dutch, a precondition of their manumission. Some intermarriage occurred between freed slave women and Europeans (Thompson 1990:45,47). Most freed slaves resided in Cape Town, where they had the same rights as other settlers until the 1760s. But after the 1790s they had to carry permits (passes) if they left town (Thompson 1990:37, 44-45). By contrast to their freed counterparts, slaves had to carry passes when moving between farm and town (Marais 1939:117).

The British, like the Dutch before them, did not initially consider

---

2. Some argue that baptism of indigenous populations, due to uncertainty about their subsequent civil and political standing, was not standard practice before 1742, when Georg Schmidt baptised five Khoikhoi at Baviaanskloof (Genadendal) mission station. The Council of Policy prohibited him from continuing, ostensibly because he was not an ordained minister (South African History Online n.d. m).

expanding their colony eastwards. Instead of incorporating the indigenes who resided on the other side of the Great Fish River by extending the Colony eastwards, the British wanted to expel them. The British launched a major military campaign between 1811 and 1812 to push more than 20,000 people (particularly the Gqunukhwebe and Ndlambe) eastwards beyond the river. British soldiers, their indigenous auxiliaries,[3] and settlers faced various amaXhosa groups along the newly constituted frontier. Grahamstown (founded 1812) formed the focal point in a line of military forts (*Encyclopædia Britannica Online* n.d. b.). Five thousand British settlers were landed along the eastern seaboard in 1820 to populate and pacify the Fish River frontier. Missionaries received permission to establish stations there for the same reason.

Ironically, the arrival of settlers provoked more tensions, contributing to the social and economic changes that would alter colonial thinking about expanding the Colony eastwards. The new arrivals founded various settlements in the eastern Cape from 1820 on, including Port Elizabeth (1820) on the coast, and Bathurst (1820) inland. Among the more prominent causes of ongoing conflict were contestations about available land. The arrival of British settlers and the prominence achieved by commercial sheep farming in the Cape economy of the 1840s contributed to more aggressive British military campaigns (*Encyclopædia Britannica Online* n.d. d.). The British authorities occasionally used the wars to fulfil the expanding labour requirements of the Cape Colony by capturing and relocating defeated populations. This practice created in 1835 the so-called Fingo in the Colony, comprising thousands of Rharhabe and Gcaleka women and children (*Encyclopædia Britannica Online*. n.d. d.). Later, Britain would war against other indigenous groups elsewhere, such as the amaZulu during the 1870s in Natal.

The arrival of British settlers coincided with "imperial attempts to create a 'free market' in labour." This meant extending equality before the law to slaves and Khoikhoi through measures such as Ordinance 50 of 1828 (allowing Khoikhoi to choose their employers) and the emancipation of slaves in 1834. The Masters and Servants Ordinance of 1841 largely restored settler control over labour by criminalising breach of contract and desertion (*Encyclopædia Britannica Online* n.d. c).

Meanwhile, motivated by the negative economic consequences of the

---

3. The British inherited the Khoikhoi corps from the Dutch and re-organised them as The Cape Regiment under British officers (Mills 2005).

British emancipation of slaves, descendants of Dutch settlers set out after 1835 on the Great Trek. More than six thousand men, women, and children had migrated north- and eastwards beyond the borders of the Cape colony by 1840 (Thompson 1990:67). These so-called Voortrekkers founded small colonies throughout southern Africa, including the republics of New Holland (1837, renamed Natalia in 1838), the Holland-Africa Republic (1852, renamed South African Republic 1853), the Orange Free State (1854) and the Zuid-Afrikaansche Republiek. The discovery of minerals on a large scale—diamonds in 1867 and gold in 1886—enticed Britain into two conflicts with the Boer republics (1899-1902). Britain's eventual victory led to the establishment of the Transvaal Colony and Orange River Colony as British crown colonies in 1902. British settlers were deposited in Natal, an eastern coastal region to the north of the Cape Colony, between 1848-1862 (Silva n.d.). Natal became a crown colony in 1843, and an independent colony in 1856. The Cape Colony received independent government in 1872.

Limited racial integration of institutions was an ideal pursued during the British colonial periods, as mirrored in the emergent mixed urban conglomeration typified as 'Colonial City.' Yet socio-economic class continued to structure social and spatial relations. Residents who occupied high socio-economic status, and who were usually white, lived in the core of the Colonial City as exemplified by Cape Town. Others at the other end of the scale, whether white or not, were usually located at the urban periphery. This initial residential pattern gradually changed as higher status whites moved to outlying areas adjacent to roads, while working class residents moved to the urban centre. Despite such conditions, colonial Cape Town was "the most racially integrated city in Africa before 1948" (Krige and Donalson 1999). While not all colonial urban areas in colonial South Africa necessarily exhibited similar residential patterns as Cape Town, some did. Bathurst, a rural village created in the Eastern Cape to accommodate British settlers, "contained 1,240 people of all colours" in 1830.

Most denominations in the Cape colony held racially-mixed congregations to be an ideal throughout the 17th and 19th centuries (Hinchliff 1968:210; Gish 1985:23; Loff 1983:22; Villa-Vicencio 1988:26; Goedhals 1989:108; Pato 1989:172). The ideal of incorporating all racial groupings was expressed by the Dutch Reformed Church (established 1665), as well as the Methodist Church (established 1814), Catholic Church (established 1834), and the Anglican Church (established 1848 as the

Church of England) in the Cape Colony.

Many denominations existed in the Colony for some time before they were formally established. The first recorded appearance of Catholics was a 1685 Jesuit visit to the shore under the Protestant Dutch rule, under which Catholics were allowed to operate from 1804 to 1805, then forbidden, then allowed again under British rule in 1820. The first Vicar Apostolic (E. Slater) was appointed in 1816, but not allowed to stay. The first resident bishop (Raymond Griffith) arrived only in 1838 (Brady 1951:115-116).

In the case of the Anglican and Catholic Churches it is easiest to date the official commencement of the denomination from the arrival—not appointment—of the first bishops: the Catholics then date to 1838, the Anglicans to 1848. The Methodists, who first appear in 1806, can be dated to the arrival of their first clergy in 1814. The first Roman Catholic Church building was erected in 1820, in Harrington Street, Cape Town. The oldest surviving church is Saints Peter and Paul, erected in 1841 at George (Agathangelus 1951, plate between pages 8 and 9).

The Anglican Church was the colloquial name of the Church of the Province of Southern Africa, which split from the Church of England in South Africa in 1870. So the Church of England refers to the numerically smaller denomination that retains the original title, while the other (larger) branch became the Church of the Province of Southern Africa, renamed the Anglican Church of Southern Africa in 2006.

The Catholic Church "recognized no colour bar from the earliest times, all Catholics sharing the same building and joining in the same worship." Catholic parishes at the Cape during the 1880s "included both European and coloured" (Brown 1960:204). This inclusiveness in Catholic circles was based on the assimilationist thinking exhibited in the Spanish and Portuguese colonies of the South and Central Americas, where mission was "an extension of Christian civilisation" (Brown 1960:204). Likewise, Anglican clergy had baptised the 'heathen' since the first British occupation of 1795, including blacks and freed slaves. But "no-one had instructed them and they were dispersed" by the 1820s (Lewis and Edwards 1934:5; Hinchliff 1968:4). Newly arrived Anglican clergy in ca. 1848 reportedly said "'it is to be hoped that masters and mistresses and others having influence over the coloured population will...induce them to attend'" (Langham-Carter 1977:56).

The inclusive ideal is reflected in the writings and actions of various church leaders, and surfaces in the awareness of laity as well. In 1842 Catholic priest Aidan Devereux (later Bishop of the Eastern Vicariate in South Africa) "noted that the Protestants made efforts to prevent the coloured population from coming near him" (Brown 1960:47). In 1856 the Roman Catholic bishop of Natal, Marie Jean Francois Allard, O.M.I. (1806-89), wrote to Father Jacobus Hoendervangers (resident priest at Bloemfontein in the Free State) that as " 'to colour, the Catholic Church pays no attention to it. Jesus Christ died for all men without distinction' "[4] (Brain 1990:71, footnote 75; Brown 1960:58,180-181). East of Cape Town in Mossel Bay of the early 1880s, Dutch Reformed laity "insisted that black [D.R.C.] members should rather join the Lutheran Church[5] or the Anglican Church" than attend the white church (Loff 1983:22).

But was the inclusive ideal translated into reality and did it become an established norm? South African church historians almost unanimously claim that racially-mixed congregations existed in the colonial periods, yet seldom supply empirical evidence. Some historical data even seem to point to a negative conclusion. For instance, the first archdeacon of the Church of England in the Eastern Cape, Nathaniel Merriman (1809-82), noted with disapproval that only whites attended Trinity Church,[6] Cape Town in 1848, which "looked just like a smart London congregation" (Goedhals 1989:108). If racially united congregations could be shown to have existed, they would demonstrate that the norm of racial segregation that came to dominate most South African denominations by the 1960s ran counter to the initial ideal of many denominations.[7] If examples cannot be found, the belief that such congregations existed could be assigned to a self-justifying ideology that existed within "English-speaking" churches.

Evidence certainly suggests that special services in the Anglican churches (then still the Church of England) were racially-mixed. This

---

4. Allard was responding to a request for an official statement regarding Catholics and black-white interaction (Brown 1960:180; Allard's Letterbook 322-323 is quoted in Brain 1990:71, footnote 75).

5. The remark may refer to congregations free from Boer control founded by German ministers in villages (Brown 1960:198).

6. Trinity, along with Saint John's Wynberg, and Saint Peter's Mowbray, represented the Erastian faction which would later feature in the 1870 split between bishops John William Colenso (1814-83) and Gray, and so between the Church of England and the Church of the Province in South Africa (Lewis and Edwards 1934:119).

7. For a contrary view, compare Jim Kiernan (1990:9).

was true of baptisms and some communion services, for instance, of 'Malay' converts. 'Malays' are descendants of Muslims exiled from Batavia (Indonesia) by the Dutch East India Company. By 1820 they numbered 3,000 at the Cape. Malays had been baptised at Saint George's Cathedral before the appointment of Robert Gray as Bishop of Cape Town in 1847 (Lewis and Edwards 1934:95). At least 33 of 57 adults baptised in Saint George's in 1849 were not whites (Saint George's baptism register; South African Church Magazine 1850:28). These comprised 16 "heathens" (i.e. black Africans); 12 Malays; one whose mother had been Malay; one Chinese; and three whose origins were "unknown" (Saint George's baptismal register; South African Church Magazine 1850:28).

During Bishop Gray's fourth visitation tour in 1850, he baptised fifteen "natives" and confirmed seven at a church meeting in the western Cape settlement of Melville, present-day Knysna (Lewis and Edwards 1934:61). Similar baptisms and confirmations took place at George, where Dutch Reformed missionary Niepoth, with the 300 "coloured people" he represented, applied to Bishop Gray for admission to the Church of England. Niepoth said that the D.R.C. did not allow coloured people to receive joint communion, baptism, or to be buried in D.R.C. church ground. The Dutch Reformed minister at Pietermaritzburg made a similar objection to the joint confirmation of "coloured people" (i.e. blacks) by the bishop (Gray 1853).

At Stellenbosch, South Africa's second oldest town, located northeast of Cape Town, a " 'Mozambique Servant' " by name " 'Nana Maria' " was baptised in Saint Mary's Anglican church on September 28, 1851. She apparently worked for Reverend Frederick Carlyon, the first rector of Stellenbosch parish. Four "non-Europeans" are named among 19 communicants at the 1855 Easter service at Stellenbosch (Hunter 1952:19).

Malay converts attended communion at Saint George's Cathedral in 1854, sitting in the free seats during matins or evensong prior to the building of the Anglican mission chapels in Cape Town (Lewis and Edwards 1934:96). Archdeacon Thomas Fothergill Lightfoot (1831-1904) said that the coloured converts (including Malays) met for regular services in the chapel-school in Upper Buitengracht Street, but until the building of Saint Paul's Mission Chapel in 1880 "resorted to the Cathedral for the Sacraments" (Lewis and Edwards 1934:96). This means a sizeable number of coloured communicants participated at Saint George's, as the Buitengracht congregation numbered 200 by 1861 (Lewis and Edwards 1934:109). In 1877 Lightfoot reported that "a great many coloured people" attend Saint George's "because Greenpoint Church will not hold them" (Barnett-Clarke 1908:183). Anglican settlers regarded the completion of Saint Paul's Mission Chapel favourably, as they thought it would drain away some coloured people. A racially-mixed Anglican service was held on 12 June 1892 at Saint Philip's Mission Chapel in English. The congregation included a "large proportion...[of] Kaffirs of various tribes", who gathered to witness the ordination of Henry Mdeleleni, a Fingo [Mfengu] catechist for twelve years (Cape Church Monthly 1892:3).

Special occasions in the Catholic church also reflected similar arrangements. In 1864 Catholic bishop Thomas Grimley (d. 1871) of Cape Town included eleven blacks in a May procession (Brown 1960:180). Such evidence confirms that congregations were mixed for special occasions, at least.[8] A particularly remarkable event occurred in 1909, when an unnamed Dutch Reformed Church minister visited the African Methodist Episcopal Church's conference at Aliwal. African Methodist Episcopal bishop Albert Johnson reported that he asked "for one of our ministers to be sent to preach to his people on Sunday night...We sent Rev. E. Jonas a native of Hottentot blood, who reflected credit upon the Church and natives" and who "uses elegant Dutch" (Johnson 1909:135).

Aside from these special events, some colonial congregations in Cape Town were certainly integrated from their founding, while others further afield probably were, too. The integrationist ideal mirrored the realities of the eventual urban settlement at Cape Town, a pattern characterised as 'colonial city.' Wherever the conversion of indigenous peoples, slaves and exiles coincided with similarly interracial urban areas, the likelihood that other congregations were mixed increased.

In Cape Town, Saint John's Church in Wynberg, for example, was integrated since its founding in 1830, as was Saint Paul's Anglican Church in Rondebosch (founded 1834). In 1830 people of all colours in the rural village of Bathurst in the Eastern Cape petitioned for an Anglican church there (Lewis and Edwards 1934:19). Although we do not definitely know that the resulting congregation was mixed, it does seem probable. In 1850 a "Hottentot" (Khoikhoi) baptised at Cape Town was one of the subscribers for an Anglican church building at Bur-

---

8. Occasional interracial contact in church services continue sporadically today.

gersdorp, so that he could have a church to go to "without fear of being turned out" (Lewis and Edwards 1934:60; Gray 1853). Funds for building churches were raised through selling subscriptions or shares.

The ideal of racial congregational integration was practiced until as late as the early 19th century. In 1828 Bentura Johannes, a "bastaard" employee of a white Dutch Reformed Church member, became a member in the Somersets-Hottentots Holland (today Somerset West) D.R.C. (Loff 1983:11-12). This was in line with a April 29, 1829 ruling by a government-appointed official at the synod of the Cape Town Presbytery that there could be no discrimination at Communion, and, by implication, not within the church either (Loff 1983:16, Bosch 1983:31). Similarly, Ordinance 50 of July 1828 declared that all free people were equal before the law. The relationship between the Dutch colonial government and the Dutch Reformed Church was such that church decisions had to be ratified by the government before they could be enforced. To ensure compliance, a civil servant was appointed to attend all official church meetings (Loff 1983:16). A Khoikhoi congregation in Stockenström (Eastern Cape) became the first black congregation to join the Dutch Reformed Church after it left the London Missionary Society in 1831. Over the next two decades at least forty-five whites became members in this congregation (Loff 1983:18), so that it was mixed for an extensive period.

But by the 1830s residential and institutional segregation along racial lines were emerging. The upper wealthier and white classes of Cape Town, a municipality since 1840, had already moved to the outskirts of the town by 1879 (see Tankard 2004). Social distance now coincided with geographical segregation, so that the central areas of Cape Town could be described as " 'not inhabited by white men' " (Bickford-Smith 1989:50, quoting A. Trollope). Social segregation also mirrored the Anglican pew-rent system that enabled the rich to sit more to the front in elaborate seating, while the poor (white or black) sat in plain, open-backed seats. British authorities applied segregated residential areas at East London (in 1848), Port Elizabeth (1855), Durban (1871), Kimberley (1880s), and in Cape Town (1901) (compare Maylam 1995).

Bishop Gray reported in 1850 that "the local [Natal] government, acting under the instructions of [the Third] Earl Grey ... is about to fix the whole coloured population in ten locations [reserves]." Similar arrangements had been mooted since 1847 (Gray 1853).

These actions provided a precedent for the legal segregation of rural areas (Natives Land Act of 1913), residential space (Natives Urban Areas Act of 1923), and access to amenities that followed in the Union period. Apartheid legislation was the logical extension of these policies.

Segregation fitted with the shift from a mercantile to an industrialised economy with an accompanying increased need for cheap black labour (Saayman 1997). The educational policies of the Cape and Natal colonies were altered to produce labourers instead of an "idle" educated black gentry. In the Cape Colony, for instance, this was exactly the opinion of Langham Dale, Superintendent-General of Education in 1884 (Saayman 1997). In 1894, Cecil John Rhodes (1853-1902), then Prime Minister of the Cape Colony, promised to introduce industrial schools in the place of mission schools whose graduates became agitators against the government. In the compounds of De Beers Consolidated Mines in 1910, "Natives" were instructed in " 'the dignity of labour' " (Saayman 1997). In Natal the fear of competition from African and Indian artisans contributed to the government instituting an emphasis on training Africans "to the lowest level of skill necessary for the labour market." This was in direct contrast to the educational policies in the Natal colony during the 1880s, which had required educating black Africans as artisans. Mission schools such as Adam's College at Amanzimtoti had followed suit. John Langalibalele Dube (1871-1946) established the Zulu Christian Industrial School in 1901 at Ohlange, Natal, for similar purposes, inspired as much by notions of educational equality as by African-American institutions (Sechaba 1982).

Even in mixed colonial congregations the status of other race groups clearly differed from those of whites. Differentiated participation occurred at congregational as well as polity levels in the Dutch Reformed Church, Church of the Province of Southern Africa, and Catholic churches. In 1754 and 1794 blacks—probably slaves[9]—that attended a Dutch Reformed Church were forbidden by church leaders to linger in the foyer of churches after services (Loff 1983:20). Communion practice also varied. Black Dutch Reformed Church members sometimes received it with white members, and sometimes separately (Loff 1983:12). At the towns of Stellenbosch and Caledon in the 1820s white men received communion first, then white women, and lastly black members (Loff 1983:11,22). In the Anglican church no steps were taken to ensure full black representation in decision-making bodies.

---

9. Loff does not distinguish between indigenous blacks and slaves.

Black Anglicans were represented by white delegates at the 1863 and 1867 diocesan synods (Goedhals 1989:109). No black delegates attended the first Provincial Synod in 1870—a pattern eventually repeated in the political realm, where whites represented black voters (Goedhals 1989:109). In congregations having financial means (i.e. being a pew-renter) was initially as much a qualification for voting in elections of the vestry (church council) as was being a communicant in good standing.

Status differences and segregated Christian congregations contributed to conversions to Islam among black Africans. In 1838 the Anglican priest J. D. Sanders wrote of the "great gulf between black and white" which causes conversions to the Muslim faith, as "among Mohammedans the coloured are treated as equals. " ' 'Slam's kerk is de zwart men's kerk,' they said" (quoted in Lewis and Edwards 1934:95).

So where the ideal found concrete form, it was often contradicted or at best skewed in practice; in differentiated seating arrangements, staggered communion practices, segregated services, and by the equation of white civilisation and culture with Christianity (compare Villa-Vicencio 1988:43,47,54; Maimela 1988:323). Separate slave-master sections existed in many churches prior to the final emancipation of slaves in 1838. Already by 1837 Dutch Reformed Church custom was "separate congregations where possible, otherwise a separate section of the church for black people, usually at the back of the church, sometimes under and sometimes on the balcony" (Loff 1983:19). Racially segregated seating became and remained unofficial Catholic practice and was only phased out in the 1970s. By 1951 a Catholic priest could write that there was "nothing wrong" with segregated seating ("special places") "for Europeans, Coloureds and Bantu", provided "they are all admitted to the same communion rail" (Schimlek 1951:159). At Saint Mary's Catholic cathedral in Kimberley, for instance, segregated seating continued from its opening in 1951 through to the 1970s. The Anglican pew-rent system resulted not only in a rich/poor division, with fewer free seats for white and black poorer people, but caused church officials to hold prejudiced attitudes against those who could not support the building in such ways.

At the same time, black converts to Christianity were expected to conform to western standards of education, morality, and culture, enforced by the format of church services (compare Goedhals 1989:107,109,110;

Cochrane 1987:25,26; Villa-Vicencio 1988:56). Catholic bishops Patrick R. Griffith O.P. (d. 1862) and James D. Ricards (d. 1893) took it for granted that blacks "would accept the ways of the whites along with their language...[but] there would be no segregation in religion, and it would not be absolute in social matters" (Brown 1960:200). And Father Bernard Huss set out in 1915 to " 'teach the Bantu to think white' " in an effort to root out "the animistic and magical outlook" (Brown 1960:261). After 1910 the "pattern of social life" for blacks was gradually conformed to the requirements of the ruling class (Brown 1960:263), as it had been during the colonial period, although then not legislated as such. In effect, due to Protestantism's strong national links, Black Christians became incorporated into the nationality of a particular denomination (Brown 1960:198): English for Anglicans, German or Swedish for Lutherans, or Scottish or Dutch for Calvinists. Despite Griffith's words, he actively opposed intermarriage between those who were white and those who were not. The ordination of black priests in the Catholic church started in 1898 with Edward Mnganga (1872-1945), followed by three others. Yet because Bishop Dr. Charles Jolivet O.M.I. (1826-1903) of Durban opposed the ordination of blacks, none was ordained again until the 1920s (Denis 1995).

Increasing institutional segregation and class differentiation among the lower classes during the 19th century exerted an escalating pressure on the integrationist ideal in denominations. *De facto* segregation had existed in schools "from the first half of the 19th century" and by the mid-1880s had extended to hospitals, prisons, and asylums (Bickford-Smith 1989:48; compare Brown 1960:224). The Anglicans had schools for the offspring of coloureds in the Cape Town suburb of Bishopscourt, and for those of African chiefs at Zonnebloem (Hinchliff 1968:36). The effect was to separate poor whites from other groups (Bickford-Smith 1989:48). This developing ideology of racial discrimination disguised as liberalism was driven partly by the increasing industrialisation (e.g. of mining) and the 'mineral revolution' of the 1870s. The discovery of copper, diamonds, gold, coal increased government resources and so the competition for them.

The liberal sentiments, which influenced British churches in South Africa from the 1880s, emphasised the worth of individuals regardless of race—but, paradoxically, maintained white power and social control (Goedhals 1989:111). Liberal convictions include:

"a belief in the importance and dignity of the individual

without regard to colour, culture, creed and sex; emphasis on equality of opportunity, freedom of thought, conscience, speech, movement and association, and the rule of law; and the conviction that society can achieve political stability, economic prosperity and social justice by human effort and evolutionary pace" (Goedhals 1989:112).

Among some missionaries (e.g. James Stewart (1831-1905) of Lovedale) this idea was expressed in paternalistic terms, with whites regarded as adults, and blacks as children (Saayman 1994:16). Among the general populace, opposition to Indian migrants had resulted in public demonstrations at Durban in 1896 and a petition at East London in 1897 (South African History Online n.d. b.).

When the Cape became self-governing (1872), segregationism was ascendant in the denominations, as most surrendered the ideal of inclusive local congregations. Segregated congregations became the rule well into the 1980s. When colonial segregation hardened into apartheid policies, the churches were already compromised by more than 70 years of segregated practice (Cawood 1964). In a supremely ironic twist of history, the initial ideal of mixed services was now inverted.

By the late 19th century upper class features had contracted to coincide with being white and British. While the constitutions of the Cape colony (1853, 1872) discounted discrimination on class or colour lines, they distinguished between 'civilised' (i.e. British) and 'uncivilised' (i.e. African; compare Tankard 2004). Prior to Anglo-Boer wars, the constitution of the Boer republic of the Transvaal denied any '"equality between Black and White in church and state."' Similarly, the Free State's constitution confined civic rights to whites only (Mbeki 1964).

Segregationism in the Cape colony had political, economic, and demographic roots that became visible also in other parts of colonial South Africa. The colour-blind franchise initially co-opted "the more prosperous black peasants and artisans" (*Encyclopædia Britannica Online* n.d. c.). When a larger black working class emerged, white support for the political status quo slowly faded. As all male British subjects in the Cape Colony could in principle vote, an estimated 47% of the electorate by 1887 consisted of black Africans. Consequently the Cape Parliament introduced the Parliamentary Voters Registration Act (1887) and the Native Franchise Act (1892) to reduce the number of qualified black voters by changing property qualifications (Mbeki 1964). Similar political conditions obtained elsewhere. The Natal Constitution of 1856, for example, introduced such complex rules for determining franchise criteria that only "three Africans and 251 Indians ever acquired voting rights." By contrast, by 1896 there were 9,309 white voters (South African History Online n.d. b.).

The hardening of white racial attitudes coincided with the ascendancy of the Afrikaner Bond (founded 1879) in colonial politics. White prejudice was fuelled by the perceived challenge of Malays to the position of the white mercantile class. Increasing numbers of black migrants from the Eastern Cape and Mozambique altered the demographics of Cape Town between 1875 and 1902 and contributed to white intolerance towards others (Bickford-Smith 1995:44).

From the late 19th century onwards legislation was gradually introduced in colonial South Africa to stem the upward mobility of those 'other than whites.' The simultaneous evolution of racism legitimated the political division and control of labour supply (Bickford-Smith 1989:47-48). AmaXhosa who wanted to work in the Cape Colony had to carry 'passes,' legal documents that permitted them entry (Tankard 2004). The slave economy of the colonial periods presented a precedent for a racial division of labour. While race initially did not matter because whites, blacks and coloureds could all be found at the bottom of the labour pool, slaves were without exception black. Sir George Grey (1812-98), governor of the Cape Colony (1854-60), created 'locations' and 'reserves' for some amaXhosa (Tankard 2004).

Locations (ghettoes), hostels, and compounds for blacks were implemented by municipal authorities and mining companies alike in Cape Town and Kimberley in 1901 and 1886, respectively. Local authorities also took the first steps towards controlling black urbanisation (Krige and Donalson 1999).

The gradual "racial structuring of society" had been anticipated in the division of mission work along racial lines almost from the start (compare Saayman 1990:29, Gilliomee n.d.:9). In the Dutch Reformed Church, ministers were at first responsible for bringing in converts; but in 1824 missionaries were appointed with the sole purpose of preaching to the (black) heathen (Cawood 1964:20; Kritzinger 1994:180). The results were segregated services and later on segregated buildings—the convention not only in the Dutch but also in the separated settler parishes and 'native missions' churches of the Anglican, Methodist, and Catholic traditions (Goedhals 1989:109; Hinchliff 1968:194; Brain

1991:133-136). The settler/mission distinction can be deceptive: mission churches were white-dominated and so captive to the interests of the ruling class, despite noble intentions and occasional pro-black advocacy by white clergy (Cochrane 1987:14,21,22). From the black perspective, there was little difference between Brit and Boer (Villa-Vicencio 1988:43).

By 1881 the Dutch Reformed Church founded separate missionary branches, such as the Dutch Reformed Mission Church that was formed for 'coloureds.' At Springbok in 1867 an Anglican missionary notes the existence of a mission congregation that met at different times (morning and afternoon) in the same building as the 'European' congregation. The mission services were in Dutch (Lewis and Edwards 1934:101). Ultimately this resulted in white (mostly urban) churches alongside black 'location' congregations or rural missions. Catholic missionary work across the Orange river after 1840 followed a similar segregationist pattern, as I describe in more detail in Chapter Three.

The role of mission policy in the supply of labour for which segregation was necessary reveals the political economy of the second half of the 19th century. Labour needs dictated by political interests determined mission policy, as it would in the 1920s (Villa-Vicencio 1988:72). Missions' emphasis on 'economic individualism' and tithes functioned to co-opt black peasants into a labour market controlled by whites, as much as government taxes did (Goedhals 1989:106; compare Kiernan 1990:15,16; Cochrane 1987:24). Through learning new agricultural methods Africans also learnt "'capitalistic approaches to the apprehension of self and society'"(Saayman 1994:14, quoting De Kock 1992:126-127). In addition, a market was created for items manufactured by the British, as John Philip (1775-1851) of the London Missionary Society noted (Villa-Vicencio 1988:44). Missions to the Batswana in the northwest in particular exemplified this approach (Kiernan 1990:16-17). While mission schools, hospitals, social services, and missionary interventions on behalf of blacks undoubtedly had benign effects (Villa-Vicencio 1988:52; Saayman 1990:33), mission also had negative impacts on integration as an ideal.

After blacks were deprived of their land by the frontier policies, mission stations and schools contributed to the provision and distribution of labour for agriculture and public works, just as they would in the early 20th century (Goedhals 1989:106, Villa-Vicencio 1988:50,59; compare Cochrane 1987:74,84). Missionaries sometimes aided the process through which tribal land was lost. The Wesleyan William Shaw fulfilled this role in relation to parts of the land of the Basuto (Villa-Vicencio 1988:57).

The four Anglican mission stations established with grants from Cape governor George Grey in 1854 near Grahamstown exemplifies the links between mission and empire (Saayman 1994:13; Ramphele 1989:179; Cochrane 1987:20,26; Villa-Vicencio 1988:56), and between mission and capitalism (Saayman 1994:14). These missions had the express purpose of pacifying the amaXhosa (Goedhals 1989:106; compare Ntlha 1994:140; Hinchliff 1968:48). Similarly the Bethelsdorp Mission Station was used to "lure Khoikhoi away from the rebellion led by Klaas Stuurman" (Villa-Vicencio 1988:59). The concept behind the founding of the Catholic mission at Marianhill (at the instigation of bishop James Richards) was that "the missionaries would bring the advantages of material civilisation and so obtain more easily a hearing for their religion" (Brown 1960:104).[10] Marianhill exemplified the European middle ages.

Apart from economic effects, missions also had cultural effects. Mission land was often an alienated enclave on which blacks became foreigners in their own land, a pattern particularly prominent among missions to the Nguni (Kiernan 1990:18; Saayman 1994:14). Cultural resistance to conversion meant that inland only those on the edges of tribal society were converted (Kiernan 1990:18). Resistance to mission by the amaZulu was accompanied by a definite reluctance to accept European values (conveyed by Catholic mission) as superior (Brown 1960:206). A lesser-known possible etymology for 'Kaffir' is the isiZulu word for converts: iKhafulo, those " 'spat out' by society" (Kiernan 1990:18). It was not until the forceful co-option of resisting cultures (amaZulu, baPedi) into the imperial culture "more benign to the missionaries" that larger scale conversions became possible (Kiernan 1990:19, Saayman 1994:14). In this way the transformation of the material conditions and social structure[11] of African society preceded (and was requisite for) the replacement of the ideology of traditional society

---

10. Brown paradoxically denies that material changes contributed significantly to conversion among tribespeople, suggesting that material changes ("improvements") followed *after* conversion (Brown 1960:214-215).

11. The missionary insistence on an end to polygamy exemplifies one such structural change (Brown 1960:206).

(Maimela 1988:314; Brown 1960:104,206). The Anglican church after 1891—when William Carter became Bishop of Natal—pursued a modified policy of placing catechists within villages (Hinchliff 1968:192). The Catholic bishop Allard had also attempted this in 1854 (Brown 1960:205,207).

And so by 1872 most denominations had surrendered the ideal of inclusive local congregations to the developing sentiments of segregation. Within the Dutch Reformed Church a growing resistance to integrated communion services, coinciding with and fuelled by rising Afrikaner nationalism based on economic issues (Gilliomee 1989), ultimately led to a 1857 decision to allow segregated communion services in separate buildings for different races (Kritzinger 1994:180). The Dutch Reformed Church decision eventually solidified into three separate missionary branches: the Dutch Reformed Church in Africa (1859) for blacks, the Dutch Reformed Mission Church, founded in 1881 for coloureds, and the Indian Reformed Church in Africa (1947). Although each branch had its own polity, they were in effect controlled by the white Dutch Reformed Church, which controlled finances, clergy supply, and ratified decisions (Kinghorn 1990:59).

The Dutch Reformed Church's decision was presumably allowed through Ordinance 7 of 1843, which freed the church from interference by the government (Loff 1983:17). The racism of the whites was framed in terms of the cultural-religious distinction between 'born' Christians (i.e. Europeans) and recent converts (mostly slaves) (Loff 1983:12). This reaction eventually led to the preclusion of Bentura Johannes from communion with whites, and prompted the white members of the Stockenström congregation to establish their own (white) congregation in 1862 (Loff 1983:17-18). The Stockenström congregation, later designated coloured, remained within the Dutch Reformed Church until deciding in 1957 to become part of the Dutch Reformed Mission Church (Cawood 1964:23).

Some Dutch Reformed Church churches had already been ignoring the 1829 ruling (Loff 1983:11,22). Like the "English-speaking" churches, the Dutch Reformed Church mirrored the ideals of the dominant society (Villa-Vicencio 1988:22; Saayman 1990:28; compare Cochrane 1990:95). That similar situations existed elsewhere is supported by the actions of Henry Bousfield (1832-1902), Anglican Bishop of Pretoria. In 1879 Bousfield "dealt sharply with one congregation which attempted to exclude Africans from its services" (Hinchliff 1968:155).

The ideal foundered first in rural areas—especially on the frontier—where armed insurrection broke out in 1801 at Graaff-Reinet to prevent evangelisation of blacks, as it would put them on equal footing with settlers (Villa-Vicencio 1988:26). Colonial authorities, as much as church polities and laity, thus often countermanded the expressed ideal of racial integration. Congregations of other denominations also were segregated, e.g. the Methodists and Wesleyans (compare Bickford-Smith 1989:48). Archdeacon Merriman witnessed the turning away of three Malays from an 1848 service at Saint George's (Anglican) Cathedral in Cape Town (Goedhals 1989:108).[12] The significance of Merriman's description is that other races were willing to attend white congregations, while whites resisted this. So despite the ideal of non-segregation, "the practice of the [Anglican] church" became divided along racial lines (Goedhals 1989:108). The churches had aided the destruction and alienation of African traditional society (Villa-Vicencio 1988:52) without extending the full benefits of Western (industrialised) society. Nor were black converts treated any differently when they joined congregations.

The "English-speaking" denominations remained under "home" rule from abroad,[13] from where its ministers also came (Goedhals 1989:122; Cochrane 1987:86; Hinchliff 1968:245).[14] Blacks were not usually permitted to become clergy. Such negative practices were rooted in 19th century attitudes of white colonists, who regarded mission as "the work of white priests and black evangelists" aimed at blacks. The perpetuation of this perspective contributed to the dominance of white priests, while removing the influence of the church from the socio-political sphere controlled by whites (Goedhals 1989:109). In the Church of the Province of Southern Africa, for instance, the idea that blacks could also evange-

---

12. The first recorded instance of a black person receiving Anglican communion was 10 June 1849, long before significant numbers of blacks started affiliating in the 1870s (Goedhals 1989:110).

13. The Church of the Province remained under rule of the British church until constituting itself separately in 1870 (England and Paterson 1989:22). In 1953 all bishops were white and had been born in England; by 1980 only one diocesan and four suffragan (assistant) bishops were black; by 1988 nine out of 18 diocesan bishops and five suffragan bishops were black (Goedhals 1989:121; Pato 1989:172).

14. In 1963 less than half of about 85 clergy in the Grahamstown diocese were South African-born (Hinchliff 1968:245).

lise whites did not emerge before 1987 (Goedhals 1989:122).

Black Christian resistance to racist conditions in churches took many forms, most notably breakaway movements and hostility to mission. For instance, Nehemiah Tile formed the independent Tembu National Church in the Transkei 1884 (Oosthuizen 1990:102; Hope and Young 1981:37). Missions such as the Swiss Presbyterians established other black churches independent of white control before the turn of the century. African independent churches varied in form from copies of their mainline predecessors to syncretism (Cochrane 1987:89). Hostility to missions was illustrated in 1860 by attempts by some blacks in the Grahamstown area to stem contributions to missionary work (Goedhals 1989:108).[15] Retributive attacks were carried out on converts to Christianity in British Natal and in Zululand (Kiernan 1990:18).

Segregation had by the end of the 19th century developed into "the dominant political emphasis in colonial policy," combined with a labour-repressive economic system of capitalism (Cochrane 1987: 48,62).[16] As social mirrors of their times,[17] the churches often embedded "imperial ideals and colonial administration" (Goedhals 1989:107; Maimela 1988:325). Church membership of the "English-speaking" churches implied the extension of paternalism in return for submission to the British government, as noted of missionary policy generally, and Anglican policy specifically (Cochrane 1987:88; Mosala 1988:315; Goedhals 1989:107).

Racial segregation and integration in congregations clearly preceded the spatial segregation of urban areas; yet those that sought to remain integrated tenaciously held on to an opposing ideology. These contesting trends also divided other colonial institutions, such as education, politics, urban planning, and economics.

---

15. This anti-missionary sentiment was again expressed more than a hundred years later (1970s), in a call across Africa for a moratorium on European missionaries (Goedhals 1989:122)

16. In Cochrane's revisionist analysis, racism has a political economic basis and is driven by conflicting class interests (Cochrane 1987:43).

17. As industrialisation took off, Anglican and Congregational (Union) churches promoted a Verwoerdian principle of educating blacks for labour (Cochrane 1987: 68).

The Union Norm of Limited Institutional Segregation, 1910-47

During the Union period national and municipal authorities sought to institutionalise limited segregation, a quest that produced the urban formation typified as Segregation City, surrounded by segregated hinterlands. A quarter of South Africa's population of 1,5 million were urbanised by 1911 (Fundneider 1998; 1910/1-50 Krige and Donalson 1999). The establishment of the Union of South Africa (1910) had integrated the four colonies into one political unit, but offered no further advancements to blacks, coloureds, or Indians. Segregation City mirrored the gradual introduction of policies to achieve spatial segregation of race groups.

The first steps towards establishing segregation as a co-ordinated systematic policy was taken by the Lagden Commission (1903-05) in the Transvaal. The Commission's recommendations on segregated land ownership, locations, and influx control was applied by successive Union governments. Under Prime Minister Louis Botha's government (1910-19) the recommendations were implemented in the Mines and Works Act (1911) and the Natives Land Act (1913). The Natives Urban Areas Act (1923) introduced under Prime Minister Jan Smuts's government (1919-24) also utilised the recommendations (Tankard 2004). These Acts directly shaped the urban areas of the Union period, although the Land Act, for example, still awaited implementation by 1918 (Dubow 1989:39). Smuts was still influenced by a liberalism in continuity with the colonial period which allowed for the absorption of 'civilised' blacks into the social and political structures.

The Stallard Commission recommended in 1922 that urban areas remain an exclusive white domain, to which people of colour should be admitted only as temporary workers. Granting them permanent urban residence would imply extending equal rights (Mbeki n.d.). Government allowed individual local governments the discretion to implement relevant national policies such as the Natives Urban Areas Act (1923), which guided municipalities in providing housing for black workers. Johannesburg declared itself a white area in 1924, and the City Council constructed separate black locations after 1927. In 1935 Port Elizabeth followed Johannesburg's example (South African History Online n.d. a.).

Accordingly, Segregation City emerged between 1923-1948, exhibiting limited racial integration of core city areas and some outlying suburbs. City authorities continued to remove black residents to the periphery under the Natives Urban Areas Act. Measures to control black influx into urban areas were increasingly tightened (Krige and Donalson 1999). Amendments to amending existing legislation such as the Urban Areas Act (1930) confined the movement of blacks and others even more.

J. Barry M. Hertzog's government (1924-39) instituted a more repressive segregationist regime, illustrated by the Native Laws Amendment Act (1937). The Act automatically reserved all urban areas for white usage (South African History Online n.d. c). Such legislation eroded what little social and political rights blacks and others may have obtained during the colonial period. The Land Acts (1913, 1936) furthered the creation of black reserves while appropriating most land for white use. Urban Areas Acts (No. 21 of 1923, No. 25 of 1945)[18] introduced influx control for black males under the responsibility of local authorities, who could remove blacks from a particular area. The Acts segregated urban areas, and restricted the rights of ownership of black urban residents (Carruthers 2000). By 1936, blacks generally could not buy property from whites.

Although the integrationist sentiment was subordinated in churches by the early 20th century, it was not eradicated but resurfaced on special occasions as a theme. Methodist minister Seth Mokitimi,[19] for instance, urged churches to promote racial integration in his 1942 address to the Christian Council of South Africa[20] (Gish 1985:13).

The practice of integration that had been established during the colonial period continued in modified form in certain congregations for some time, as did the custom of mixed services on special occasions. Some congregations retained a blend of white and coloured parishion-

---

18. The Urban Areas Acts were partially repealed by the Abolition of Influx Control (No. 68 of 1986), and in full by the Abolition of Restrictions on Free Political Activity Acts (No. 206 of 1993). The Land Acts and Group Areas Acts were repealed in 1991, along with 189 sections and acts supporting racial discrimination in land legislation for rural areas (South African History Online n.d. c).

19. In 1937 Mokitimi was the housemaster of a young Nelson Mandela at the Methodist Church's Healdtown Institution.

20. The Christian Council functioned from 1936 to 1968, when it was replaced by the South African Council of Churches (RICSA 1998).

ers until the late 1940s, such as Saint Mary's Catholic cathedral in Cape Town (formally, the Cathedral Church of Our Lady of the Flight into Egypt). Saint Mary's could do so due mainly to the mixed nature of neighbourhoods around the cathedral. The different 'races' that attended Saint Mary's sat in separate places by choice, an unconscious pattern that mirrored the old master-slave divisions. There was little conscious social mixing outside Masses, and coloured members were not represented in lay leadership (Nolan 1993). Similar seating arrangements existed in Catholic parishes elsewhere, such as at Saint Mary's Cathedral (founded 1886) at Kimberley. When that building was opened in 1951, a coloured and Indian parish was joined to the white one, but the 'races' sat separately.

Outside of the churches, vestiges of integrationism was evident in the formation of racially-mixed industrial unions between 1928 and 1946. Registered and unregistered unions participated in joint strike actions during the same period. Black and white workers still worked together on the shop floor in the textile and sweet industries, for example. The Industrial Conciliation Act (1924) prevented black pass-carrying male workers from representation in industrial councils. Consequently, registered trade unions could only include whites, coloureds, and Indians. Unions in the garment, leather, furniture, and canvas industries began to admit Indian and coloured members in the late 1920s. The Garment Workers Union admitted black men in 1926, but split into a white and a black section later. In 1928 black women in a Johannesburg laundry went on strike in solidarity with a victimised white woman. In 1930 the multi-racial South African Trades and Labour Council formed, which called for non-racial unions. Co-operation and solidarity between the registered and unregistered unions continued after the depression. The Transvaal Textile Workers' Union resolved in 1935 to create one non-racial union for all textile workers (South African History Online n.d. k). Similarly, non-racialism was entrenched in the Federation of South African Women (1954) (Lazerson 1994:151-2). Between the 1950s and 1970s the South African Congress of Trade Unions and the Federation of South African Trade Unions respectively continued the non-racialist tradition (Lazerson 1994:247).

The discussion so far points to the changing contents of what was understood by non-racialism in different historical contexts. In the 1950s, non-racialism emerged more organically from debates in black circles as how best to organise against segregation. By the 1970s, it had achieved a life of its own as a principle for establishing a future society. White political activists began to see their participation in grassroots organising in the townships as a symbolic assertion of non-racialism (Lazerson 1994:250,251,259).

Despite continued forced removals, then, some congregations could continue well in to the 1960s to draw in people of colour from the surrounding neighbourhoods. Saint James, a congregation of the Church of England in Kenilworth, Cape Town, represents one such example. Saint James' opened its doors on 22 October 1968 — ironically, "in broken-down buildings that once belonged to the Africa Evangelistic Band." That section of Kenilworth had been subject to Group Areas removals, but "pockets of the original inhabitants still remained." Consequently the congregation was attended by people of colour from the start to the present (Retief 2005).

Yet across many denominations those who were not white faced considerable resistance to being appointed as clergy, which mostly precluded them from entering higher office (compare Goedhals 1989:108; Maluleke 1994:94; Balla 1994:163).[21] For example, while the Swiss Mission (today, the Evangelical Presbyterian Church) was founded in 1875, the first black to be ordained as minister was Jonas Maphophe in 1910 (Maluleke 1994:94). By 1941 black Church of the Province clergy were still not represented at diocesan chapter, provincial or diocesan synods (Goedhals 1989:117). And white Anglican ministers in 1943 resisted the election of James Calata as bishop of Saint John's diocese (Goedhals 1989:116,117). Mary Magdalen Monyane, first black woman in an Anglican order, was "sent to a white community for three months only" during the same year (Denis 1995). Only in 1963 was Seth Mokitimi appointed as the first black head of a major denomination, the Methodist Church (Gish 1985:74). In the whole history of the Methodist Church of Southern Africa since 1806, only seven black presidents had been appointed by 1988. The ratio at Methodist conferences by 1978 was 70 whites to 41 blacks (Gish 1985:4,69).

When blacks were admitted to the ministry, they were trained in segregated seminaries and appointed only to black parishes. Black

---

21. The initiative of black evangelists (such as Josefa Mhalamhala, who took the gospel to Mozambique in 1882) deserve recognition. From 1873 to 1875 their solo work lay the foundation for Swiss missionary work in South Africa (Maluleke 1994:94).

Christian resistance to increased segregationism in the churches fuelled black independent breakaway movements and internal criticism from black clergy from the late 19th century on. Lay criticism of a colour bar in the Church of the Province of Southern Africa emerged at the 1923 Provincial Missionary Conference, for example (Goedhals 1989:116). Until the late 1970s black clergy were often paid less than their white colleagues (Hinchliff 1968:207;[22] Cochrane 1987:186; Villa-Vicencio 1988:36). In the Methodist Church of Southern Africa black ministers received a lower stipend until 1976 (Gish 1985:69).

In the Roman Catholic Church the massive influx of blacks into the previously white denomination as a result of mission work[23] neither changed the leadership's make-up nor the character of the institution (Villa-Vicencio 1988:36). Black Catholic candidate priests were trained at Saint Mary's Major Seminary established at Ixopo, in present-day KwaZulu-Natal in 1929. The seminary was later renamed Saint Peter's in 1981 and moved to Hammanskraal in present-day Gauteng, to function as an integrated training facility for priests (Denis 1995).

A fully-fledged racist ideology had emerged and was applied in various legalised forms before the National(ist) Party came to power in 1948, entangling colonial and post-colonial churches.[24] 'Apartheid' may first have been used in the 1929 Dutch Reformed Church Synod to describe the principle of racial separation in mission work (Oosthuizen 1990:105). In the pre-apartheid period until 1930, segregation in Anglophone churches enforced and duplicated the division of labour into racial categories (Cochrane 1987). Both English and Afrikaner ruling classes committed themselves to the supremacy of whites in the political economy (Villa-Vicencio 1988:46). In effect, the Anglican church before 1911 was "almost a state church" in South Africa, as in Britain (Cochrane 1987:154). Bishop Gray, for example, was appointed by the Colonial Office in 1847 (Retief 1999). The reactions of these churches to the social upheaval of the 1920s remained the position of the ruling class, and of the mine owners and mining capital (Cochrane 1987:132).

---

22. The exception was always the diocese of Cape Town, which paid "all its clergy at the same rate" (Hinchliff 1968:207).

23. Catholic mission started after industrialisation, which drove blacks of the land to the mines. In the Transvaal, these happened after 1890 (Villa-Vicencio 1988:36; Brain 1991:70-71).

24. For an insightful picture of the theology of the white colonial church, see Maimela 1988:324-327.

The Apartheid Norm of Complete Segregation, 1948-89

When nationalist white Afrikaners ascended to power in 1948 under D. F. Malan, they declared South Africa to be an independent Republic. The Apartheid period saw the institutionalisation of complete social, residential, and labour segregation (Prinsloo 1999) as norm that would produce Apartheid City between 1949-1960. Racially exclusive institutions crystallized, political power for coloureds diminished,[25] cities were residentially segregated,[26] contact between whites and blacks were severely curtailed, and individual prejudice against blacks were common among whites.

Black urban residents had trebled between 1921 and 1936 (South African History Online n.d. a.). Urbanisation accelerated further during the Second World War, so that about 42% of the population lived in urban areas by 1951.

Malan's government enforced racial social segregation by promulgating legislation, including the Population Registration Act (1950, scrapped 1991) that defined the race groups to which the whole population was then consigned. In what amounted to a caste system, blacks occupied the lowest rungs in the hierarchy of access to social, political, and economic resources. The Industrial Conciliation Amendment Act (1956) reserved certain categories of jobs for whites, supporting education legislation such as the Bantu Education Act (1953) that prepared blacks for 'appropriate" manual labour occupations. The state withdrew its subsidies for church schools, effectively closing most black schools.

Separate ethnic educational institutions excluded blacks from white universities, for example, with very few exceptions. The Group Areas Act (1950, scrapped 1991) allocated separate urban spaces to different races. Other legislation severely curtailed or completely prohibited types of social interaction between designated race groups. The Prohibition of Mixed Marriages Act (1949, repealed 1986), for instance, forbade intermarriage between race groups. Sexual intercourse between

---

25. Parliamentary disenfranchisement of coloureds occurred in 1951, provincial in 1961, and municipal in 1971 (Pinnock 1987:162).

26. By 1970 "at least 208 new towns for coloureds and 76 for Asians had been proclaimed," most designed to "enclose people in hostile environments" with few access roads which could be sealed off (Pinnock 1989:159).

individuals from different races was criminalised and policed. The Bantu Authorities Act (1951) extended the provisions for separate administrative structures for blacks introduced in the Native Affairs (1920) and Native Administration Acts (1927). The pace of black urbanisation coupled with influx control measures contributed to the creation of various squatter settlements.

The government's removal of municipalities' discretionary authority to implement racist legislation as they saw fit accelerated the emergence of Apartheid City. In apartheid theory, cities and towns were now the exclusive residential domain of whites. Apartheid City was an urban mirror of the complete segregation envisaged by national policies, and endured beyond 1990 (Fundneider 1998:36; Krige and Donalson 1999). The implementation of the Group Areas Act saw coloureds and Indians relocated from mixed urban areas to newly created racially homogeneous peripheral suburbs, and blacks to adjacent so-called 'locations.' Each white town or city had its own accompanying satellite ghetto some distance away. Industrial buffer zones usually separated black locations—intended as dormitories for male labourers—from white areas. Locations lacked infrastructure—apart from rudimentary train and bus depots to transport workers to the white city—as it did formal commercial activity. Separate local authorities administered white city and black location.

Variants of Apartheid City appeared later in the form of Homeland City (post-1960) and Apartheid-City-in-Transition (post-1985). By 1960 prime minister Hendrik Verwoerd's apartheid government had created black ethnic cities (such as Botshabelo) in the so-called homelands—black labour reserves in rural areas, part of South Africa's unequal racial subdivision. Apartheid-City-in-Transition emerged as the final variant between 1985 and 1987 (Krige and Donalson 1999). Rapid urbanisation, accompanied by the gradual informal and limited formal integration of formerly homogeneously white core city areas, forced P. W. Botha to abandon the Urban Areas Act—which controlled black influx—in 1986.

As status differentiation became legally fixed along racial lines in the twentieth century, the churches followed suit, as Cochrane (1987) demonstrated. In 1951 the Catholic priest Francis Schimlek could write that "the [Roman Catholic] Church does not preach absolute equality between white and black" but only equality "in the highest order of things;" by which he understood joint access to communion (Schimlek

1951:159). The ideal of integrated churches would not reappear until the 1950s; it would take to the end of the decade before it would be recast in concrete form.

By 1964 most denominations admitted that "people of different races do not normally worship together in the same church" (Cawood 1964: 58,61,52,76,92). This was as true for the Anglicans as it was for the Methodists, Catholics, and Presbyterians. With some exceptions, segregated congregations, enforced by a segregationist ideology, would become the prevalent organisational option for most denominations well into the 1980s.

So once again non-racial ideals expressed by denominational leadership failed to affect the composition of either decision-making bodies or local congregations. Black Anglicans had to wait until 1960 for the first black bishop (Alpheus Zulu, appointed as assistant (suffragen[27]) bishop to Zululand), and until 1986 for the first black archbishop, Desmond Tutu (Goedhals 1989:120,124; Cawood 1964:16,56; Hinchliff 1968:240). Although the Presbyterian movement started in 1824, a black presbyter of South Africa's seven regional presbyteries was not elected until 1952, in Port Elizabeth (Cawood 1964:89,91). By 1964 the predominantly black Evangelical Lutheran Church in Southern Africa-South East Region still had a white bishop as sole leader (Cawood 1964:87). On the positive side, the Church of the Province had since 1964 "a number of African archdeacons [official with oversight over clergy and laity of groups of parishes] whose archdeaconries include white priests and lay people, for example Pretoria" (Cawood 1964:58).

The Catholic Church paradoxically pursued an open denomination with parishes that catered for specific ethnic groups. Until fairly recently, black Catholic priests were appointed only to black parishes, and found advancement in the hierarchy difficult. The Catholic hierarchy contained those that opposed and those that supported apartheid. Catholics in general harboured a lingering fear of ruffling government feathers, stemming from past state antagonism to their denomination. Catholic leaders took longer than other denominations to publicly condemn apartheid.

In 1970 five black priests protested that despite their ordination, " 'we have been treated like glorified altar-boys' ". Included in their number

---

27. Unlike diocesan bishops, suffragen bishops cannot be members of the Synod of Bishops, nor vote in it (Cawood 1964:56).

was Smangaliso Mkhatshwa, later (1980) appointed as secretary of the Southern African Catholic Bishops' Conference (Denis 1995). Bonaventure Dlamini was appointed to Umzimkulu in 1954 as the first black South African Catholic bishop, but without much support, he eventually resigned in 1967 (Denis 1995). When white priests were later appointed to black parishes, they often served as the voice of conscience in times of state-controlled violence. The South African Catholic Bishops Conference—a voluntary and consultative body of bishops, vicars and others, established in 1947—played a similar role. The Bishops Conference in 1957 "became the first church body to theologically reject apartheid" (Villa-Vicencio 1988:36; compare Oosthuizen 1990:109). In 1991 about 8% of all Christians claimed to be Catholic.

When leadership opened to blacks at a higher level in the Roman Catholic Church, Church of the Province of Southern Africa and the Methodist Church of Southern Africa, the same did not happen in local congregations. The frequently expressed ideal of racially-mixed congregations was not realized. White congregations found they could ignore the more radical statements by black church leaders, who in turn found themselves restrained by the dependence of churches on white funding (Villa-Vicencio 1988:152; Maimela 1988:325). The far more conservative stance of laity as opposed to clergy had long been a feature of white congregations in mixed denominations (compare Hinchliff 1968:240).

Racially-mixed churches, rare before 1948, became even more so after the National Party gained power and gradually eliminated the mixed neighbourhoods that supplied a racial mix of congregants. Legislation was passed which forbade whites to enter black areas unless they had obtained a permit, and controlled black entrance to white areas through passes. The link between racially-mixed churches and their mixed neighbourhood (especially in the Cape) was noted in 1964 (Cawood 1964:10,59), and illustrated by Saint Mary's Catholic cathedral in Cape Town. Some mixed neighbourhoods persisted with their congregations until the late 1970s. An exceptional few outlasted the declaration of the neighbourhood as officially white, such as Saint Paul's Anglican church, Rondebosch.

Historically various attempts were made to rectify the segregation of local congregations while, ironically, proving the extent of segregation. The most important included:

1. **calls for interracial contact within the churches**, e.g. at the

1948 Non-European Christian Conference on Race Relations. In 1958 the Methodist Conference resolved that it will remain "one and undivided" (Gish 1985:13, Cawood 1964:50). Such calls were translated into action through mixed study groups and pulpit exchanges, e.g. in the Methodist Church of Southern Africa (Gish 1985:27). But this seemed not to bear fruit at local level, with the Methodist president of conference admitting in the 1970s that most congregations were mono-racial (Gish 1985:71)[28];

2. **calls for interracial co-operation outside the churches**, reiterated by a 1949 conference on living in a multi-racial country held by the Christian Council of South Africa in Rosettenville, Johannesburg (Gish 1985:16). Similar conferences followed sporadically—for instance, in October 1956 and in December 1957, hosted respectively by the Interdenominational African Ministers' Conference and the Anglican church. South African clergy also attended racially-mixed conferences outside South Africa, such as that held by Moral Rearmament in 1953 in Lusaka. Later, this practice of meetings outside of South Africa was extended to contact with banned liberation movements. In 1968, for example, the African National Congress met with Catholics in April, and with Lutherans in November;

3. **calls for mixed congregations**, e.g. Canon John Collins of Saint Paul's Cathedral (Church of England, London) who in 1953 implored Church of the Province of Southern Africa bishops to appoint "'at least one church in each diocese where no colour bar of any sort whatsoever operates'" (Clark 1989:150).[29] At the World Council of Churches second assembly in 1954, member churches were asked to remove segregation in congregations (Cawood 1964:123). The 1960 Methodist Church of Southern Africa Conference accepted an

---

28. There is a long tradition of conferences on religion and race relations; John Dube, for example, in 1926 participated in the International Conference of Christian Missions in Belgium, which dealt with this topic (Akinwumi 2002).

29. Collins was responding in a sermon to Trevor Huddleston's request to publicly oppose government policies (Clarke 1989:150). Collins founded the International Defence and Aid Fund for Southern Africa (1956), which covered legal costs of anti-apartheid activists and supported the families of detainees.

education programme that recommended "the possibility of establishing in one of our city circuits a racially inclusive church as a pilot scheme." By implication, one did not exist at that time (Cawood 1964:51). And a 1962 Methodist pamphlet encouraged 'multi-racial' worship (Gish 1985:72, see 7,13,24,71). A document entitled "Towards Inclusive Congregations" was submitted in 1970 by Reverend Peter Storey to the Methodist Renewal Commission, based on his successful attempts to integrate Buitenkant Street Methodist Church in District Six, Cape Town, as I describe more fully below. Storey outlined a three-year plan to convert an inner city congregation to one that is 'racially-inclusive.' In 1981 the Methodist Church of Southern Africa's 'Obedience '81' conference, a grassroots meeting of 800 Methodists, resolved to demonstrate racial unity at local congregational level (Gish 1985:47-8);

4. **calls for the internal unification of denominations**, such as that issued by Methodist president Stanley Mogoba at his induction in October 1988 for the creation of a non-racial church (South African Institute of Race Relations 1988/89:726). The Presbyterian Church of Southern Africa's Church and Nation Commission called on members "to work and pray for a non-racial church that will faithfully reflect Christ's unity for His church" (South African Institute 1988/89:728). In response the Methodists formed geographic rather than racially based circuits, while black Anglicans did eventually achieve improved representation at provincial and diocesan levels (Balia 1994:164; Charton 1994:155).

The Methodist Church of Southern Africa in 1972 and the Catholic Church initiated internal racism investigations, as did the Church of the Province in 1973 (Gish 1985:76; Prior 1982; Charton 1994:154). Whether such measures changed anything is doubtful; by 1976 Methodist president Abel Hendrickse wrote a letter to be read in all churches urging examination of internal racist trends (Gish 1985:41). The Church of the Province admitted racial polarisation existed in its own ranks by the late 1980s (South African Institute 1988/89:725).

The early forms of a Black theology anticipated by Nehemiah Tile crystallised as the religious counterweight to the Black Consciousness movement that emerged by 1968 (Cochrane 1987:220; Balia 1994:163;

Mukuka 1997). Black Consciousness proposed that blacks free themselves from the psychological effects of subjugation by creating their own institutions. Black theology analysed the experience of oppression by reflection on scripture passages relating to liberation.

Influenced by Black Consciousness, black pressure groups formed to demand internal change in churches, such as the Black Methodist Consultation in 1976, which hosted seminars on topics such as the Africanisation of the Church (1980) under Stanley Magoba (Gish 1985:80; Balia 1994:163; Denis 1995; Mukuka 1997). The Consultation wished to reduce the dominance of white leadership in the denomination, as whites chaired ten of the twelve Methodist districts at the time (Theilen 2003). Black Catholic priests formed the Permanent Black Priests' Solidarity Group in 1971, which replaced the Saint Peter's [Seminary] Old Boy's Association (founded 1966, Denis 1995; Mukuka 1997 gives 1976). The numerically small Solidarity Group also included black Anglican priests, and participants regarded themselves as the theological vanguard of Black Consciousness. In 1977 the lecturers and rector of Saint Peter's Catholic Seminary marched on police headquarters at John Vorster Square, Johannesburg. They were protesting against the banning of Consciousness organisations (Mukuka 1997). The Solidarity Group became part of Ministers United for Christian Co-Responsibility during the 1980s (in which *Johweto* leadership would participate). In similar challenging vein, black participants in a 1980 South African Council of Churches conference on racism presented white Christians with an ultimatum to take concrete actions "to demonstrate their willingness to purge the church of racism" (Villa-Vicencio 1988:150).

By 1994 several attempts to unite the racially divided 'missionary' branches of Christian churches had been completed, with varied measures of success. The predominantly coloured Dutch Reformed Mission Church (established in 1881) and the black Dutch Reformed Church in Africa (established in 1859) combined in 1994 to form the Uniting Reformed Church. By 2011 the white Dutch Reformed Church still had not joined. Such measures also exemplify attempts to shape the social base which has determined the form and content of the churches as social institutions in the first place, and so demonstrate the dialectic relationship of religion to society (compare Villa-Vicencio 1988:128).

But despite the attempts at denominational unification, the composition of lower level organisational structures were hardly affected, including congregations (Charton 1994:155). Until the 1970s, regional structures of denominations mirrored the legalised division of white vs. other race groups, and that of the Afrikaans or English vs. other ethnic groups (Gish 1985:7). Denominations were segregated by race, or were united but inwardly divided along racial lines. Internal segregation could take quite complex patterns, as the Methodist Church of Southern Africa illustrates. So the Methodist Church's annual synods (that deliberate regional policy) became 'multi-racial' only in 1973. Yet in the Cape District, Methodist synods had always been integrated. "In other Districts, the Ministerial Session (when ministers only met) had been integrated for many years before 1972, and only the Representative Session (when lay delegates joined in) was the segregated part of the Synod" (Storey 2005 b).

A 1977 study[30] found that 94% of Christians polled felt that the church practiced racism ('racialism'). Polarisation was most evident between those who had never experienced joint bi-racial (black/white) worship (Lutheran World Federation 1977a:456).

By the 1960s integrationism had acquired a new imperative in the form of non-racialism—the desire to eradicate race as means of social classification. Outside South Africa non-racialism transformed the liberation movements from racially exclusive organisations in which whites could either not be formally admitted or could not be elected to executive positions. Inside South Africa non-racialism was the hidden hand in the churches that strengthened calls to racial integration and contributed to deliberately racially-mixed congregations emerging. According to Nelson Mandela, non-racialism became an A.N.C. 'principle' in the 1950s, second only to representing the political aspirations of black Africans. Certainly, the preamble to the Freedom Charter stated that "South Africa belongs to all who live in it, black and white" (Rosenberg 1996). On the other hand, non-racialism did not prevent segregated political organisation, deemed necessary as a defensive and in line with historical experiences (Lazerson 1994:215[31]). Most

---

30. The study was conducted by the Ecumenical Research Unit under Trevor Verryn, on behalf of the S.A.C.C. (Lutheran World Federation 1977b:455). The Research Unit was probably the first church research organisation in South Africa.

31. The African National Congress's National Executive Committee in 1959 stated that the primary purpose of the Congress was *not* to build a non-racial society. The context was the debate on forming one Congress instead of the four racially based organisations that comprised the Congress Alliance.

commentators argue that non-racialism as principle arose in South African communist circles around 1928 during the debate about whether to implement a black republic in South Africa. Julie Frederikse (1990:8) points to the origin of non-racialism in the International Socialist League, "the first political group to attempt to organise non-racially." After the League broke away from the white Labour Party in 1915, it promoted "full rights for all," accepting "all South Africans without distinction of colour or class." By contrast, Robin Petersen (2000) argues for the "sustained use and genesis" of non-racialism as concept in the Non-European Unity Movement. The Movement coined the slogan "non-racialism, not multi-racialism" in the 1950s to oppose the multi-racialism of the African National Congress and the nationalism of Africanists (Petersen 2000). The eventual pervasiveness of non-racialism as organising principle is illustrated by a Pan Africanist Congress broadcast from Dar es Salaam in 1990 that copied the Non-European Unity Movement's slogan (Briston 1998).

During the dark years of apartheid, deliberately integrated local congregations emerged in defiance of the political system.

The idea of deliberately initiated integrated congregations did not formally surface inside South Africa until 1958 when Reverend R.J.D. (Rob) Robertson suggested to the General Assembly of the Presbyterian Church of Southern Africa that a racially-mixed congregation be established in every major South African city (*Dispatch Online* 1997). The Assembly "registered not the slightest interest" (Robertson 1997:4). In 1961 Robertson requested that the General Assembly allow him to carry out such a project, for which he would reside in the racially-mixed North End area of East London (founded 1847) in the Eastern Cape. At the time, the Presbyterians had launched a programme to promote more white-black contact between congregations (Regehr 1979:162). Accordingly, the 1961 Assembly gave Robertson the go-ahead.

The founding meeting of Robertson's racially-mixed North End Presbyterian Church took place in 1962 (Robertson 1994:2; Regehr 1979:162). North End's racially-mixed congregation met near the border of lower income white and coloured areas, and also drew blacks from a nearby township (Storey 1994). Some 42 people attended the services, with roughly equal representation from blacks, whites and coloureds. The session (church governing body, elected for life) comprised two black, one coloured and three white elders (Robertson 1963:9; Cawood 1964:95). The congregation disbanded in 1970, with two mixed groups being absorbed into all-white congregations—which in turn became and remained mixed as late as 1981 (Hope and Young 1981:124; Robertson 1994:2). Marjorie Hope and James Young suggest North End dissolved because it had been "only a pilot project" and that the members had "no wish to form another church."

Meanwhile other similar projects had emerged. Saint Peter's-by-the-Lake Lutheran Church, Johannesburg, was deliberately constituted in 1961 by whites, a black couple, and an Asian couple with their three children as founding members. Saint Peter's was affiliated with the German-background white Evangelical Lutheran Church in South Africa-Transvaal in 1964, as the Lutheran denominations then were "organised along ethnic lines". The members became dissatisfied with this arrangement as they felt that the denomination's persistent use of German isolated churches from English-speakers and from the African context (Lutheran World Federation 1977a:458, 459,461; 1977b:455, 457-8).

Robertson's example stimulated a similar attempt at Buitenkant Street Methodist Church, a coloured congregation[32] of 400. The church's building was situated in District Six,[33] a predominantly coloured suburb of Cape Town. The minister at Buitenkant Street between 1966 and 1972, Reverend Peter Storey, had corresponded with Robertson about the idea of a mixed church. In August 1968, Robertson gave Storey his 1961 and 1968 memos to the Presbyterian Church of Southern Africa's General Assembly. By 1966, the Group Areas removals of coloured people that would transform District Six into a white residential area had just begun. Meanwhile Buitenkant Street's youth had met with their white counterparts at Seapoint Methodist Church, an encounter that left them feeling inferior. A group formed to explore the empowerment of the gospel, which led to the design with Storey of a course called "My brother and me." Advertising drew white Methodist participants from other churches. The course ultimately became a conduit through which some 60 whites joined the Buitenkant Street Methodist (Storey 1994). Storey also initiated other projects which included all races, such as The Carpenter's House, a community centre (Boston University 1999).

---

32. The congregation has since amalgamated with the Metropolitan congregation.

33. The Sixth Municipal District of Cape Town was declared in 1867, with residents comprising "a mixed community of freed slaves, merchants, artisans, labourers and immigrants," according to District Six Museum's website (www.districtsix.co.za).

Robertson later integrated Saint Antony's United Congregational and Presbyterian Church. Saint Antony's was founded in 1975 in a former Anglican church building in the mixed Johannesburg suburb of Pageview (Hope and Young 1981:124). A Presbyterian minister, Ian Thompson, had started a ministry to mainly homeless people in an empty Anglican building in Pageview. A support/advisory committee was formed which included Storey. This committee later invited Robertson when Thompson left. An average of 40 congregants attended Saint Antony's, and worshipped using a 15-page roneo'd songbook comprising different ethnic languages. Members met during the week in one another's houses in Johannesburg suburbs like Vrededorp, or even in Soweto (*Pro Veritate* 1976:14). This was perhaps "the first hymnbook with mixed languages," according to Storey. Saint Antony's eventually merged with Saint George's Presbyterian Church in the Johannesburg inner city suburb of Joubert Park.

Early deliberately mixed congregations of the 1960s depended on proximity to mixed urban neighbourhoods that had almost completely disappeared by 1976, adding impetus to the emergence of a context-independent type of deliberately mixed congregation around 1985. For example, when the Central Methodist Mission in Johannesburg started integrating after 1976, the immediate neighbourhood was still predominantly white. Chapter Two relates how blacks who travelled to Johannesburg initially integrated Central Methodist Mission. But by the late 1980s informal disregard of the Group Areas had signalled the gradual integration of Johannesburg's inner city areas, from which most whites eventually fled to the suburbs. White congregants who travelled from white suburbs to Central's building, now set in a predominantly black residential and commercial area, had fully reversed the process by 1994.

As the term indicates, context-independent congregations integrated through the efforts of coloured, black or Indian congregants who travelled to meetings in white areas. Historically, congregants who continued to worship in church buildings now located in the designated white zones from which they had been evicted during apartheid set the precedent. Saint Mary's Anglican cathedral (formally, Cathedral of Saint Mary the Virgin) in central Johannesburg integrated in 1957, nine years after the formal inception of apartheid as regime. Such practices ensured that by 1964 Catholic and Anglican cathedrals were racially-mixed islands adrift in a sea of apartheid segregation;[34] for instance, Cathedral of the Sacred Heart in Pretoria and Saint Mary's Catholic cathedral in Kimberley (Cawood 1964:10; Brain 1991:157). Cape Town's Central Methodist Mission integrated through amalgamation with Buitenkant Street Methodist Church, not through drawing members from the immediate area. The minister of the Cape Town church, David Newby, had been on Peter Storey's Johannesburg staff in 1986. The Cape Town case is remarkable in that the coloured Methodists of the Buitenkant Street church offered to amalgamate with the white congregation at Central, then known as Metropolitan. The amalgamation probably saved the white congregation from closure, as it was losing members who had moved to the suburbs.

Despite the apparent complete triumph of apartheid, a number of secular and Christian precedents existed for black-white interaction, integrated organisations, and interracial events. Anglican priest Trevor Huddleston lived in the freehold area of Sophiatown for six years from 1943. Reverend Nico Smith in 1981 reputedly became the "first white person to obtain official permission to live in a black area."[35] Smith left the Dutch Reformed Church and resigned as theology professor from the University of Stellenbosch to serve a black church in Mamelodi, 10 miles outside Pretoria (*Carte Blanche* 2000). Smith founded an organisation to foster interracial contact called Koinonia (-1994). Koinonia's programmes drew small groups of people together in one another's homes for meals, for dialogue and interaction over a set period. In 1988 Koinonia organised the Christian Encounter in Mamelodi, a four-day event that drew 215 people to live in the homes of people on the other side of apartheid's barriers. Among the participants was Alexander

---

34. The Rhenish and the Anglican churches, located on Stellenbosch's town square, represent two notable examples at a smaller scale.

35. This claim by *Time* magazine is doubtful, depending on whether the stress is on Smith's primacy or legality. Other whites had lived in townships before Smith did. The Reverend Dale White lived in Kliptown, Soweto, between 1972 and 1992, while associate priest at Saint Paul's Anglican Church in Jabavu, Soweto (Truth and Reconciliation Commission 1996). Missionaries had lived in black territory; later, white Catholic priests were assigned to black parishes. White unionists like Betty du Toit worked in black townships during the 1950s; as did white members of the South African Congress of Democrats like Bram Fischer during the 1960s (Lazerson 1994:101, 104). During the 1980s white medical doctor Ivan Thomas served the black informal settlement of Crossroads, near Cape Town.

Venter of the Johweto Vineyard (see Chapter Four). Whites lived for the duration in black homes, and blacks in white homes (Livas n.d.). Koinonia's predecessor was Church Women Concerned, started in the early 1970s by Methodist Shirley Turner in Cape Town. Turner arranged for equal numbers of African, Coloured and white women to spend weekends together to effect reconciliation through political, social, and spiritual solidarity (Gaitskell 1992:381).

African Enterprise is another Christian organisation that set precedents both as a racially-mixed organisation and as organiser of large-scale interracial events such as the South African Congress on Mission and Evangelism in Durban (March 1973), and most notably the South African Leadership Assembly (1979). The post–event processes of the Leadership Assembly drew whites into black townships for dialogue and fellowship meetings. Like other evangelistic para-church organisations in South Africa, African Enterprise conducted integrated outreaches into black areas.

With regards integrated secular organisations, the Liberal Party "was the only legal multi-racial party in South Africa" from 1958 on. The Party was founded by Alan Paton and others in 1953, and Paton was the elected leader between 1955 and 1968. The party dissolved in 1968 with the promulgation of the Prohibition of Improper Political Interference Act (1967), which declared multi-racial parties illegal. The management of *Contact*, the party's magazine, reflected the racial mix of the party as Paton and Jordan Ngubane sat on its initial board of directors (Vigne n.d.; see also 2005). Another multi-racial organisation that emerged in 1955 and initially connected religious affirmation with political orientation was the Black Sash women's organisation. The name derived from their practice of wearing black sashes to signify the passing of the constitution with the removal of black voting rights. By the late 1950s the Sash had left behind its white middle-class origins to combine with the African National Congress Women's League, the Federation of South African Women, and the Mothers' Union of the Anglican church in protest against the introduction of compulsory reference documents for African women (Gaitskell 2002:383).

The transnational anti-apartheid organisations that emerged after the late 1950s were also racially integrated, often including deported or exiled South Africans as participants or founders. The impetus for such organisations included the Sharpeville massacre (1960), calls for boycotts from Albert Lutuli (1961), and the Rivonia treason trial (1963).

Abdul Samad Minty, later Deputy Director General of the South African Ministry of Foreign Affairs, helped to found the Anti-Apartheid Movement in Britain in 1959, for example (Reddy 1999). The goals of the Anti-Apartheid Movement was to turn global sentiment against the South African regime and to support the struggle of the liberation movements by implementing boycotts and sanctions.

By 1986, students had established racially-integrated communes at some campuses, such as the University of Natal in Pietermaritzburg. Political activists increasingly began to organise along integrated lines in the 1980s, whether in exiled political movements such as the A.N.C., or in national student bodies such as the left-leaning National Union of South African Students.

By 1985 a variant on context-independent mixed congregations had emerged, as some whites were now willing to cross into designated black areas from which legislation still barred them until 1989. This reversed the usual situation where blacks and others travelled from townships to integrate church meetings in designated white areas. Chapter Four shows an example of how blacks initially travelled in 1985 from Soweto to Vineyard church meetings in a school hall set in a white Johannesburg suburb. They eventually successfully challenged a small number of whites to travel to Soweto for meetings instead, from which the Johweto Family Vineyard eventually emerged.

The Reformed Confessing Community is another example of an integrated congregation that arose from the unusual willingness of whites to travel into another area. In this case, the whites travelled to church meetings of an (Indian) Reformed Church in Africa congregation in Laudium, a designated Indian area 14 kilometres southwest of Pretoria. In 1987 a small group of about 20 whites and Indians broke away[36] from this congregation along with one of their (white) ministers—the Rever-

---

36. The split was partly due to a 1982 objection by Kritzinger to being paid from funds supplied by the Dutch Reformed Church to the Indian Reformed Church in Africa. Kritzinger, full-time minister at Laudium from 1979-81 and part-time until 1986, suggested that he support himself through part-time work at the University of South Africa. The Indian Reformed Church in Africa synodical commission then revoked his status as minister, which the Laudium congregation refused to accept. A second contributing factor was the leadership style of a later full-time minister, Reverend N. Shunmugam. In 1987 parishioners felt that Shunmugam had objected in an authoritarian manner to "having politics in church." Two other congregations also left the Indian Reformed Church in Africa around this time.

end Klippies Kritzinger, and later called themselves the Reformed Confessing Community. The small congregation first met in a school hall in Laudium, initially using the Indian Reformed Church in Africa's liturgy and structures, but then deciding to create these anew. Instead of accepting the old offices (such as "deacon"), they asked themselves what the essential functions were that needed to be done in a congregation. Action committees were formed around each function, with the leaders forming a 'service council.' They also experimented with different liturgies. But members of the Community always wanted to rejoin the broader Reformed establishment, and so they had not officially constituted as a separate congregation. Members had established good relations with black Reformed churches, and did not want to be cut off from the issues facing black Reformed people. In particular, they wanted to be part of the uniting process between the black Dutch Reformed Church in Africa and the coloured Dutch Reformed Mission Church. The moderators of both these denominations told the Reformed Confessing Community that they had to join a congregation of either denomination if they wanted to be part of the unification process. Reformed Confessing Community members perceived the Melodi Ya Tshwane[37] congregation in central Pretoria as a more favourable option than joining Nico Smith's large black Atteridgeville congregation. The size of the latter led some members to fear that they would lose their unique congregational identity. Some Indian members had already left the Reformed Confessing Community due to the considerable distance between Laudium and Atteridgeville.

Attempts to unite various racial groups in churches did not always meet with success. The Methodist Church of Southern Africa had attempted to unite previously racially segregated local (Circuit) structures since 1976, without total success—despite the initial target date of January 1996. Both the Anglicans (Anglican Church of Southern Africa) and Methodists had tried to integrate white congregations with black ones that had been meeting at different times in the same building. These euphemistically termed "afternoon services" were held primarily for domestic workers in vernacular languages under the authority of a black clergy-person based in a nearby black "township" congregation.

---

37. Melodi Ya Tshwane (the song of Tshwane) was the name given to the pre-colonial Pretoria area by men listening to the birds as they brought their cattle to drink at the Fountains. Evangelist Piet Mabuza had suggested the name for the congregation.

The majority of English-speaking congregations continue to exhibit little or no integration due to the lasting effects of geographic separation. In some cases in Cape Town, less than a kilometre separated such racially segregated congregations from one another. Lack of integration is not limited to English-speakers: Afrikaans-speaking churches like the Dutch Reformed Church remain hesitant to unite with the black and coloured Uniting Reformed Church.

The Post-Apartheid Norm of Institutional Integration, 1990-99

State attempts to institutionalise complete integration marked the post-Apartheid period inaugurated in 1990 and cemented by the first democratic elections in 1994. Parliament scrapped all remaining legislation that prevented social integration and introduced new policies that encouraged it. Legislation was introduced that mandated the racial and gender integration of the labour force and promoted black economic empowerment through shared ownership of companies listed on the stock market. In this changed context, segregation in South African churches slowly yielded to integrative external and internal forces.

By 1994 South African churches could be classified in terms of a fourfold racial matrix that juxtapose racial integration in congregations with the denomination's stance on integration. The matrix allows localised organisational structures (congregations) to be compared to regional organisational structures (denominations). This strategy permits a clearer understanding of how we can apply "integrated" and "segregated." An integrated denomination draws affiliates from all race groups, whether or not all are represented in every congregation. An integrated congregation is attended by individuals who can be said to belong to different racial groups. Segregated denominations could become integrated through amalgamation with another segregated denomination. Denominational leaders could proclaim a new openness to other races. But without altered structures and practices, a denomination can be open to all racial groupings in principle, yet remain segregated. The exclusion of blacks from appointment as clergy, and later from decision-making bodies in denominations that allowed them to affiliate, represent a case in point.

The major categories that can be constructed using the matrix, as demonstrated in Figure 2 (see next page), include (a) segregated congregations of segregated denominations; (b) integrated congregations of segregated denominations; (c) segregated congregations of inte-

Figure 2:
Segregation-Integration by Congregation and Denomination, 1994

Segregated Congregation + Segregated Denomination	*Integrated Congregation + Segregated Denomination*
• African Methodist Episcopal • Afrikaanse Protestantse Kerk • Apostolic Faith Mission of South Africa • Dutch Reformed Church • Evangelical Presbyterian Church • Nederduitsch Hervormde Kerk • Presbyterian Church of Africa • Presbyterian Church of Southern Africa • Seventh-day Adventist Church*	• Dutch Reformed • Seventh-day Adventist Church*
Segregated Congregation + Integrated Denomination	*Integrated Congregation + Integrated Denomination*
• Assemblies of God Church • Church of England in South Africa • Evangelical Lutheran Church of Southern Africa • Gereformeerde Kerke in Suid-Afrika • United Congregational Church of South Africa	• Apostolic Faith Mission of South Africa • Church of the Province of Southern Africa • Dutch Reformed Church • Methodist Church of Southern Africa • Roman Catholic Church • Uniting Reformed Church

* See p.65 for a description of the complex Adventist arrangements.

grated denominations; (d) integrated congregations of integrated denominations—few in number. Each category can be subdivided further.

In a first category belonged **racially-homogeneous churches**, segregated congregations that mirrored segregated denominations.

Denominations that had been racially segregated since their founding comprised one subcategory here. These may have resulted from how different missionary societies worked exclusively among particular ethnic groups, such as the Evangelical Presbyterian Church.[38] But wholly black churches also arose out of secession, in reaction to racist theology and eccl esiology. The African Methodist Episcopal Church, the numerous varieties of African Independent Churches, and the Presbyterian Church of Africa (founded 1898 by Pambani Mzimba) count as examples. Exclusively white denominations had been formed, such as the reactionary Afrikaanse Protestantse Kerk, which broke away from the Dutch Reformed Church in 1986 when the latter opened its membership to all races (South African Institute 1988/89:732).

Article 3 of the Nederduitsch Hervormde Kerk's constitution restricted membership to whites; although it had helped to organise the Hervormde Kerk in Suidelike Afrika as a small "independent" black wing in 1977 (South African Institute 1989/90: 292; Villa-Vicencio 1988:26). While white churches in this subcategory deliberately excluded other races, black churches did not.

Historically divided and racially-defined "missionary" sub-denominations make up a second subcategory. Examples include the Apostolic Faith Mission (founded 1910), the Full Gospel Church of God in South Africa (1951), and the (Indian) Reformed Church (established 1947).

Churches that were officially open to all races, but whose congregations remained racially segregated constitute a third subcategory. An example of a mainly black denomination was the Evangelical Lutheran Church of Southern Africa (1975). The predominantly white Presbyterian Church of Southern Africa and the Dutch Reformed Church[39] fell on the other end of the racial scale.

A second category comprised **segregated congregations of integrated denominations**. One subcategory included *denominations with joint unity at higher polity levels*, such as the Assemblies of God (established 1917). For instance, the Gereformeerde Kerke in Suid-Afrika

---

38. First known as the Swiss Mission in South Africa; then as the Tsonga Presbyterian Church (1962); then by its present name since 1982 (Maluleke 1994:94).

39. The exception that proves the rule is Saint Stephen's D.R.C. congregation, Cape Town, which is coloured (Cawood 1964:23). Kritzinger maintains that all Reformed churches "have members from more than one racial group" (Kritzinger 1994:183).

(established 1859) had one white "national" and two black synods which together met in a General Synod, which in 1988 already consisted of 75% black representatives (South African Institute 1988/89:734). A second subcategory included *congregations of previously segregated denominations that had recently united*. The Uniting Reformed Church (1994) was a typical example, representing an amalgam of the predominantly coloured Dutch Reformed Mission Church (established 1881) and the mainly black Dutch Reformed Church in Africa (formed 1859). A third subcategory consisted of *denominations that were officially "open" to other races, but had attracted few members of other race groups* to their local congregations. The Evangelical Lutheran Church of Southern Africa remained mainly black, just as the Dutch Reformed Church stayed mainly white.

A third major category in the matrix included **integrated congregations of segregated denominations**. Typically, this concerned denominations that had not as yet amalgamated, such as certain white Dutch Reformed congregations in the Goodwood-Parow circuit (now part of Metropolitan Cape Town) attended by coloureds. Breakaway congregations of the (Indian) Reformed Church in Africa, e.g. the former Charisma Reformed congregation in Lenasia could also be included. Neither the Dutch Reformed nor (Indian) Reformed denominations had as yet joined the Uniting Reformed Church. Before the amalgamation between the Dutch Reformed Mission Church and the Dutch Reformed Church in Africa, its parent denomination, the Melodi Ya Tshwane congregation in Pretoria also fell into this category. In the Seventh-day Adventist Church, local congregations were open to all races, but regional conferences and national unions were segregated. The exception was the Transvaal conference, which included coloureds. After 1991 the national unions of the South African Adventist Church began to integrate in response to a call by their denomination's executive committee. In 2002 the committee made the same call to South African conferences, which still had not completed integration (Krause 2002).

A final category was made up of **integrated local congregations of integrated denominations,** of which few examples existed in 1994. A first subcategory here would encompass so-called mainline denominations, such as the Central Methodist Missions in Johannesburg, Durban, and Cape Town. Selected parish churches of the Roman Catholic Church (e.g. Saint Francis Xavier, Christ the King, both in Johannesburg) also qualified for inclusion. So did certain congregations of the

Church of the Province of Southern Africa, and of the United Congregational Church of Southern Africa. A second subcategory comprised congregations of the independent Pentecostal and Charismatic groupings. Rhema Bible Church in Randburg (founded 1979) of the International Federation of Christian Churches served as Pentecostal example, here. Integrated congregations linked with the Associated Christian Ministries[40] represented Charismatic cases, including Johweto Vineyard in Soweto; and Stellenbosch Christian Fellowship in Stellenbosch.

The white flight from inner cities that marked the post-apartheid cities contributed to the rise of context-independent integrated inner city congregations, of which arguably the most remarkable is the numerically small Melodi Ya Tshwane congregation, initially part of the (black) Dutch Reformed Church in Africa. Black women domestic workers in 1992 took the first deliberate steps to establish Melodi Ya Tshwane. Their dream to have a black church in the heart of Pretoria arose from their experience of having to travel by public transport all the way from Pretoria to Mamelodi to attend Nico Smith's Dutch Reformed Church in Africa congregation. The women presented their idea to Smith, and the Melodi congregation was formally established during a service in Kilnerton Methodist Church on January 12, 1992. Smith invited the Reformed Confessing Community to join the women from Mamelodi. By 1993 Melodi was meeting in a church building of the former white Meintjeskop Dutch Reformed Church in Arcadia, Pretoria.[41] Meintjeskop congregation had ceased to exist as a white congregation because of dwindling numbers. Melodi drew leaders from all genders and races, and the various cultures and languages of members were reflected in the songs and style of worship. Services started with informal singing, with the seated members calling out the

---

40. In 1989 Associated Ministries became the Association of Vineyard Churches South Africa.

41. Melodi's ministers included the reverends Frans Mnisi, Louis Thobela, Nico Smith, Klippies Kritzinger and evangelist Piet Mabuza. The ministers and laity served the congregation and its fourteen outlying wards in the Eastern Pretoria area. Each ward elected two members to serve on the church council of 28, and to preach to them. Melodi had two kinds of members: those who come to the Sunday service in the city, and those who went to one of the fourteen ward services at three p.m. on Sunday throughout Pretoria. Such ward services resulted from apartheid laws which forbade blacks to start a church, or own a church property in white areas.

names of favourite songs, which were sung without instrumental accompaniment from a loose-leaf white songbook. The songs were in seSotho and English. Although the liturgy formally remained Reformed, discussions or testimonies in African style sometimes took the place of sermons. Melodi is currently part of the Uniting Reformed Church.

By 1994 some racially homogeneous denominations had initiated dialogue towards integration, signalling the rising wave of integrationism that was increasingly embodied in the policies of the post-apartheid regime. The Baptist Convention (mainly black) and the Baptist Union of South Africa (mainly white and coloured) united in 2001 to form the South African Baptist Alliance. Despite good intentions, amalgamation of previously segregated denominations sometimes took several years. For example, the black, Indian, and coloured branches of the Apostolic Faith Mission had already united by 1990. Although the white branch of the Apostolic Faith Mission had discussed the possibility since 1989, unification only happened in 1996. Similarly, although the black, coloured, and Indian subdenominations of the Full Gospel Church of God had by 1990 decided to merge into one integrated association, the white group only joined in 1997 (South African Institute 1989/90:292). Certain cases of unification remain incomplete. As noted, the predominantly white Dutch Reformed Church has not yet joined the Uniting Reformed Church, despite mooting the possibility since 1994. Such extended processes have as much to do with the time-consuming methods by which denominations make decisions as it has to do with entrenched prejudice, as can be illustrated by the Uniting Reformed Church, which itself took from 1974 to 1986 to emerge.

AN EXPLANATION FOR RACIAL INTEGRATION AND SEGREGATION

All that remains in this chapter is to synthesise an explanation that accounts broadly for various forces that affected integration and segregation in churches. Such an explanation will have to account for differences and similarities across time and space in terms of factors that may have effected such change. We need to keep in mind that congregations embodied agents who themselves contributed to the creation of social actions and beliefs. The increasing dominance of segregationism in South African churches was spurred by the experiences, economic standing and social status of congregants inside and outside their churches. In turn, their lives were directly affected by the views, policies, and practices of secular and ecclesial leaders, with whom they may have agreed or disagreed. During the colonial period, whether congregants resided in the Cape Colony or in Natal, or one of the Boer Republics, would make a difference to their perspectives. If they lived in the Cape Colony, for instance, their views on interracial interaction would differ according to whether they lived at the Eastern Cape frontier or in the Western Cape.

The journals of Bishop Robert Gray provide us with insight into the tensions between denominational leaders, clergy, and congregations that reveal the contestation between integrationism and segregationism. Gray obviously favoured racially-mixed congregations, yet more often than not found segregated congregations on his journeys. His reports showed that the same divisions existed in the Dutch Reformed Church. Yet while Gray commented negatively on segregated white congregations in the Cape Colony, he was in favour of spatial segregation between the "coloured people" of Natal and the white settlers.

2

Resisting the Apartheid City:
Central Methodist Mission, Johannesburg

INTRODUCTION

Since its founding in 1891, Central Methodist Mission's congregation and programs closely reflected demographic shifts in central Johannesburg and political change in South Africa. Close ties with the city constantly surfaced in the congregation's collective consciousness and in its various publications. The 70th anniversary brochure's motto "Your church, as old as the city" (Webb 1951) was echoed in a 1992 pew bulletin: "Serving the church in the city for more than a century." Some initiatives by the congregation actually anticipated later events and structures in the city. The congregation's racial integration after a strategic intervention in 1976 occurred before demographic transformation washed over the inner city nine years later. Similarly, the establishment of the Deaconess Society in 1890 anticipated the establishment of later secular welfare organisations.

But at various times the congregation experienced severe disjunctions between its public identity and the politics of its context. Central was founded as an English congregation that catered to British subjects. Yet the congregation was located in the independent Boer region of the Zuid-Afrikaansche Republiek (Dutch for South African Republic). At the time of the church's founding, the Zuid-Afrikaansche Republiek was poised for a second conflict with Britain, commonly known as the Anglo-Boer War (1899–1902). Tacit support among congregants for British forces was inevitable. Less than a century later, Central's leadership would signal a more blatant opposition towards the apartheid government, by opening church property for meetings banned by the state.

Within the history of the congregation, the successive ministers and buildings emerge as equally important to Central as its ties with the city—and as closely interwoven. The number of ministers who fulfilled roles within South African Methodism and the wider South African ecumene tied Central to faith communities beyond its walls. Symbols that attest to these wider linkages are still scattered throughout the building. At the same time the church building rooted the congregation in a neighbourhood that largely determined its programs. The programs drew the congregation as much into the realities of the apartheid city as it drew residents into a sacred space where those realities could be challenged. Program and neighbourhood were synchronised with the transformation of the inner city from a segregated colonial settlement to an apartheid city. A few white churchgoers managed to sustain the commute from their suburbs that initially allowed the congregation to remain unaffected by this demographic shift. Ultimate change came to Central when the vision of an alternative society, promoted by a visionary clergyman, drew conflict with the forces of apartheid right into its own building.

METHODISM AND RACE IN THE OLD TRANSVAAL

The high plateau across the Vaal River (hence the *Trans*vaal) assumed several political forms under white rule. The Voortrekkers established four Boer republics here in a region bounded by the Vaal River to the south, the Limpopo River to the North, and mountain ranges to the east. The Boers united their small independent states into the Zuid-Afrikaansche Republiek (Z.A.R.) in 1852, with Pretoria as capital (founded 1855). The British annexed the amalgamated Z.A.R. in 1877, but was defeated by a Boer uprising between 1880 and 1881.

The Methodist presence in the region dates to before the formation of the Boer republics, and before the arrival of Methodist missionaries, too (Millard 2003). Local residents of the region who had travelled to the Cape and Natal had encountered Wesleyans there, and had returned to establish Methodist meetings. A Methodist mission station for indigenous people was founded near Maquassie[42] in 1823 by Reverends Samuel Broadbent and T.L. Hodgson (Hall 1961:1) on behalf of the Wesleyan Methodist Missionary Society. Their successors, Reverends James Archbell and John Edwards, in 1833 "led some 12,000 Barolongs, Griquas and Korannas to better grazing lands they had acquired for them" near the present town of Thaba Nchu (founded 1873) in the east-

---

42. Also known as Makwassie (founded 1891), near Wolmaransstad in what today is Northwest Province, southwest along the N12 from Johannesburg.

ern Free State (Hall 1961:1).

David Modibane Mogatla (also known as Magatha or Magatta), a moTswana refugee from the amaZulu conquests of Mzilikazi, was converted at the Wesleyan Methodist mission station at Thaba Nchu. Mogatla was given permission to preach by Methodist missionary William Shaw in about 1852, and eventually returned to Potchefstroom (71 miles southwest of Johannesburg) as an evangelist. Although the magistrate ordered Mogatla to be beaten, and prohibited him from preaching, he carried on in Natal, and in Sekhukuneland in northern Transvaal (present day Limpopo Province) (Millard 1999). Mogatla twice met Commandant Paul Kruger, later president of the Zuid-Afrikaansche Republiek. Kruger wrote a letter permitting him to preach at Potchefstroom. Mogatla returned to Potchefstroom in the 1860s, where his work drew a visit in 1871 from Reverend George Blencowe, Methodist missionary at Harrismith in the Free State (Hall 1961:1). Blencowe had already visited the Transvaal twice before. After Blencowe glowingly reported Mogatla's work to him, Natal chairperson Frederick Mason caused Blencowe, George Weavind, and William Wynne to be sent to Potchefstroom in 1872 to establish "the first European Society."[43] Weavind was sent to Pretoria in 1873, where he was later joined by Reverend James Calvert (Hall 1961:2).

The first Transvaal Methodist Synod,[44] the policy-making organ of a Methodist district, was held in Pretoria in 1882. Reverend Owen Watkins acted as superintendent for the whole Transvaal. The Transvaal region, established in 1880 by the Missionary Society, was treated as a single circuit[45] within a larger district that included Swaziland (Hall 1961:2–3). Weavind "opened up" the mining town of Barberton for Methodist work in 1885–86, preparing the way for Reverend William Meara as the first resident minister there in 1899 (Hall 1961:3). Weavind and Meara would later be appointed as ministers to Central.

---

43. 'Society' in this context is a Methodist term for 'congregation.'

44. Synod is an annual business meeting of a District, attended by ordained (ministers, deaconesses) as well as lay members of the Methodist church (circuit stewards, lay representatives of Quarterly Meetings, lay Connexional Officials, members of District Committees, District Presidents of Women's Auxiliary, Women's Association, and Women's Manyano). Elected lay members of Conference and the general president of the Women's Auxiliary may attend if they reside within the District.

45. A number of congregations (societies) together comprise a circuit, whose affairs are administered by a Quarterly Meeting.

By 1887 the Transvaal Synod meetings were racially segregated, partly due to the length of time it took to examine black lay preachers on probation. The segregation led Mangena Maake Mokone (1851–1931), one of only two ordained black Wesleyan ministers at the time, to initiate the Ethiopian Church in October 1892 in the black residential area of Marabastad, in Pretoria. Some of the reasons Makone identified as necessitating schism would continue to haunt the history of South African Methodism, particularly the unequal stipends paid to black and white ministers. A white minister, Geoff Underwood, preached the dedicatory sermon[46] at the official opening of the Ethiopian church in 1893 (Millard 2003).

The history of Methodism in the old Transvaal region demonstrates the joint efforts of black and white Methodists, but also the internal racial differentiation that would dog South African denominations for most of the 20th century. Despite interracial cooperation, the typical pattern of mission settlements for indigenous peoples and congregations for white settlers demonstrates that racially-integrated congregations apparently were not part of early Methodist experience in the region. As in other denominations, black Africans were not as a rule appointed to denominational leadership positions.

Since apartheid's inception in 1948, the Methodist Church had vocally opposed discrimination and segregationist policies (Dandala 1997). Successive synods echoed this opposition. The 1977 Methodist Conference[47] rejected the establishment of "independent" homelands for black Africans. The Transkei government then banned the Methodist church in 1978, and seized Methodist properties (Dandala 1997).

Public opposition to apartheid was often accompanied by a critical self-examination of Methodism's own compromised position. In particular, racially segregated administrative districts and local congregations received formal attention, as did racially differentiated pay scales for ministers. Regardless, "both black and white congregations were locked into their own separate cultural worlds instead of...informed by one another" (Dandala and Harris 1997). In a submission to the Truth and Reconciliation Commission in 1997 the denomination admitted to a

---

46. Underwood used the same text (Gen. 28:19) as was used at the 1794 opening of the first African Methodist Episcopal Church (a breakaway from Methodism) in Philadelphia (Millard 2003).

47. Conference is the governing body (legislative, executive) of the Methodist Church, as well as the final court of appeal in matters of discipline.

divergence between official opposition to apartheid and informal complicity. In this regard the submission echoed a 1976 declaration that Methodists "had not sufficiently shown the possibility of an alternative to racial discrimination and group selfishness" (Dandala 1997).

Methodist societies (congregations) complied with the racial segregation anticipated by earlier regimes and encoded under apartheid. Methodist services in the white suburbs of Johannesburg, for instance, reflected the class and race distinctions of city and society. While whites attended morning and evening services, their black servants met for vernacular afternoon services in the same building.[48] Coloureds, Indians, and whites met in their own congregations in their racially-delineated suburbs. Similar patterns existed for most other denominations.

The Methodist Church of Southern Africa eventually introduced measures to erase the use of racial terminology in church matters. Anticipating post-apartheid state legislation, quotas were set for equity in gender and racial representation in the decision-making organs of the denomination. Since the mid-1970s the denomination attempted to unite circuits by reordering them geographically rather than racially, as before. Similarly, the class- and racially segregated congregations that used the same building at different times were encouraged to explore organisational and financial co-operation. At Central, such attempts resulted in a united leadership that oversaw separate "sections." The Central Section included the activities and church services of Central's morning and evening congregations. The Fordsburg Section was joined to Central in 1987, comprising four "afternoon societies" (Braamfontein, Ophirton, Crown Mines, Central) attended mostly by black workers[49] (Central Methodist Mission 1991:2,47).

FROM MINING CAMP TO COLONIAL CITY (1886–1909)

Johannesburg and the congregation today known as Central Methodist Mission were linked from the start, as the first Methodist church was built three years after the city was founded in 1886. Johannesburg's ori-

---

48. This arrangement seems very similar to that between Anglican and Dutch Reformed Churches in the mid-19th century, as Bishop Gray's dairies show.

49. Central's working class congregants included migrant labourers, domestic workers, retired mine workers, Soweto families, and nurses (Central Methodist Mission 1991:47).

gins lay in shanty towns that mushroomed across three farms (Braamfontein, Doornfontein and Turffontein) after the discovery of gold along the 30-mile long Witwatersrand (Afrikaans, "white water reef"). Small-scale diggers rushed to set up camp, first Ferreira's Town on the farm Turffontein, then the adjacent Marshall's Town. Various farms were proclaimed open diggings by the government of the Z.A.R. in September 1886, including Langlaagte and Wilgespruit[50] (City of Johannesburg. n.d. b). The Z.A.R. government then laid out a triangular village at Randjeslaagte between the three farms. The boundaries were formed by Marshall's Town in the south, End Street to the east, and West Street to the west, with Clarendon Place at its apex to the north (Manoim 2003).

Methodists were among the residents of Johannesburg's early shanties. Their meetings in each other's homes constituted "probably the first religious meetings to be held in Johannesburg" (Clegg 1936:1). A Society was formed in January 1886 under Weavind, who travelled from Pretoria to the north, a fifty mile journey that took two-days by ox-wagon.

Methodist laymen "Father" John Dednam and A. John Thornhill Cook[51] started holding regular services at Ferreirastown in 1886 in "a workshop belonging to Mr. E. O. Leake" (Clegg 1936:1; Hall 1961:3; Central Methodist Mission 1991:1). From an initial 300 souls, Ferreiratown's population mushroomed to 6,000 (Manoim 2003). The "earliest records of the Methodist Church in the Transvaal" show the population of Johannesburg to be 8,000 in 1886 (Webb 1944:1), rising to 80,000 by 1895 (Beavon 1997). Ferreirastown was included on the preaching plan of the Pretoria Circuit, with monthly services conducted by Weavind and Reverend Courtney James. Cook and Dednam also began to hold services on the farm Concordia near Baragwanath (present-day Soweto) (Hall 1961:7). Concordia remained on Central's preaching plan until 1931 (Hall 1961:1). By March 1886, fortnightly services were held (Webb 1944:1).

Methodists living in the area appealed to England for a minister, and so Reverend Frederick Briscoe from Pretoria was appointed in April 1887 as resident minister. Briscoe served the area from his ox-wagon for six months. Methodist congregations met wherever they could, including the Theatre Royal and a temporary tin chapel (Hall 1961:3; Webb 1944:1).

---

50. The farm Langlaagte was gradually transformed into such Johannesburg suburbs as Mayfair, Fordsburg, and Sophiatown. Wilgespruit overlapped with the present-day city of Roodepoort, west of Johannesburg (Manoim and Davie n.d.).

51. Ancestor of a recent Central leader, Jonathan Cook.

Meanwhile, tensions between Boer and Brit escalated due to the discovery of gold, with output catapulting from £80,000 in 1887 to nearly £8,000,000 in 1895. Mine owners were without exception British, and many miners were also from abroad (Library of Congress 1996). The British declared themselves offended by racial discrimination in the Boer republics. People of colour living in the Z.A.R. were not only denied franchise and property rights, but Act No. 3 of 1897 also forbade racial intermarriage (South African History Online n.d. b).

Central's first incarnation was as the Wesleyan Church Hall, a stone church completed and opened in July 1889 at the corner of President and Kruis Streets, Johannesburg (Hall 1961:3; Central Methodist Church 1967:1). The cornerstone was laid in April[52] 1887 by Johannesburg's Landdrost, Captain Johannes von Brandis. The building was "patterned along the lines of the great Central Halls of England, with a ministry which combined evangelistic preaching with social upliftment" (Central Methodist Mission 1991:1). From about 1886, Central Halls rather than churches of traditional design were erected across England at places such as Westminster, Manchester, Birmingham, and Bristol (Webb 1956:1; Cracknell and White 2005:43).

The President Street Church, as it came to be known, was remembered as "the centre of education, cultural activities, and hearty Sunday Services." The Wesleyan Hall was opened in September[53] 1887, seating 300 and costing 900 pounds (Central Methodist Church 1967:1; Webb 1944:1). A Day School was opened in 1888, with a chapel added soon afterwards (Webb 1944:1). Other churches were then built in nearby Fordsburg and Jeppe suburbs (Central Methodist Church 1967:1). The Witwatersrand became a separate circuit in 1890, with Reverend William Hudson appointed superintendent of the Johannesburg circuit in 1893 (Hall 1961:3). Five ministers served at the Hall between 1887 and 1893.[54]

A typhoid outbreak in 1890 killed many Johannesburg residents, including forty Methodists. The collapse of the share market led to decreased business and the departure of many city residents (Webb 1944:1). The leadership responded by founding The Wesleyan Deaconess

---

52. Or July, according to Clegg 1936:1.

53. The bronze plaque in the foyer gives the date of opening as July 1887.

54. Central's clergy during the colonial era included Reverends F. J. Briscoe (ca. 1887), R. F. Appelbe (ca. 1887), W. Hudson (ca. 1893), J. S. Morris, Thos. Wainman (ca. 1893) (Clegg 1936:1; Webb 1944:1; Central Methodist Mission 1991:1; Hall 1961:3).

Institute in 1890[55] as "the caring arm of...Methodist Central Hall," making it the oldest welfare organisation in Johannesburg (Central Methodist Mission 1991:35). The first Deaconess (a "Sister Theresa") was employed by Reverend Fuller Appelbe (1890–95) to work among the poor of Johannesburg (Central Methodist Mission 1991:1; The Deaconess Order:1). Yet the enlargement of the Hall three years later hints that the congregation grew, regardless (Hall 1961:3). Central also soon developed a reputation for choral music, via a Johannesburg Wesleyan choir with instruments, founded in 1895.

Johannesburg's spatial development soon exhibited areas segregated by class and race, although some rapidly acquired a more integrated character. The city's planners—first representing the Z.A.R. government and, after 1902, the Transvaal Colony—wanted to implement residential and commercial segregation. Black Africans were prohibited by the 1885 Gold Law from living on or owning land "proclaimed for mining" (Parnell and Pirie 1990:130). The Z.A.R.'s Regulations for Towns (proclaimed 1899) forbade persons of colour to use sidewalks (South African History Online n.d. b). More than 29,000 blacks were housed in mining compounds by that time (South African History Online n.d. l). Even by 1892 there had been as many as 53 companies employing 3,400 whites and about 34,000 blacks (Simons and Simons 1968).

Poorer workers lived in the Brickfields area, with segregated sections planned for Afrikaners, Indians, Malays, and black Africans. The Kaffir Location (sic) for black Africans adjoined a "Coolie" (Indian) location in Brickfields. Other "coolie locations" were established for Indians from Natal at Braamfontein, Fordsburg and Jeppe in 1899. At the time, about 17,000 Indians resided in the Z.A.R.. Some owned residential and business property along the western side of central Johannesburg (South African History Online n.d. b; South African History Online n.d. f). A Malay Location was established for coloureds in Brickfields. Later they would be housed in Newtown, the name given to the area after the destruction of Brickfields in 1904 (City of Johannesburg. n.d., Beavon

---

55. The Deaconess Society was only accepted by the British Conference in 1910; The Deaconess Order within the Methodist Church of Southern Africa was only officially founded in 1944. A Deaconess College had been established at Ilkley in the United Kingdom (The Deaconess Order n.d. :2). The Deaconess Society functioned as an "umbrella welfare organisation for [all Central] ministries which raise moneys [sic] from the public" for "the work of the Methodist Church in Johannesburg and Soweto" (Central Methodist Mission 1991:2,35).

1997). Vrededorp, by contrast, was primarily inhabited by white Afrikaners (South African History Online n.d. d). Racially-mixed working class areas had developed along Johannesburg's peripheries by the 1890s.

A second conflict broke out between Britain and the Boer Republics on October 11, 1899, ostensibly after disagreements about the limits of franchise for English-speaking immigrants. Such immigrants had comprised the majority of the white population since 1890 (Library of Congress 1996). By the turn of the century "more than £60,000,000 of capital had been invested in the gold industry," mostly by European investors. Gold mines employed about 100,000 Africans (most from Mozambique), and Johannesburg had 75,000 white residents (Library of Congress 1996). As a result of the war, black Africans were evacuated, and most Indians left "for Cape and Natal Colonies, Mozambique and India" (South African History Online n.d. b). At Central, clergy contemplated evacuating to Pretoria.

The British captured Johannesburg in 1900, and achieved final victory in 1902, with the Z.A.R. becoming the Transvaal Colony (Library of Congress 1996). The Treaty of Vereeniging the same year confirmed the withholding of franchise from black Africans that had been Boer practice. Subsequently, Lord Alfred Milner's Transvaal government enforced many discriminatory acts. Milner sought to prevent Indian refugees from the Boer War from returning to their businesses and residences in Johannesburg, for example. The gradual erosion of Indian rights led many to protest against the implementation of legislation in 1907 that required them to register and carry identification documents (South African History Online n.d. b).

By contrast to the elimination of black and Indian residential areas, white suburbs—such as Jeppe and Malvern—were laid out to the east of Johannesburg by the municipality and mining companies in 1903 (South African History Online n.d. d). In 1904 Brickfields was destroyed due to a reported outbreak of bubonic plague, and all residents were relocated more than 10 miles to a site adjacent to the Klipspruit Sewage Works. By this act Klipspruit became Johannesburg's first black township (South African History Online n.d. f) and the foundation for what would become Soweto.

GROWING IN STATURE DURING THE UNION PERIOD (1910-48)

An enlarged Methodist Central Hall was proposed by the Transvaal Synod of the Methodist Church in 1913. According to Central minister

Henry Goodwin, quoted in the Johannesburg newspaper *The Star* on February 3, 1916, the extension was partly due to the " `crowded congregations...under the Reverend Glyndwyr Davies' ministry' ." At the time the Central Hall was "heavily in debt." The Wesleyan Methodist Missionary Society in 1914 accepted the proposal to enlarge the property on condition that the debt be redeemed. The Society offered to pay off £20,000 if overseas funds were matched by an equal local effort. Central minister and superintendent of the Central Circuit Henry Goodwin agreed to raise funds locally (Hall 1961:5).

The foundation stone was laid on the corner of Pritchard and Kruis Streets in April 1917, and in November 1919 the church moved to its new building "just opposite the entrance to the Courthouse." The debt of the Pritchard Street building was £35,000 (Hall 1961:5).

Central Hall's growth in public stature is reflected in the dignitaries that attended the opening ceremony over the November weekend. Participants included the Governor General and the President of the Methodist Conference, The Right Honourable Viscount Buxton and James Pendlebury, respectively. Prime Minister Jan Smuts addressed a men's fellowship (the Brotherhood) at an afternoon meeting that also included the mayor of Johannesburg (G.B. Steer, 1919–20), and Professor Jan Hofmeyr (later deputy prime minister). The presence of Canadian-born J. Albert Johnson, presiding bishop of what was then the 14th Episcopal District of the African Methodist Episcopal Church, ensured that at least one black person participated in the event. Smuts' address noted the need to discover a way of dealing with black-white issues.

The opening was celebrated by the "splendid singing of the choir" under Wansborough Poles (Webb 1956:2). Under the Reverend William Meara (1920–34) an impressive organ was procured in 1928, and Rupert Stoutt appointed as organist and choir master in 1924, although he actually served in this capacity from 1920 until the 1970s (Hall 1961:5). Meara was an Irishman who had arrived in South Africa on June 9, 1899. His first appointment was to Barberton, then to Central in 1920 as superintendent of the Central Circuit.

South Africa's racial problematic hovered only on the fringes of Central's collective awareness between 1889 and 1976. A "rummage" sale advertised for Friday 16 May 1930 was "for natives only;" and probably contained the leftovers from the previous day's "jumble" sale which had been advertised "for Europeans only." No indication is given of the removal of blacks from the inner city to Orlando location that year

(South African History Online n.d. g), named for city mayor (1925-26) and Methodist layman Edwin Orlando Leake (1860-1935). Leake chaired the city council's Non-European Affairs Department between 1930-31.

By contrast, missionary endeavour was evidently important to the congregation. A number of pamphlets from the 1920s call for contributions and advertise meetings. The strike of 1922, when white miners who had seized control of Johannesburg had to be quelled by the air force and army, received no attention. The principal of the Methodists' Kilnerton Institution spoke at a May 1927 "missionary anniversary service." In 1931 Meara reported "consistently larger" congregations "than any year of our history." Evangelism and ministry "to the poor and needy" peaked during the Depression of the 1930s. Meara told of "fifteen young men and women seeking the Lord" on a Sunday evening (Meara 1931:6). As well-known as Billy Graham in his time, but far more socially-engaged, Donald (later Baron) Soper,[56] appeared at Central Hall from July 25-30, 1937. Soper had been appointed superintendent of the West London Mission, London, in 1936. At Central Hall, Soper gave a series of evening sermons on such subjects as materialism, fascism and pacifism (Central Methodist Church 1971:12). Soper may have used the new Wesley Hall which had been completed in 1935.

As befitting a denomination controlled by the British Methodist conference, Central maintained strong links with Britain, demonstrated not only by the appearance of Lord Soper, but also by the work of the Deaconesses. Central Minister Joseph (Joe) Webb had studied at Cambridge in the 1920s, where he had befriended Soper (Central Methodist Church 1971:12). And Deaconess Sister Edna Peters from Leeds replaced Sister Annie D'Urban, who broke down under the strain of filling a position previously occupied by two Deaconesses.

Reverend Joe Webb was appointed superintendent at Central in 1942, when the congregation's programs reflected the Second World War years. Saturday night entertainment were laid on for soldiers in the Wesley Hall, as were teas after Sunday evening services in the Conference Room. Sister Vera Temple (1939–43) had people over for visits to the Deaconess' apartment in nearby Villiers Court (Webb 1943:2).[57]

---

56. Soper also spent time in Cape Town, Durban and Pretoria, according to a 1937 church bulletin advertisement.

57. A welcome by the deaconesses to a Royal Air Force serviceman in ca. 1941 is described on a BBC website, *Memories of Frank Lund* (http://tinyurl.com/l3wkd).

Webb made an effort to keep in contact with Central members on service, sending out a monthly letter and 200 parcels in December 1942 (Webb 1943:1). Central's membership numbered a "flourishing" 500 in 1943. Attendances at Sunday School peaked and were also good in the Women's Auxiliary, the Women's Bright Hour,[58] and Young People's Guild. Webb proposed a Youth Institute in 1943, which would consist of a games room, a reading and writing room, and a library for use by young working people (Webb 1943:2).

By November 1944 the membership stood at 627, with missionary subscriptions at £420 the "highest ever" (Webb 1944:2). Webb made his first of several pleas for the necessity of appointing "additional ministerial staff,"[59] noting the pressures emanating from his dual roles as chairman of the district and superintendent of the Hall. Two full-time secretaries[60] looked after administration. A Tuesday evening fellowship in the Conference Room was well-attended. An Easter youth camp was held at Grasmere, where a five-acre campsite was purchased on a ten-year lease.

The Saturday night entertainment for soldiers was abandoned due to the introduction of a 9 o'clock curfew. As Sister Vera had meanwhile married, members of the Royal Air Force and South African military were now entertained at the Manse on Saturday and Sunday afternoons rather than in the Deaconess' apartment. An apartment "at the top of the Hall" was converted "as for a club," and the first meal was to be prepared there on November 8, 1944. Other plans included adding "one more floor to Wesley Hall for our expanding youth work," and more seating. Purchasing a permanent public address system—instead of hiring one—was envisioned, to relay services to the Wesley Hall; presumably, for overflow congregations (Webb 1944:2,3).

Central Hall was also becoming known through various broadcasting activities. In 1944 the Central Hall Choir under Stoutt had recorded hymns for the South African Broadcast Company's religious programmes. Stoutt's organ interludes were used to introduce and end epilogues. Central was allotted "three broadcasts per thirteen Sundays." As a result, Webb not only received many letters from, but also con-

---

58. The Bright Hour is a fellowship for elderly women, started by the Deaconess Society.

59. Webb speaks of help "in this regard" by Reverend A. A. Kidwell; who must have served in at least a part-time capacity at the Hall in 1944 (Webb 1944:2).

60. Mrs. F.M. Price, Mrs. H.C. Stocks.

ducted personal interviews with, people "who normally never go to church" (Webb 1944:3). In 1945 Deaconess Sister Mary Caley served a probation period at Central before going for training in England, where she was ordained at Liverpool in 1947.[61] After her return to Central she was employed by the Deaconess Society in varied appointments until she retired in 1982 (The Deaconess Order n.d.:2).

By November 1946 Webb's idea of a youth centre had finally been concretised, with the Centre opened by Johannesburg's only woman Mayoress, Mrs. J. McPherson (1945–46), in June. Matt Eddy was appointed as Director of Youth Services and as manager of the Book Depot (Webb 1946:1). Webb proposed in 1951 that in addition to himself "at least one junior minister" be appointed. The Sunday School boasted 245 children and 42 teachers that year, and youth met in four age-differentiated groups during the week (Webb 1951:3-4; Central Methodist Hall 1966 a:14).

Because of Webb's popularity, the Pritchard Street Hall frequently overflowed, and in 1946 it was decided to build yet a bigger building (Webb 1946:2). In 1949 Webb issued "A plea for regular giving", a brochure encouraging members to use an envelope system to contribute on either a monthly basis to a Sustentation Fund, or to a Weekly Offering System (Webb 1949).

Central Hall's growth in stature in Johannesburg society and South African Methodism between 1919 and 1942 can be gauged by several factors. First, Central's property was extensively used for Methodist gatherings and annual celebrations of the anniversary of Methodism in Johannesburg, as well as for other Christian events. A "Universal Week of Prayer" was held at Central in January 1930. The Great Jubilee Rally of Rand Methodism in November 1936 (in the presence of the president of conference, A. A. Wellington) and a February 1938 Central Circuit Rally was held in the Wesley Hall.[62] In 1943 lunch hour prayer services were conducted in Wesley Hall by ministers from different denominations (Webb 1943:2). Second, the congregation's anniversary celebrations were often held simultaneously with that of Johannesburg Meth-

---

61. In November 1944 Webb noted that Caley and Woolcott was welcomed "as Deaconesses" during the year ending June 30th, 1944 (Webb 1944:2; compare 1943:1). If Webb is correct, either Caley's probation period started in 1944, or the dates 1945 and 1947 are incorrect.

62. Berea, Central, Orange Grove, Norwood, and Turffontein societies were represented at the Rally.

odism in Central's building. A pamphlet from Meara's time proclaimed in large bold print the 42nd anniversary of Johannesburg Methodism, and in small print in brackets underneath, 9th of Central Hall. Third, successive Mayors of Johannesburg participated regularly in Central's functions, and the exchange of roles and buildings were sometimes reciprocated. Mayor Penry Roberts (1933-34) chaired the 47th anniversary of Methodism in November 1933. Mayor M. Freeman (1934-35) chaired the 15th Central Hall anniversary meeting in November 1934. Mayor Donald Mackay (1936-37) officiated at the 1936 jubilee. He was followed by Mayors J.S. Fotheringham in 1937, J.J. Page in 1938, T.A.M. Huddle 1939, and so on, into the 1940s. An undated pamphlet, distributed to "church members," indicates that Reverend Arthur Clegg (1934-d.1941) chaired a Good Friday "evening of sacred music" in the City Hall during an event arranged by the Witwatersrand Church Council.

FROM AWARENESS OF APARTHEID TO OPPOSITION (1949-90)

For most of its existence Johannesburg's central area comprised a white business and residential district. In the grand scheme of apartheid, black Africans could only enter the city during the day as labourers who served white employers. At night, most had to return to the conglomeration of black locations known as Soweto, constructed southwest of the city. Other blacks lived on the Johannesburg's outskirts, in major hostels, or in servants' quarters on top of buildings. Until the early 1980s the city remained part white–collar business (banking, insurance, law courts) and part white residences. Some 166 apartment blocks could be found in the central and northern parts of the inner city, according to a survey of an area between President, Wolmarans, Sauer, and Nuggett Streets by Central evangelism team director Dave Ching. None existed south of President Street (Ching 1988:1,2).

The spatial patterns in apartheid Johannesburg were similar to those elsewhere in urban South Africa,[63] due to several interacting factors. Black urbanisation, fanned by industrialisation during the two world

---

63. Population movement, social dynamics, and layout do vary between South Africa's four major cities. By contrast to Durban and Johannesburg, for instance, in Cape Town white traders dominated trading in coloured areas. In District Six, 200 white businessmen owned properties valued at R2 million in 1962, employed 2,000 people and boasted an annual turnover of R4,5 million (Pinnock 1989:162).

wars, and the rigid legal system that arose to control it after 1948, directly impacted all South Africa's urban areas. Ironically, legislation to effect spatial segregation had the exact opposite result. Black urbanisation increased in the 1960s when the state evicted blacks from rural areas that had been declared white. Some black reserves were excised in favour of the consolidation of "homelands," and legally-designated illegal squatters were also evicted (Mabin 1991:36). People of colour were evicted from areas which they had historically inhabited due to the implementation of the Group Areas Act.[64] A case in point is the forced removals in Johannesburg of people from the previously predominantly "Malay" area of Pageview (Pinnock 1989:162).

Black African urbanisation was paralleled by a general outflow of whites from central residential districts to the suburbs[65] (compare Mabin 1991:36). Young white families were drawn out of the inner cities when the apartheid state subsidised suburban housing. Whites were simultaneously also pushed out by the effects of rent control, which "decreased profitability of apartment buildings for landlords." White landlords began to neglect services to apartment buildings. An overall decline of residential stock resulted that rendered the inner city unattractive for the middle–income Indians and coloureds who had succeeded whites as residents by the early 1980s. Lower rents drew lower income blacks, who had to endure even worse services due to relations with landlords that generally worsened (Beall, Crankshaw, and Parnell 2001:47).

Other patterns found in Johannesburg also typified urban areas elsewhere in South Africa. Shopping areas were relocated from the central business districts to the suburbs during the 1970s. Large shopping malls were built in the northern municipalities of Sandton (1973) and Randburg, as well as the eastern municipality of Bedfordview (1978) (Beavon 2000). Meanwhile, industries were moved to the south and south–west of the metropolis. Johannesburg's central business district was gradually converted from a shopping and residential area to an office park; as happened in Cape Town, for instance (compare Pinnock 1989:166). Between the 1940s and 1980s most of what little natural features had remained in the inner city (such as trees and parks) were

---

64. Group areas were declared "on the basis of land-ownership and not residency" (Pinnock 1989:162).

65. Central Cape Town's white exodus occurred in 1951, coinciding with an influx of 22,000 'non-whites' (Pinnock 1989:161).

eradicated through building programmes. Today the area of central Johannesburg lacks " 'any natural character at all' " (Storey, quoted in Scott 1981:18).

By the early 1990s Johannesburg's inner city was already inhabited predominantly by black Africans, with the exception of a few whites who were too old and poor to move. The latter included a Mrs. Preyer, the oldest surviving member of Central's congregation.

Aware but not there (1949–75)

A realistic evaluation of Central's relations to socio-political issues should be gauged against the major events that directly affected inner city Johannesburg at various times. Such relations can also be measured against responses to apartheid by Christian organisations in general, and by South African Methodism in particular. Any evaluation should ultimately consider the very effective propaganda campaigns waged through state-funded media to foster ignorance among the general populace about the truths of apartheid. The South African Broadcasting Corporation's television and radio services, and—for a while—*The Citizen* newspaper were used quite effectively in this regard. Opposing voices inside and outside South Africa were discredited by the state through the same means.

The attitudes of Central's members and ministers to racial issues of the day seem ambiguous, at best. Webb, for instance, was remembered by the oldest white member of the congregation as a popular, down-to-earth speaker. Not only was Webb famed for his broadcasted sermons, but also campaigned "for racial justice and understanding" (Preyer 1993[66]). But Webb's pronouncements on racial issues were quoted and used in Alexander Steward's book *You are wrong, Father Huddleston* (1956), an attempted rebuttal of Anglican priest Trevor Huddleston's book *Nought for your comfort* (1956). Huddleston had condemned South Africa's racial policy in his book by describing its effects on the freehold area of Sophiatown, part of his parish.

The Men's Fellowship reported visits to "the Johannesburg locations and Kilnerton Training Institution" in 1951. Yet, no word appeared in congregational publications about the April 1959 march on the Johannesburg City Hall in opposition "to the government's attempts to ban

---

66. Mrs. Preyer was a long-standing member who had attended Central for 46 years (1945–1991).

black students from campus" by 3,000 "students[67] and lecturers of the University of the Witwatersrand in their academic gowns" (Schoonakker 2004). Nor were there any references to the Methodist Church's condemnation of apartheid legislation at the annual conference in Kimberley later that year (*Contact* 1959 a).

The April 1966 meeting of the Men's Fellowship heard of black malnourishment (affecting 80% of labourers on the Rand) and high infant mortality rates (Webb 1951:8; Central Methodist Hall 1966 a:10). In 1966 the "Young And Not So Young" women's fellowship heard from (minister's wife) Mrs. Cook "a vivid account of her life at an African College." The Sunday School collected money "to buy a bicycle for an African Minister in one of the townships" (Central Methodist Hall 1966 a:8,12). Comments about black impoverishment and the desire for freedom by all races were bynotes in missionary appeals (such as the District Missionary Fund campaign in 1930) and editorials by Central's ministers (Pitts 1966). The "alarming number of deaths while in custody of African prisoners" deserved one sentence in the congregation's 1969 newsletter, in contrast with the two pages devoted to the "manpower" shortage suffered by the Methodist ministry (Central Methodist Church 1969:7).

By 1961 Central was touted as the "leading Methodist Church in Southern Africa." Due to the endeavours of Meara, Webb, and choir master Stoutt, Central also had a reputation as "Methodism's leading place of worship" (Central Methodist Mission 1991:1; Hall 1961:5). The Hall had been renovated and re-opened in 1956 to include a floor of offices, "a new system of ventilation and air conditioning", a small sidechapel, and new seating (Webb 1956:2; Hall 1961:3).[68] Prominently positioned choir stalls were built into the present sanctuary, but the choirs were all-white. A coloured choir member since 1985 told me that "no other race was allowed until Stoutt's death in 1985." Despite such attitudes among prominent laypersons, in August 1963 a wide group of churches met at Central Methodist Hall to "discuss the formation of a multi-racial inter-denominational institute." On Sunday 15 December

---

67. Theresa Heinz Kerry (nee Simoes-Ferreira), later the spouse of U.S. senator John Kerry, participated in the march while a student at the University (Schoonakker 2004).

68. During the five months that the congregation was excluded from the premises during restoration, services were held in the Plaza Theatre (Webb 1956:4; Hall 1961:3) in Rissik Street.

1963 the Christian Institute was launched at the Central Hall, with C.F. Beyers Naudé giving his inaugural address as director (Mayson n.d.:2, Naudé 1963).

Reverend Stan Pitts (1965–75, d.2003) was appointed to replace Webb, who died of cancer in 1972. Pitts was remembered as "popular and sincere...The congregation came first—he knew what was happening and came to visit when there was trouble." But Webb was a hard act to follow, and Pitts "did not have the same appeal." Pitts was the last minister to regularly visit members (Preyer 1993).

Central's present six-storey building was completed in 1966. The congregation said their farewells to the old building with closing services on 29 May 1966. Reverends Pitts, Webb, and Ernle Young were present. Then the congregation, arranged in fellowships or groups, walked one block east to the new building at the corner of Smal and Pritchard Streets, adjoining the Supreme Court. The procession was headed by the Mayor and Mayoress, and Pitts laid the foundation stone (Central Methodist Hall 1966 a:4,6,10,14). On May 31 volunteers started moving equipment, files and furniture to temporary church offices in Pritchard House as well as into the new building. The half-finished new building was still being completed, and in August 1966 services were still being held in the finished basement (Central Methodist Hall 1966:1). The building programme coincided with a 1966 fund-raiser in the guise of a Christian Stewardship Campaign, which Pitts presented as an opportunity to "re-dedicate ourselves" and "fulfil the purposes of God for our Church set in the midst of the City." Hostess Chairman (sic) Daphne Pitts explained that the Campaign followed on a visitation programme in which "almost 125 women" had visited "nearly 1,500 families" (Central Methodist Hall 1966 b).

The newly named Central Methodist Church was officially opened with a dedication service on 15 October 1967, remembered in a Pew Bulletin with that date and in a commemorative brochure. The motto of the church was "As old as the city itself." The building had a restored organ[69] from the Central Hall and, rare for South Africa, cushioned, tip-up seating for 1,012. According to Pitts the new name was chosen because "many of our people" had "reiterated wishes...that our new place of worship will be more a "Church" than a "Hall" (Central Meth-

---

69. By 'new' Pitts probably meant a "new three manual console and pedal range...to make all note and pedal movements automatic" as described in the Commemorative brochure of 1967 (Central Methodist Church 1967; cf. 1966 a:1).

odist Hall 1966:1). This may have indicated a class shift among members. The Hall was later demolished.

Central's newer building, still in use today, contained numerous halls, rooms, and deliberate symbols which linked to the congregation's history and its faith tradition. In the 1990s the foundation stones (1889, 1917, 1935) and copper depictions of past buildings were prominently on display in the building. From the main lobby, a staircase led down to the Wesley Hall, an auditorium containing a stage and seating for 500. Wesley Hall played a significant role in Central's engagement with apartheid's security forces. Another stair wound up to the Minor Hall (seating 200) on the mezzanine floor. The main sanctuary was located on the first floor, along with a lounge (the old Coffee Room). The second floor contained the old parlour and a gallery overlooking the sanctuary. Offices, board room and an apartment occupied the third floor, and offices and a second apartment the fourth floor. The fifth floor offered accommodation for cleaning staff.

Secular and religious symbols were visible in the chapel off the lobby, which one entered via a door with handles in the shape of two fish worked in brass. High small stained glass windows in the chapel reminded worshippers of the connection with Christians past and present. The stained glass windows depicted the shields of the four authors of the gospel, the Old Testament (a rose), four missionaries (Andrew, Peter, Philip, Paul), John Wesley, "World Methodism," "World Christianity," Christ (a crown, a red cross), and the Holy Spirit (a descending dove). Around the altar rail, kneeler cushions offered 12 tapestry symbols of "the community in which we live" (Mining, Industry, Commerce, Building, Farming, Hospitals, Education, Science, The Home, Music, Transport, Sport).

Symbols were also displayed in the main sanctuary on the first floor, where seating was arranged in a six-sided semi-circle. At the front, on a raised platform surrounded by rails, were an altar table, a lectern to the left of the centrally placed pulpit, a baptismal font (also to the left). The altar rails were in the shape of an octagon. Choir stalls rose in three rows above the pulpit to the organ screen stretched across the central part of the main sanctuary; the top stall was level with the second floor gallery. The organ screen reached to the ceiling, divided into nine sections—four flanking a large copper cross. The eight screen sections had small, blue (Jerusalem) crosses near the top, each surrounded by four even smaller white crosses. The Jerusalem crosses represented the centrality of the cross, while the four white ones symbolised "the outreach of the gospel to the four corners of the earth," according to the commemorative brochure. Octagon-shaped panels decorated the rest of the screen, symbolising the "binding of the family of God together." The ceiling was six-sided (hexagon), with recessed lights. A stained glass window to the right of the organ screen depicted the ascension and repeated the hexagon shape of the ceiling. In all, twelve stained glass windows portrayed scenes from the life of Jesus.

Central Methodist Church's prominent stature over time was reflected by the succession of ministers who eventually served as presidents of the Methodist denomination in South Africa. Meara was elected to this office twice after he had left Central (1937, 1945), while others included Titcomb, Goodwin, Webb (thrice, starting in 1950; see Hall 1961:5), Pitts (twice), Peter Storey (1984), and Mvume Dandala (1997).

Into the crucible (1976–81)

When Reverend (later Bishop) Peter Storey was appointed superintendent minister of Central Methodist Mission in 1976, he publicly declared to his large white congregation that he wanted to racially integrate the church. The same year high-school students had revolted in Soweto against apartheid education, and were met with overt violence by the state under John Vorster (prime minister, 1966-78).

Storey is "seventh in a family line of South African Methodist ministers dating back to 1820" (Boston University 1999). His family life and experiences as a young minister shaped Storey's opposition to apartheid on theological grounds. Storey's father was probably "the first Church leader to not only denounce apartheid, but to declare it a 'sin against God, Father, Son and Holy Spirit' in 1957—an action that brought down upon him the wrath of Prime Minister Verwoerd" (Storey 2005 b). Storey senior denounced apartheid in his own congregation. From such and other examples Storey garnered his own theological conviction that an emphasis on personal salvation must be accompanied by calls for social justice. Australian Methodist minister Alan Walker, who had conducted evangelistic crusades in Johannesburg and Pretoria in 1963, was a particularly deep influence in this regard. As a young man Storey had spent two years at Walker's Central Methodist Mission in Sydney (1965–66). Storey indicated that "Walker was known for his integration of personal and social religion and was blistering in his attack on South African apartheid" (Storey 2005 b). But as Chapter

One related, Storey's integrative intentions were first stimulated by Reverend Rob Robertson and his North End congregation in East London.

Storey's declaration drew Coloureds and Indians to attend Central (Storey 1993:1), but also led to a decline in white attendance.[70] Central's remaining white members by now mostly resided in Johannesburg's suburbs, from where they continued to travel in to Central (Storey 1992:4). A few whites still did in 1992, because of their desire to belong to a racially-mixed congregation. While 40% of the congregation had been white by 1991 (Storey 2005 b), 22% remained by 1992.

At the core of Storey's deliberate attempts to mix Central was the six-day "My brother and me" course, run over six Tuesdays in 1976. The goal was to enable "whites to face their prejudice in the presence of blacks." Storey described the experience as not different from the progression of conversion: "proximate intimacy, confrontation, repentance and confession, commitment." Participants had to undertake to attend the whole course, "otherwise most would have left when it became uncomfortable in the third week or so" (Storey 1994). "My brother and me" courses continued to be offered "at Central and various other venues, including weekend courses held at retreat centres...into the 1980s" (Storey 2005 b).

Storey consistently preached on socio-political themes, while using the worship service to pull people back to the Bible and doctrine. Storey "saw change coming, saw the social injustices...he stressed social consciousness and our obligation to other people." Compared to his predecessors "he was more of a policy-maker; and a lot of things the minister used to do now fell on the shoulders of the people" (Preyer 1993). Evangelism team leader Dave Ching said "Peter Storey's greatest gift is being prophetic, seeing where God is working in the wider world" (Ching 1992a). F.L.O.C. director Wendy Young's impression was that "without Peter Storey, Methodists would have lost their place in the city" (Young 1992).

Storey's intent to cross racial barriers was concretised by the appointment of two black staff members. Lindi Myeza, a female social worker, served from 1976 until 1982 as Central's first ever black staff member

---

70. Methodist minister Colin Morris had a similar experience in 1959 in Northern Rhodesia (Zambia). His preaching against racial segregation, and in support of universal franchise, emptied his flourishing white congregation in Chingola (*Contact* 1959 b:7; see Barrow 2001).

(Central Methodist Church 1982:7).[71] A part-time black minister, Sizwe (Tom) Mbabane, was appointed to reach out to black workers housed on top of apartment blocks around the church building (Storey 1992:4; Central Methodist Church 1980 a:1). Mbabane started black-language services on Sunday afternoons in 1980 (Central Methodist Church 1980 b:12). At the same time Helen Muller, a member of the congregation, started two pre-school centres in the black city of Soweto. *Thlokomelong Jabavu*, one of these, was still in existence in 1992. Lionel Lennert became the first coloured to serve as Society Steward in 1985 (Central Methodist Church 1985:3). Storey's anti-apartheid preaching was accompanied by public roles that opposed the State's race policies: as presidents of first the South African Council of Churches (during the 1970s) and, later, of the Methodist Church (during the 1980s). The implications of Storey's role and appointments must be seen against the wider socio-political canvas of revolt (1976) and State repression through various States of Emergency (e.g. 1985; Storey 1992:4).

Storey initiated The Academy for Christian Living in March 1977, under leadership of Muller (Central Methodist Church 1978:1). The Academy provided adult Christian education courses in the Bible, skills, personal growth, and expositions on current issues. The idea was inspired by similar programmes run at Church of the Saviour in Washington D.C., which Storey had visited. Course attendance regularly averaged 80 people. Myeza taught in the Academy for Christian Living, despite objections "to a black woman preaching to us" (Preyer 1993).

By 1982 interest in the Academy had tapered off and it was eventually halted — an experience that puzzled and pained Storey. He suggested that participants stopped coming because the inner city area around Central was increasingly seen as unsafe. Five assaults had taken place over four months in Central's building during the early 1980s, despite arrangements with the police to provide safety. The global petrol crisis that also impacted South Africa at about this time also played a role. Another contributive factor was the decision to alternate the Academy's classroom activities with small Growing in Faith Together groups which met in people's homes.[72]

All these may have made people reluctant to come in to the inner city

---

71. Myeza had in 1972 acted as literacy trainer for the Women's Association of the African Independent Churches (Myeza and Te Siepe 1972).

72. GIFT also fulfilled unexpected functions: four of the five people who had joined Central from the defunct Civic congregation met in a western suburbs GIFT group.

to attend Academy meetings (Storey 1994). The idea of the Academy was later incarnated in the School for Christian Living, an internal education programme for church members (Central Methodist Mission 1991:24). Many participated in the Academy because they had been visited by Central's evangelism team in an expression of care. Former director Dave Ching traced the origins of the evangelism team to 1981. During that year, "as many members of the congregation as possible" were involved in going out to invite people to special occasions, such as Easter services (Ching 1992b:4).

Noticeable growth of black membership started only in 1978, after an intentional three-step plan to symbolise concern for the real needs of urban (particularly black) people (Storey 1993:1-2). The three-step plan coincided with the 1978 campaign to encourage church members to give "to God through Central Church." The campaign highlighted the ministries of Central, which included "homeless men who gravitate to this city church" and a "special fund for the unemployed...in the present economic recession." The giving scheme was dubbed "Adventure in Giving," as "giving is an adventure in gratitude and faith".

The first step to increase black attendance was the black/white contact programme "My Brother and Me",[73] and the other two steps were of equal stature in the context of the apartheid city.

The second intentional step was to open the first restaurant to cater for all races in Johannesburg in April 1978 as "an act of defiance against the ban on mixed amenities" (Storey 2005 b). At the time, the Separate Amenities Act (1953) still prohibited such places (Storey 1993:1, 2002:120 footnote 1; Scott 1981:7,18). Storey recalled that "the authorities attempted to shut us down...we skirted the race laws by becoming 'a place for the preparation of food' " rather than a 'restaurant.' While the former required "only health department approval," the latter was directly affected by the Separate Amenities Act (Storey 2005 b).

Conceived in 1977 and funded from external sources, the People Centre restaurant in Central's basement[74] was open five days a week (Scott 1981:6). Joan Rudolph, the first director, became Central's first full-time lay staff member (*What a Family* 1978:2).

---

73. The format of "My Brother and Me" anticipated similar programs for fostering interracial contact later during the mid-1980s, most notably those run by Nico Smith's Koinonia organisation and by African Enterprise.

74. The first manager, Joan Rudolph, was later succeeded by Beth Logan, then Wendy Young, before Rudolph returned to see the Centre through its final years.

White volunteer members served black patrons in the People Centre in a racial role reversal that provided a startling symbol of the congregation's intentions. A young black male patron commented in 1981 that people "were learning to get on quite naturally" (Scott 1981:13). An elderly white man "felt that the solution to the country's ills had to follow the lines which the restaurant was modelling". A middle-aged black "commented that he had been given the opportunity to form relationships with whites more than before through his contact with the People Centre" (Scott 1981:14). A sign advertising the restaurant was placed in Smal Street outside the church building. Some 1,045 patrons per week were using the restaurant by 1981. Some 48,7% (510) was black, and 44,5% (465) white (Scott 1981:1, 11–12). A number of older white people found a place where they could find companionship as patrons or volunteer helpers (Scott 1981:18). The Centre catered for church functions, such as the 95th anniversary dinner. By 1991 the Centre had six full-time staff and six regular volunteers, with an annual budget of R135,000—but patrons had declined to 600 to 800 per week (Central Methodist Mission 1991:36,37). Instead of increasing, as Storey had hoped, the number of volunteers had declined slightly to five by 1992, as had the restaurant staff, who consisted of a cook (Eva Philips), cashier (Lulu Zazini) and two washers of dishes. In any case, volunteers were mainly older people, who realised the work was "about service." There were seldom younger volunteers, perhaps because of transport and parking problems (Rudolph 1992).

When it closed in 1993, the People Centre had amply fulfilled its envisaged function of moving the frontier with the city from the doorstep of the church into the building itself. Closure was prompted by a fall-off in patrons and the financial losses that resulted. Storey suggested that the Centre was the source for Central's first black worshippers.[75] He maintained that people "who went there first...after a while decided...to attend worship" (Scott 1981:24). The people drawn in were not the " 'churchy' " type who would usually enter the building. As the needs of city people were brought to the attention of church people, the People Centre also served Central (Storey, quoted in Scott 1981:17). Several patrons volunteered to work at Central's reception desk on

---

75. Of respondents polled in the restaurant in 1981, 14,3% were involved in Central activities (Scott 1981:11). The reliability of the data is highly questionable, due to the extremely small sample (21 out of 1,045 patrons), and do not show clearly whether blacks attended Central activities because of the restaurant (Scott 1981:8,11,15,24).

Sundays (Scott 1981:23). Due to their experiences with the People Centre, blacks " 'felt totally free to use the church's facilities' " and some had approached him for counselling, Storey said (Scott 1981:19). Rudolph aimed to serve people with dignity regardless of who they were (Rudolph 1992).

Yet the interactions between black restaurant staff and black patrons, between black staff and white director and volunteers, inadvertently demonstrated a paradox facing those who want to undo racial structures. They also have to overcome their own captivity to the very norms that they were inverting. Some volunteers did not return because they felt it was "just kitchen work, and they employ [black] people to do that" (Rudolph 1992). Very few black volunteers came forward, perhaps because many who visited the Centre were unemployed, and could not afford to work without remuneration (Rudolph 1992). Participants in such projects often had to traverse vast class and ideological distances to reverse the racialism—and associated paternalism—that dominated South African society. A full-time white worker's comment illustrated this:

> I tried to get black staff to assume responsibility, but it didn't work; they couldn't. A pity, because I wanted to grow them. Perhaps they were from the older school, but the first thing they did [when confronted with a difficulty] was to call me. We talked about it, but they could not handle it. They would get manipulated and intimidated by [other] blacks.

Storey's intentions prompted some 200 white members to leave. A white member described them as "those who did not like so-called political preaching." Some whites who remained purportedly said that blacks were acceptable " 'as long as they behave'—but they would not have said the same thing about whites" (Preyer 1993). Comments by a member who stayed show the struggle that now emerged among some whites: "We had to accept it—I did not feel happy: it changed the atmosphere...also in the [women's] clubs we did not feel free to talk—for example about a murder—as they would know it is about a black man." More whites eventually left when younger white couples, once they started families, began to attend the churches in the local suburbs where they now resided.

Storey's actions and Central's programs created a growing reputation of credibility that drew in congregants who differed racially and ideologically from Central's previous all-white congregation. In conjunction with the contact programs, white members (and others) were made to meet with blacks, to work through their prejudice, and so a climate of acceptance was gradually established within Central.

The actions and resultant racial mix also created a supportive network of ideas with strong boundaries. As a result, Central became integrated before Johannesburg did. Central's black component had surpassed the 20% mark by the mid-eighties, when black Africans began to live in inner Johannesburg's apartments. Central was "able to welcome new black residents with an already integrated community" (Storey 1992:4; 1993:2). Blacks slowly started attending, among them interracial couples (Preyer 1993). For example, by 1981 Blacks attended Workers' Worship during Wednesday's lunch hour in the chapel. A "small group of coloured folk" sat "in the back left corner" by 1982 (Young 1992). A "non-racial young adults' group" (*Khululeka*) had been established by 1989 (Ching 1989:1).

Storey himself stressed that "integration could not have happened at Central without Scripture, a theology of hospitality and justice, and emphasis on the Wesleyan convictions about the 'allness' of God's grace...No determination on my part to see an integrated Central could have happened without the sermons...and teaching that fed and grew people, both black and white." He pointed to the School for Christian Living and the curricula developed for home groups as examples of sustenance for those involved (Storey 2005 b).

The siege years and beyond (1982–90)

The final deliberate integrative step taken by Storey was arguably the most radical: to allow various persecuted bodies prohibited from meeting under security legislation (e.g. the Internal Security Act) to hold protest meetings in Central's building. Trade union meetings were held in the Wesley Hall in the basement during the eighties, sometimes disrupting other programs. The Congress of South African Trade Unions (Cosatu, launched 1985) in particular was actively campaigning against apartheid at the time. At first, Cosatu co-operated loosely with the United Democratic Front alliance (1983–1991), with which it later established the Mass Democratic Movement (founded 1989). In another notable protest meeting at Central in 1987, 3,000 strikers of the South African Railways and Harbours Workers' Union crammed into the building. The workers were part of a nation-wide strike involving about 18,000 employees, that intended to address racial discrimination and state repression of black trades union (Visser n.d.:7). Storey recalled that "most of them had marched with knobkieries and sticks of one kind or another and my staff and I had to 'disarm' each of them on entering...we never permitted weapons of any sort in the building" (Storey 2005 b).

When the Unlawful Organisations Act (1960) banned black African political movements in 1961, some church leaders became the voice of the oppressed by default. As their buildings provided space for political and related meetings, they too became targets for security force actions. Dean Edward King attempted to offer sanctuary in Saint George's Cathedral in Cape Town to protesters that were being beaten by police in 1972 (Barron 1998). Political gatherings were held on church premises, partly to circumvent the government's prohibition of private gatherings with the 1974 Riotous Assemblies Amendment Act. In 1982 the Internal Security Act allowed magistrates to prohibit any gathering for 48 hours (Maho 2002). Despite such measures, churches continued to be used for United Democratic Front meetings in 1984, for instance (Lazerson 1994:263).

Consequently, some churches fared even worse than Central. On November 17, 1985, for example, a mass meeting was held in a Methodist church in Mlungisi about a consumer boycott which was bankrupting white-owned shops in nearby Queenstown. Arriving in an armoured vehicle, police fired tear gas into the Mlungisi church (Colman 1991). In April 1986 the state prohibited all outdoor and some indoor meetings. A Roman Catholic Church hall in Ackerville township near Witbank was "gutted" on the night of May 21, 1988 "before a Cosatu meeting there" (Congress of South African Trade Unions 1999). What is remarkable about Central is that unlike the other examples mentioned here, its church building was located in what at the time was still legally a white area.

The practice of permitting political meetings on Central's premises continued until late in the 1980s, as exemplified by a Mass Democratic Movement meeting at Central on August 17, 1989. The meeting was part of a national defiance campaign to integrate all segregated amenities by invading them (*Roca Report* 1989). "The Wesley Hall was used at the d.rop of a hat," remembered Rudolph. The massive crowds did "just what they wanted to" and the noise discouraged some people from using the People Centre restaurant. After complaints, a staff meeting agreed that the Hall would only be used after 3 p.m. (Rudolph 1992).

The Sanctuary upstairs continued to be used for lunch-hour protest meetings (Storey 2005 b).

Many confrontations followed with the police who wanted to invade Central property to effect arrests and disrupt meetings. Storey describes the period as "the siege years" (Storey 1992:5). All the ministers were arrested after one such stand-off. Central's treasurer and former circuit and society steward Ken Roberts lead the call for their release at John Vorster Square police station. The ministers were also involved in a march on John Vorster Square—this time without arrests (Storey 1992:5). On one occasion the police entered the building "and sat on our communion rail, training their guns on the 800 people in the Sanctuary" (Storey 1992:5). On another, security police allegedly defaced the church walls in 1988 prior to a commemoration of the June 16 uprising (Storey 2002:115). Storey remembered that "tear gas was also used at least once to disperse a Detainees' Parents' Support Committee meeting in the People Centre" (Storey 2005 b).

Religious institutions like Central who supported the anti-apartheid movement indeed came under siege by the regime's security forces, as did all activists during the 1980s. The Security Branch of the police, for example, initiated an internal network known as Strategic Communications (StratCom). StratCom's purpose was to discourage political opposition by spreading disinformation and creating perceptions which hindered anti-apartheid activities. Other methods included surveillance, intimidation, and assassination. Within StratCom a so-called church desk was responsible for church-related political activities. A lieutenant in the Security Branch, Michael Bellingham (also referred to as Bellinghan or Bellingan), in 2001 successfully applied to the Truth and Reconciliation Commission for amnesty for disrupting protest meetings at Central between 1982 and 1986 (Truth and Reconciliation Commission Amnesty Committee 1995, 1998 b, 2001).[76] Bellingham defaced Central's buildings, and tried to recruit clergy to inform on Storey (Storey 2005 a).

Opposition to Central's position also came from other sources. The government-sponsored South African Broadcasting Corporation refused Central airtime on its roster of church services "rather than let us preach the truth" (Storey 1992:5). On one occasion the Broadcast Cor-

---

76. Bellinghan also applied for amnesty for murdering his wife because "she had threatened to reveal his political role" (Truth and Reconciliation Commission 1998a).

poration cut off the service "in mid-broadcast because of our lighting of the 'Candle of Peace and Justice' on our altar," recalled Storey (2005).

Meanwhile, Central Methodist Church became Central Methodist Mission in 1985, reflecting a totally outward-oriented vision initiated by Storey in a 13-point Mission Statement which intended to move Central (a) "from a suburban mentality to identification with the city"; (b) "from a white membership to an inclusive community"; (c) "from an inward orientation to creating frontier ministries"; (d) "from traditional growth patterns to intentional evangelism." As an innovation to help raise funds, Central's property was restructured to include shops "so that property financed property," and to allow the congregation's financial gifts to be expended on ministry. Storey recognised that an inner city church could not survive purely on the giving of its people (Storey 1994). In 1984 the hotel next door was forced under municipal regulations to buy air space from Central, bringing in R325,000 and free parking on Sundays for the congregation and its staff. In 1987 the debt on the church building was paid off (Storey 1992:5).

In line with the outward vision several ministries developed, of which the most relevant included various racially-mixed ministries to the aged, the poor, the homeless, and city children. Cornerstone House, a block of apartments dedicated to care for the disabled and pensioned, housed 56 people over eight years. The building was rendered "untenable" when state agents exploded a bomb underneath the South African Council of Churches' headquarters, Khotso House, nearby (Storey 1992:4,5). From 1986 Central became partners in the City Care project with Saint Mary's Cathedral (Church of the Province of South Africa). City Care attempted "to alleviate the suffering of [about 40] destitute people in the city through providing counselling, financial assistance and a lunch-time feeding" (Central Methodist Mission 1991:43; Storey 1992:5). A social worker was employed to help carry out the work (Central Methodist Mission 1991:42). Central initiated "the first ever after-school centre in the city" (Careways) in 1973, and launched a pre-school program (For the Love of Children) in 1989, based on a ministry of the Church of the Saviour in Washington D.C. (Storey 1992:5).

As a result of the outward focus, even Central's evangelical outreaches to Johannesburg's apartment buildings in 1987 could not help but encounter the apartheid city. Some 100 residential apartment buildings could be found within a six-block radius around Central, "within one quarter of the area defined around Central" (Central Methodist

Mission 1987:1).

When an evangelism team visited a total of 1,776 apartments in 15 of these buildings, they found many tenants grimly resisting eviction in terms of the Group Areas Act through Flat [Apartment] Committees and later the Action Committee to Stop Evictions (ACTSTOP) Tenants' Association (Central Methodist Mission 1987:1,2). Aside from extending friendship, noting problems and needs, outreach participants also offered advice on where to find help, whether at Central or "other caring agencies like ACTSTOP" (Ching 1989:1). ACTSTOP, a non-governmental agency founded to help people resist evictions, had opened a Tenants' Advice Office in Central's building (Central Methodist Mission 1987:1,2). Storey led an ecumenical delegation to Europe, the United States Congress, and the United Nations in 1984 to ask for pressure to be exerted against Group Areas Act removals (Boston University 1999). In 1987 Central placed a joint advertisement called "Scrap Group Areas" in *The Weekly Mail* of October 16–22, with the United Democratic Front, National Union of Mineworkers, Johannesburg Youth Council, and Call of Islam.

Six Bible studies were established in as many different blocks in 1989, encouraging spiritual growth, mutual caring, "a healthy network," and "a sense of community" (Ching 1989:2). Two half-time evangelists (Alan Storey, Pogiso Takwesi) lived in the city "among the people they serve" (Central Methodist Mission 1991:18; Ching 1989:2). The team helped to distribute bread and soup for those sleeping on the streets as part of a winter programme organised by the *Usindiso* night shelter and several churches (Ching 1990:3).

Even where the intention behind Central's outreach programmes was conversion and aid, racial integration usually also featured. For example, a young low-income Afrikaner encountered during a visit was provided with clothes, and his loneliness addressed through inclusion in the non-racial fellowship group *Khululeka*. Although this constituted "his first contact with blacks," Ching thought his prejudice was "being outweighed by the friendship offered there" (Ching 1989:1). Conditions in the apartments included overcrowding, lack of electricity, and passages flooded with sewage (Ching 1989:1). Even black township residents whose churches participated on occasion in Central's visitation program were as "horrified" as their white privileged counterparts at inner city conditions, reported Ching. One visit in 1990 unearthed a two-room apartment inhabited by fifteen women and children. At night the children slept under the adults' beds (Ching 1990:1). About 100–125 apartment dwellers per month were visited in 1991, and outreach now extended to prostitutes (Central Methodist Mission 1991:18). Soon afterwards volunteer participation started tapering off, and increased security precautions at apartment blocks made visits more difficult.

Visitation team members discovered the lives led by inner city children and the homeless. Of 754 apartments visited in 1986, over 406 had children whose average ages fell into two sets: 1 to 10 years old, and those older than 15 (Rees 1986:1). The children often had nowhere to go after school; although some had keys, others were locked out until a parent returned. They spent the afternoon sitting on the stairs, or wandering the streets. Some could not attend school at all, due to lack of money for transport (*What a Family* 1992:3). The encounter with the growing number of homeless persons on Johannesburg's inner city streets led to a project that catered for five hundred people per week by 1992. Eventually dubbed *Paballo ya Batho*, project volunteers went out into the city at night to dispense soup and provide basic medical treatment (*Paballo ya Batho* n.d.).

TOWARDS A POST-APARTHEID CONGREGATION (1990-94)

Contact with inner city children led to the creation of a pre-school and after school care centre in which racial integration featured as underlying theme. Careways, the after-school care centre, provided refuge for children ages 6 to 12 on weekday afternoons. The aim was "to bring children of all races together in order that they learn to live alongside each other" (Central Methodist Mission 1991:41). Careways raised almost four-fifths of its budget from fees. The rest of the costs were recovered from overseas donations (congregations in the United States and the United Kingdom) and from fund-raising events involving the children and parents (Central Methodist Mission 1991:41).

A pre-school entitled For the Love of Children (F.L.O.C.) was established in June 1989 in central Johannesburg, catering for children aged 3 to 6. F.L.O.C. staff also trained home carers recruited from the surrounding apartments and from domestic workers who look after children (*Dimension* May 1989; Central Methodist Mission 1991:38). F.L.O.C. reflected the city "in the proportions of Black, Coloured, Indian, and White children attending" two years later (Central Methodist Mission 1991:38). Almost two-thirds of F.L.O.C.'s expenditure was recovered from fees, the rest coming from other sources (donations, fund-raising) (Central Methodist Mission 1991:38). Additional sponsors included groups in South Africa (Anglo-De Beers, Mobil, the Loewenstein Trust, JCI, Russell's furniture chain stores, the Perm Building Society); the United Kingdom (Saint John's Playgroup, Orpington; Harpenden Methodist Church); the United States (Foundry United Methodist Church, Washington; Dranesville United Methodist Church), and Sweden (The Federation of Swedish Liberal Women) (F.L.O.C. 1991:2). F.L.O.C. organised field trips to provide "experiences denied to children surrounded by concrete," such as discovering coloured leaves, insects, and animals (F.L.O.C. 1991:1).

By 1992 Central's staff had grown from two ministers and two secretaries in 1972 to 24 staff members and three ministers (Mvume Dandala, Philip Mvunyiswa, Janet Hudson). The budget had leapt from R60,000 in 1974 to around R700,000 (Storey 1992:5). About 58% of the congregation were black Africans, and 62.6% were women. Most children in the Sunday School spoke vernacular languages, and a call went out for teachers fluent in seSotho or isiZulu (*What a Family* 1992:2). Two of the ministers were black (Dandala, Mvunyiswa), and the third was a white woman, Janet Hudson. Hudson had been ordained in 1986 as the very first woman Methodist minister in the Johannesburg district. Three years later she was appointed to Central (Hudson 1992).

Dandala had been a member at Central while working as the General Secretary of the Missions Department of the Methodist Church. Since 1986 he had been living in the predominantly white satellite city of Edenvale to the east of Johannesburg. His move there generated friction with whites in his neighbourhood, and was reported in two daily newspapers. Dandala trained at the Federal Theological Seminary at Alice in the 1970s, before winning a scholarship to Cambridge, England for 1974–75 (Dube 1993:12). From 1975 to and 1982 Dandala was appointed to the staff of Empangeni Methodist Church on South Africa's northeast coast. The Empangeni circuit became "one of the first to become racially-integrated" in 1978. White and black societies had met in racially segregated circuits prior to this, and a 1976 Conference decision for geographic groupings was left to the circuits to interpret, with positive reinforcement from the Missions Department (Church World Service 2003; Dandala 2005). The main thrust of his ministry was to the "'desperately poor community of kwaMfeka'" (Dube 1993:12). From 1983–1985 Dandala was superintendent minister in Port Elizabeth

North, "during the height of political conflict between the United Democratic Front and the Azanian People's Organisation." He came under pressure from all sides and the police, spending some time in detention without trial " 'for accommodating students' meetings and trying to be peacemakers' " (Dube 1993:12).

In 1992 Storey was succeeded by Dandala, who became Central's first black superintendent minister. Storey had held the dual roles of superintendent of Central and bishop of the Central District (the old South Western Transvaal District) since 1984. As he could no longer manage the double burden, he became full-time Bishop at the end of 1991 (Storey 2005 b). When Dandala was approached by Storey about appointment to Central, he had mixed feelings about accepting, related in part to Johannesburg's travails. What "could I try that Peter Storey has not tried," he asked (Dandala 1992). In an interview with *The Weekly Mail* newspaper he described the job of running Central as "the mother of all challenges" (Dube 1993:12).

Dandala understood his tasks at Central to include helping "blacks feel at home—that they are not just visitors." He wanted to deal with the "real fear of the implications of major black leadership for members." Like his predecessor, he would have liked to "make the church financially viable." The difficulty that black members would experience at Central, he said, was to settle "in what was a strong white traditional church" (Dandala 1992). Dandala's early months at Central was difficult, particularly as he inherited structures and expectations not of his own making. Ironically, he experienced difficulties working with the 10-step charter that Storey had designed.

Signs of strain appeared among Central's staff and congregation, partly due to public roles played by successive superintendent ministers, partly to the strong outward focus and overcommitment of personnel. "Central is strong on the journey outward but has no inward journey," commented one worker. Of the nine mission clusters that had developed, the programmes of several no longer functioned (e.g. Ubulungisa); only functioned in a limited way (e.g. only two fellowship groups remained); or had been closed (e.g. Malihambe). The "growing measure" of financial support that Storey's overseas visits had brought for Central's work had started to dry up. The time consumed by new superintendent Dandala's public role had led to a simmering conflict among staff. The black/white ratio in the congregation came under threat, due to white flight from the city and to the symbolic weight of a predominantly black ministerial team (Storey 1993:2).

The vision of full integration had only partially been fulfilled by 1993. Meetings remained male-dominated in style and in choice of chairpersons. Blacks and women were under-represented in leadership structures, the former more so than the latter. For example, at a leaders' meeting in January 1992, 12 of the 25 people who attended were women, and three were black. Neither one of the two faith-sharing small groups that remained was integrated.

Central's leaders were aware of failures along the way. Some indicated that the mostly black congregation remained uninvolved in Central's programmes. Storey acknowledged that black congregants failed to become involved in decision-making and in "helping to carry the load" during his time at Central. He suggested that black Methodism's tradition of holding black ministers responsible for all aspects of their congregations without lay involvement could have been partly to blame. Storey believed that South African Methodism needed to change those aspects of black ministry that depended on authoritarian styles. The difficulty of black members to be informal and spontaneous during worship at Central may be related to their perception of the black superintendent as an authority figure. Another failure was the constant stop-start nature of the youth group (Storey 1994). Storey admitted that his style of leading was top-downwards. Some members commented that he had been "dictatorial" and "very authoritarian." Storey emphasised that he implemented "structures of accountability" and regularly consulted with lay leaders in formal and informal meetings. "None of the significant decisions happened without lengthy discussion and the okay of our lay leaders," he said (Storey 2005 b).

EXPLAINING CENTRAL'S RACIALLY-MIXED COMPOSITION

The question how Central became racially-mixed under apartheid requires our attention to forces that affected the decisions of those who promoted, accepted or resisted integration. As this, in turn, requires a scrutiny of external and internal forces at play between 1976 and 1990, I start below with the external socio-political and economic structures that impacted the congregation. Then I review the internal structures and agents operating within the congregation. The descriptive and particular nature of my discussion here prepares the groundwork for more theoretical and generalised extrapolations in Chapter 5. Such possibilities should be weighed against the alternating biases that nudged other

South African congregations towards either integration or segregation, as discussed in Chapter One. The absence of detailed congregational data renders speculation about the colonial to the Union periods precarious, and my conclusions should be accepted as preliminary. Note that the general factors that I identify as influencing Central's racial composition during the colonial period would also have affected Saint Francis Xavier. Similarly, factors that affected Central during the apartheid period would also have influenced both Saint Francis and Johweto, and will not be repeated in Chapters Three and Four. Instead, I will note more specific phenomena that impacted on each case in relation to their particular contexts and denominational linkages.

Several constraining factors at work in central Johannesburg from the colonial to the Union periods limited Central to being a white congregation even before apartheid became official policy. I could find no counter-evidence from Central's remarkably extensive records to suggest that Central was not a white congregation prior to 1976. Occasional exceptions did occur, most notably when a young Nelson Mandela attended Central in the 1950s, during the ministry of Joe Webb (Storey 2005 b).

During both Boer and British colonial periods potential candidates (who could have been drawn into a mixed congregation) lived at Braamfontein, relatively close to the Wesleyan Church Hall. Yet the municipal policy of removing blacks, Indians and coloureds from the central city to the urban peripheries would have reduced such potential sources of racial integration. South African Methodism's tradition of establishing mission stations for blacks and "societies" for whites would have helped to keep Central segregated. The racial bias of early Johannesburg's Methodists probably favoured white labourers, diggers, and farmers. At the time there was a general trend towards segregation in colonial Transvaal. The Transvaal Education Act No. 25 (1907) established separate schools for children of colour. Africans, Indians and Coloured were prohibited from admission to 'European' (i.e. white) schools (South African History Online n.d. b). The Act ensconced English as the only language that was a compulsory school subject.

Despite all these factors, other racially-mixed congregations did emerge during the colonial period in Johannesburg and Pretoria. But as these were located mainly in racially-mixed areas, we should compare Central to other churches in Johannesburg's central area, such as the Anglican cathedral of Saint Mary's. While Saint Mary's did not become integrated until 1957, this still pre-dates Central's integration by almost two decades.

The above review of national and local factors that promoted institutional racial segregation in Johannesburg brings us to the factors that prompted integration. Central's narrative clearly demonstrated that innovative individual agency (torey) played the primary role in moving Central beyond segregation. torey himself was embedded in a network of like-minded and supportive individuals. The initial impetus of his father and later of obertson provide examples of individual external support. Within the congregation, torey's actions were augmented by the presence of individuals—such as Rees, Roberts, Mvunyiswa, Trevor Hudson, Rick Matthews, David ewby, Helen Muller, Myeza, Mbabane and Ching—whom he had appointed. Individual agents drew on a repository of collective symbolic and ideological resources, generated by others who resisted apartheid, to integrate institutions. But agents could also add new resources or change those that already existed. The candle circled by barbed wire on Central's communion table to remember political detainees demonstrates such innovation. We also need to consider seriously the claims by Storey and Ching that the Scriptures were an important resource, particularly torey's emphasis on "the Biblical theology of hospitality, on the inclusiveness at the centre of Wesley's theology" (Storey 2005 b).

Once congregations like Central became racially-mixed, the "image of the church as a non-racial church" drew people who believed in integrating previously segregated institutions (Dandala 1992). More than a third (35%) of those that I polled in 1992 attended Central for this reason. Reverend Dandala himself wanted to be part of a racially-mixed church "because of a commitment to various races reaching out to one another...South Africa has got to be a non-racial community, and I want to be part of [such] a community on the basis of an informed faith" (Dandala 1992). He pointed out that blacks who attended Central's Sunday morning service could have gone to the Fordsburg Section's vernacular services in the same building during afternoons. Instead, they wanted to belong to a church that was for everybody.

More specifically, white congregants who continued to attend a church now located in the mainly black inner city neighbourhood had a particular symbolic impact on church membership. A black congregant said that when Reverend Mvunyiswa baptised a white child, "this shows that whites accept change...I have not seen this anywhere else"

(Ndamase 1993). Sixty-three percent of those who attended Central in 1992 had invited others to come. Presumably, they had liked the racial mix and had invited others who would also respond positively to it. Ching summarised the collective alternate vision that drew people to Central when he said:

> Racial integration is an expression of the kingdom, while mono-racial churches are a cheapening of it. In [the New Testament book of] *Revelation* all nations are worshipping God together. The Homogeneous Unit Principle[77] is heresy, especially in [racially] divided nations (Ching 1992a).

By 1992 whites were slowly withdrawing from Central's congregation, despite hearing from the black superintendent minister and other leaders that retaining the racial-mix was vital. An older member thought that adult white congregants, while continuing to attend Central, had enrolled their children in the Sunday schools of suburban churches, to which they themselves were now moving. Post-apartheid Central seemed to be in a slow transition to becoming a black church. An internal bifurcation was emerging between an increasingly black morning service and an evening service that was attended mostly by whites. This was of some concern to a regular evening service participant, who said there was a need "for more blacks to come."

My interviews with Central's congregants provided a variety of perceptions of why blacks attended. Some whites suggested that Central's leadership style was more attractive to black Africans than those of township congregations. According to this perception, authority at Central was less formal and strict. "A lot come because they are not tied down as tightly," said a white congregant. The brevity of Central's services compared to those in the townships was seen as more appealing to blacks. A black member noted that people are accepted in terms of how they dress. Although the dress code of black African congregants remained visibly more upmarket than those of whites, a black congregant argued that the 3 p.m. vernacular service had an even more formal dress code (Ndamase 1993).

Central's programs modelled an alternate social order that drew

---

77. The homogeneous unit "principle" was used by church growth advocates to justify socially and ethnically-similar congregations, viewed as producing maximal numerical growth. Missiologist Donald McGavran originated the notion, arguing that "People like to become Christians without crossing racial, linguistic, or class barriers" (McGavran and Wagner 1990:46,163,238).

people from the segregated city into an integrated experience, however limited. The People Centre provided " 'a model for the bridging of racial differences within a social setting' " (Storey in Scott 1981:18). Others came because of the involvement of their children in F.L.O.C. or the Careways after-school program. Central's reputation for social engagement, constructed by the actions of Storey and the congregation during the 1970s and 1980s, continued to draw members by the early 1990s (Storey 1993:2, 1992:4). A coloured member noted that had heard of Storey during the 1976 riots. Like others, he felt that a racially-mixed church in which people were treated the same was important: "each one could benefit spiritually from the different cultures" (Ortell 1992).

But mostly the involvement of Central's staff in the struggle for social (racial) justice gained credibility and drew both blacks and whites of the same persuasion into the congregation. Such actions built a reputation "for being the centre of protest and a haven for those who were being harassed by the security police" (Storey 1993:2). Eric and Lynne van den Berg served as typical examples of such white congregants, as did F.L.O.C. director Wendy Young. Eric, a white lawyer, was a conscientious objector and a member of the Methodist Order of Peacemakers. Lynne had been a member of the radical student organisation Students United for Christian Action, and had attended a church in the coloured suburb of Coronationville. She had heard of Storey's "anti-apartheid Christianity", and wanted to be part of a group where she would not stand out (Van den Berg 1993). She contrasted her experience at Central with that offered by Northfield Methodist which she had visited. There was "no candle and no reference to the taxi war" raging at the time (Van den Berg 1993). Similarly, F.L.O.C. director Wendy Young came because she was "looking for a church involved in wider issues." Young regularly drove past "thirteen other Methodist churches" to attend Central (Young 1992).

Despite the intentions of ministers and laity, interaction between congregants—outside of official programmes (meetings, ministries)—still appeared superficial by 1992. Interracial encounters were limited to Sunday teas after services, and in general the style of proceedings at Central still seemed both English and white. Rudolph said, "We are trying to maintain a [sense of] family; but maybe the bridge is too wide. We are trying to involve people with one another, but this does not appear to be important [to them]" (Rudolph 1992). The fact that people had few links with other congregants did not help. The Ndamase family, who lived in an apartment two blocks from the church building, could not say whether any of Central's other congregants lived nearby (Ndamase 1993). I later discovered from Central's records that about 48 other churchgoers lived on the same city block as the Ndamases. Curiously enough, Central's "white culture" and English language-orientation actually seemed to contribute to the mix. Whites, and probably Coloureds and Indians, were unlikely to attend a purely vernacular service. Some blacks seemed to prefer not to attend the traditional, more formal, black Methodist services elsewhere.

In summary, then, transition to a racially-mixed congregation was aided primarily by the decision by former senior minister Storey to move the church in that direction in 1976. The symbolic value the church acquired through anti-apartheid activities drew like-minded people of all colours. Integration was primed by the exodus of whites to the suburbs from the late 1970s and the influx of blacks into urban areas in the mid-1980s. The subsequent decline in Central's overall membership was halted by the addition of black members. Integration was also helped by the Methodist Church of Southern Africa's status as comprising the largest number of black affiliates—apart from the African Indigenous Churches. Black Methodists may for this reason have been over-represented in the black influx into central Johannesburg. The Mthandazo and the Mthemba families were representative of the 27% of those polled in 1992 who attended because Central was their nearest Methodist church. The desire by some blacks to escape more conservative black township churches, as Central's black ministers claimed, seemed to be another factor driving congregational integration.

3

Integrating the Segregated Suburb:

Saint Francis Xavier Catholic Church, Martindale

INTRODUCTION

The history of Saint Francis Xavier Catholic Church clearly illustrates the close interaction between this congregation and its ideological (political) and geographical (urban) contexts. Saint Francis began as an African Mission located in the freehold area of Martindale, on the western fringe of Johannesburg. Over time, the state's implementation of the Group Areas Act (1950) changed the parish's immediate geographical context into a white suburb. Saint Francis' historical trajectory starkly exhibits the transition from the union regime that discouraged urban integration to the apartheid state's regime of enforced segregation.

Like Central Methodist Mission, shifts in Saint Francis' composition were mediated by the spatial development of Johannesburg. The policies of the city council and the state to racially redistribute urban residents directly impacted Saint Francis' original parishioners. Saint Francis' adjacent neighbourhoods—Martindale, Sophiatown, and the Western Areas—bore the brunt of state-enforced segregation. Forced removals between 1955 and 1961 imposed involuntary segregation on black and coloured residents of these areas who were also parishioners. The historically close connection between parish and suburb surfaces in the preference of parishioners to speak of 'Martindale' rather than of 'Saint Francis.' Today the parish lies in the newly-reconstituted suburb of Sophiatown. In contrast to Central Methodist Mission's early history as a white congregation, Saint Francis began as a black parish. But despite the initial differences and widely varying locations, the two congregations shared a common mono-racial destiny, as the analysis will show.

After the triumph of apartheid in 1948, Saint Francis' parishioners continued to intermarry and to attend Mass together in quiet acts of defiance, as the parish's original marriage registers highlights. During the apartheid era Saint Francis attracted white Catholic ideological opponents of apartheid who viewed participation in rituals in a transracial context as acts of symbolic defiance, as the title of this chapter suggests. The apartheid state had succeeded in changing the black suburb into a white area, yet the stubborn resolve of parishioners to remain loyal to Saint Francis ensured a racially-mixed composition that denied complete victory to the state.

The parish marriage registers bore out the picture of different races living together and sometimes intermarrying,[78] until segregation took hold. Saint Francis' records from 1929 to 1955 show that ten couples married outside their ethnic group. Despite the Prohibition of Mixed Marriages Act (1949), 34 people (17 couples) married outside their ethnic group between 1955 and 1993 (Saint Francis Xavier Catholic Church n.d). While the Mixed Marriages Act prohibited marriage between whites and other race groups, other ethnic groups were also affected. People had to adopt the racial identity of the person they married. In all, twelve mixed marriages were registered at Saint Francis after the passing of the Act, which was in force until 1985.

The number of mixed marriages at Saint Francis are significant when compared to the national average of about 100 such marriages annually in South Africa during the 1940s. From 1983 to 1993 only one other mixed marriage is recorded, indicating the force of apartheid legislation. Most of those who were married had lived in adjacent Sophiatown. The registers also show that Saint Francis was largely a black parish until 1961; starting with the first wedding in 1933, black marriages dominated each decade into the sixties. Of the marriages between 1933 and 1955, 216 were of black persons. The registers also track the trajectory of integration in the parish. A marriage of a white couple first appeared in 1934, five years after the church building was erected; the first Indian marriage occurred in 1942.

Forced spatial segregation did influence congregational composition, as removals decreased the proportion of black parishioners, resulting in services that were eventually mainly attended by whites. A few blacks continued to travel from Soweto to the church services, despite the cost and distance.

---

78. Five interracial couples were married before 1949, and five more between 1948-55. Seven such weddings occurred between 1967 and 1983 (St. Francis Xavier Catholic Church n.d.).

CATHOLICISM AND RACE IN THE OLD TRANSVAAL

Once Catholics began to consider African tribes across the Orange River in 1840, the pattern of Catholic mission changed to segregated missions. European civilisation was considered unlikely to dominate in the transOrange regions (Brown 1960:204; see Oosthuizen 1968:15). Until the 1850s Catholics in the Transvaal region were served through occasional visits from priests from Mozambique (via Father Juaquin da Santa Rita Montanha) and from Fauresmith (the Belgian, Father Hoendervanger, Order of Premontre) (Brady 1960). Whether the Mozambique connection stemmed from Portuguese religious orders that were originally responsible for Catholic mission in Southern Africa is unclear. In any case, Catholic worship was forbidden in the Zuid-Afrikaansche Republiek until 1872, as it had been in the Dutch Cape Colony. As a result, so few Catholics lived in the Transvaal, that until 1877 a priest was sent from Natal to minister to them.

The Catholic presence in Johannesburg was closely tied to the work of the Missionary Oblates of Mary Immaculate (O.M.I), who arrived in Natal in 1852, from where they began to conduct their Transvaal missionary activities. Prior to Johannesburg, the Missionary Oblates had worked in the Transvaal at Pilgrims Rest (1857) and Potchefstroom (1870). In 1877 Bishop Dr. Charles Jolivet O.M.I. of Natal founded a mission at Pretoria. In 1886, the Missionary Oblates were made responsible for the establishment of the Catholic church over the whole of the Transvaal. The Apostolic Prefecture of Transvaal was detached from the Vicariate of Natal by Pope Leo XIII in the same year under the Right Reverend O. Monginoux, OM.I., the first Prefect Apostolic (Brady 1960; Missionary Oblates of Mary Immaculate 2002.).

The first Catholic church building in the Transvaal was erected in Pretoria in 1887 for the hundred Catholics who then resided there. From the start of the 20th century the Oblate Fathers were joined in the Transvaal by other religious orders. But the order remained in charge of the Transvaal, first as an independent prefecture, and later as part of the diocese of Kimberley (1902). In 1904 the region became the Vicariate Apostolic of Transvaal, from which the Apostolic Vicariate of Johannesburg was detached in 1948. Johannesburg was raised in status to a separate diocese in 1951, and in 2007 to a a Metropolitan Archdiocese (Catholic Archdiocese n.d.). The present Archbishop, Buti Thlagale (appointed 2003), is again an Oblate Father.

The first Catholic Mass on the diggings that later became Johannesburg was said by Father L. Trabaud, O.M.I., in the bakery of a Mr. Whelan in Ferreira's Camp. Thirty-three attended that service in February 1887, and numbers rose to more than sixty by April. By August 1887 the first Catholic buildings in Johannesburg had been erected at the corner of Fox and Small streets. The buildings comprised a residence for the priest, a small church, a school, and a small convent. Holy Family Sisters were brought from Natal to look after the school and convent. An Oblate Father from Kimberley was appointed the first Catholic parish priest of the mining camp. By 1892 a larger church had been constructed on the corner of Main and Von Weilligh Streets by the newly appointed prefect, Father Aloysius Schoch, O.M.I. Schoch built a still larger church in Kerk Street (Brady 1960).

Catholic work in the Transvaal of the 1890s became racially segregated, ostensibly due to "difficulties of language and distance." Black miners who had arrived at the gold mines on the Reef region (Johannesburg and surrounds) included Catholics from Lesotho, Natal, Transkei, and Mozambique (Shangaans) (Brain 1991:71). A priest from Maputo was responsible for visiting the Shangaans. Catholic priests served the white areas, and few could speak indigenous languages. One exception was the German, Father Willem Schwiete, who spoke isiZulu and seTswana and was involved in the mineworkers' missions on the Reef. During this period Mass was conducted in Latin and the sermon or instruction in English (Brain 1991:71,134).

Catholic ranks were swollen by the sporadic addition of immigrants and indentured labourers, including Chinese, Portuguese, and Lebanese immigrants. Chinese and Lebanese were classified Asian ("Asiatic") in accordance with the Transvaal Act (1885), and for a while Portuguese were ascribed the same status as black Africans. Throughout its history, Saint Francis Xavier drew in such people who lived on the edges of racial classification.

The Chinese were brought to South Africa as indentured labourers at the start of the 20th century (Brain 1991:114, 117). Yet the first Chinese arrived in the Cape Colony as exiled prisoners in 1660 (*Daily Mail and Guardian* 2000; Kubheka 2004). By 1904 1,380 Chinese were living in the Cape Colony alone, but further immigration to the Colony was prohibited by the Chinese Exclusion Act of 1904 (Yap and Man 1996). The Qing Court had by 1905 appointed a Consul to Cape Town to look after the affairs of Chinese residents in the country (Kubheka 2004). Between 1904 and 1907 some 63,695 Chinese were recruited to work as unskilled labour in the Witwatersrand mines (Beavon 1992). In 1908 the Chinese Association joined the non-violent campaign against the Transvaal Asiatic Registration Act which the colonial government had passed the previous year. Because the Act was perceived as being anti-Asiatic, rather than anti-Indian, opposition came from Indians and Chinese alike. While in prison in 1907 for his part in organising the campaign, Mahatma Gandhi consulted with Leung Quinn (Chinese Association) and Thambi Naidoo (Transvaal British Indian Association) before rejecting the compromise terms of the Act that had been proposed by then-colonial secretary Jan Smuts (South African History Online n.d. b). By 1910 all indentured Chinese had been repatriated (Burger 2003), but more than a thousand traders and shop keepers who had not been mine workers remained in the Transvaal (Man 2005).

Many Chinese lived in the Martindale and Sophiatown neighbourhoods, and were among those who were forced to leave. Others resided in the coloured suburb of Albertsville, from where they attended Saint Francis until 1976, when Albertsville too was designated a white suburb. As no particular area had been set aside for the Chinese, many had to live in the limbo of the so-called grey suburbs of Doornfontein, Jeppe, and Mayfair (Man 2005).

The first Lebanese immigrants came to Johannesburg with the discovery of gold towards the end of the 19th century. Originating mostly in northern Lebanon, some entered the Transvaal via Mozambique (Lebos 1997). Colloquially known as Syrians, after the administrative Turkish district where they had lived, the Lebanese experienced dual prejudice as "outlanders" who also were designated non-Europeans. The Lebanese were classified under Transvaal Act (1885) as falling under the "Native Races of Asia" in the opinion of the Rand Township Registrar. Their origin as Turkish nationals also associated them with the "Mahomedan subjects of the Turkish dominion" which Article 1 of the Act declared to be Asian (see De Villiers, Solomon and Innes 1913). Despite both the secular and Catholic press arguing that the Lebanese should be regarded as "European" (Brain 1991:258), their non-European status extended into the Union period. In 1913 Moses Gandur, a Lebanese who wanted to obtain land rights, successfully petitioned the courts to classify "Syriacs" as white (Hourani 2000). In part, the petition succeeded because Syrian Christians had already in 1907 been granted licenses to trade by the Receiver of Revenue, who explicitly stated that they were excluded from the Asiatic Amendment Law. A similar opinion was offered by the Registrar of Asiatics (De Villiers, Solomon and Innes 1913). Most Catholic Lebanese belonged to parishes using the Maronite rite, "which follows the Syriac liturgy of Antioch" (Brain 1991:178). In 1905 a Maronite Catholic Church was started in Diagonal Street, Johannesburg, and in 1908 a Maronite church building was erected in the Fordsburg suburb (Brain 1991:118, 178). Some Lebanese continued to attend Saint Francis to the present.

By 2012 the Archdiocese of Johannesburg comprised 125 parishes that served a Catholic population of approximately 800,000 (Catholic Archdiocese of Johannesburg n.d.). According to the South African Catholic Bishops' Conference, South African Catholics reside in 21 dioceses plus 5 archdioceses (Cape Town, Durban, Bloemfontein, Johannesburg, and Pretoria; South African Catholic Bishops' Conference n.d.; compare Cheney 2005).

FROM FARM TO FREEHOLD (1897-1909)

The history of Saint Francis does not start with the colonial era, although the origins of the suburb with whose fate its own would be entwined, did. The close connection between suburb and parish was highlighted by the habit among parishioners in the 1990s to speak of 'Martindale' rather than 'Saint Francis,' as I do. This practice showed that Saint Francis' collective identity was formed as much by the history of the surrounding neighbourhood as by the history of change in the wider Catholic church.

The suburbs of Martindale and Sophiatown, its adjacent neighbour, were part of 237 acres of the farm Waterval [Waterfall] that one Herman Tobiansky bought in 1897, some 7 kilometres west of central Johannesburg. Because of a lack of interest from whites, Tobiansky eventually sold plots to anybody—to blacks as well as to whites who rented their property out to black tenants and others. Martindale became a freehold area in which blacks could own land and live in Johannesburg that otherwise reserved property rights for whites. To the northeast a similar situation prevailed in Alexandra township.

FROM MISSION TO SOME TO PARISH FOR ALL (1910–48)

After the First World War, the municipality in 1918 created the Western Areas Native Township (for blacks) a mere one block west of Saint

Francis. An influenza epidemic that year provided the authorities with the pretext to move blacks from inner city areas to Western Areas. Johannesburg already had a black population of 116,120. With the establishment of Western Areas, the council for the first time assumed responsibility to provide housing for black residents (Beinart 2004). The population of the freehold areas exploded from 12,000 in 1928 to 26,000 in 1934, partly due to the industrialisation of the city after the First World War. While mine owners housed their workers in compounds close to their places of work, factory owners did not. The clearance of inner city black and mixed race neighbourhoods by the city council and the lack of alternative accommodation also contributed to the population expansion of the freehold areas.

The close proximity of various groups in the surrounding neighbourhoods contributed to Saint Francis Xavier's mix of races. Sophiatown—named for Tobiansky's wife—counted white, coloured, Indian, and Chinese residents among its mostly black population. Sophiatown had dirt tracks until the 1930s, with rudimentary sewerage services. Health care and educational services had to be provided by churches. Martindale and Newclare were from the start set aside as black suburbs. Fewer blacks owned property than rented it. Those who did own property in Sophiatown, Martindale, and Newclare formed the Non-European Ratepayers' Association in 1926. In 1933 the municipality proclaimed Johannesburg outside the freehold areas a restricted area in which blacks could not own or lease property (South African History Online n.d. a).

Saint Francis Xavier African Mission was completed in 1929 under Father Yves-Marie Saccadas, O.M.I. (1879-1946) as one of the first Black missions in Johannesburg. As it was colloquially known during this period, 'the Mission' was instigated by Bishop David O'Leary, O.M.I. (1880-1958). O'Leary, the first South African born Catholic priest, was appointed as the third vicariate apostolic of the Transvaal in 1925 (Brain 1991:205,212). As both Saccadas and O'Leary belonged to the Missionary Oblates of Mary Immaculate, the parish was initially considered an "O.M.I. Parish." By 1993 neither the priest (Vic Kotze) or the bishop (Reginald Orsmond) were Oblate Fathers. Saccadas served Saint Francis until 1944. Originally based in the Johannesburg suburb of Mayfair, Saccadas had travelled regularly to serve the Martindale area since 1926.

According to a tradition handed down within Saint Francis, most parishioners in the 1920s were blacks, with some coloureds and a small group of whites. Long-standing parishioner Haynet Alves related that she had heard this from late parishioner Betty Charles. Charles herself was "an old [coloured] woman [who had been] married to a white guy" (Alves 1993). Hymns were sung in seSotho and isiZulu, and a black choir used the balcony as a choir-loft.

The tradition about the languages used at Saint Francis and its early mix is largely borne out by the history of the convent school built there in 1931 (Brain 1991:205,212). The Saint Francis Xavier School was staffed by the Sisters of Notre Dame de Namur (Belgium) from 1932. From an initial intake of 53, the school grew to 400 children by 1933, afterwards reaching an annual enrolment of more than 1,200 pupils. Probably reflecting the mix of the church itself, the children were from amaZulu, baSotho, Batswana, and coloured descent. The Sisters received permission in 1947 from the educational authorities to start a secondary school (Sisters of Notre Dame de Namur n.d.).

Meanwhile, the Johannesburg City Council decided in October 1944 to pursue the 'Western Areas Scheme.' Newclare, Western Native Township and part of Claremont would become coloured townships, and be consolidated with Coronationville (established 1937) and Noordgesig (1940, bordering Orlando East) to provide housing exclusively for coloureds (South African History Online n.d. f). Black residents of Martindale and Sophiatown would be removed to Orlando and other areas in the South Western Townships, as Soweto was initially known (South African History Online n.d. g). Opposition from many quarters delayed the Scheme's implementation, including from the dominant party in the City Council, the United Party, and from the Transvaal Indian Congress, who objected almost immediately, in November 1944.

When Father Jean-Marie Delajod, O.M.I. (1905-70) became parish priest at Saint Francis in 1945, Mass was conducted in a mix of Latin and in isiZulu, the language spoken by most parishioners. Delajod was remembered in Saint Francis as the priest who walked to all corners of his parish during his tenure from 1945 to 1960. Portuguese parishioners were now participating in services, but the evidence about when they started to come is inconclusive. Some parishioners recalled that Portuguese began to attend services during Delajod's time, but a registry recorded a Portuguese wedding in 1934. A long-standing parishioner recalled that "Many Portuguese had vegetable farms in what is today Northcliff suburb. They sat in the first three rows—did not want to sit with the blacks." By then some whites were also attending, while coloureds (for whom Saint Francis remained the closest Catholic church) continued to come.

FROM FORCED SEGREGATION TO VOLUNTARY INTEGRATION (1949-90)

The Johannesburg City Council's reluctance to implement Group Areas was overcome when the National Party government under Hans Strijdom created the Native Resettlement Board to effect the Act in the Western Areas under guise of slum clearance. The Minister of Native Affairs responsible for the removal of the estimated 80,000 blacks from Sophiatown, Martindale and Newclare was Hendrik Verwoerd (South African History Online n.d. h.).

Opposition to the scheme continued along white and black fronts. The planned removals were actively opposed by white liberals, both inside and outside the Liberal Party. The Liberal Party's 1953 municipal by-election campaign in Ward 9 (Johannesburg suburbs of Killarney, Saxonwold, Parkview, Greenside), for example, had centered on opposition to the removals. Reportedly 30% of the white electorate who had voted for the party "opposed the removal of African inhabitants of the Western Areas. They accepted these African people as fellow citizens of Johannesburg; they opposed their removal...on moral and common-sense grounds" (*Contact* 1954). Significantly, many of the other white liberals who opposed the removal were associated with multi-racial institutions such as the Joint Councils of Natives and Europeans, as well as the South African Institute of Race Relations (Hirson n.d).[79]

Sophiatown residents combined with political organisations to form the Western Areas Protest Committee (South African History Online n.d. i.). The African National Congress highlighted opposition to the Scheme during the run-up to the Congress of the People at Kliptown. Walter Sisulu urged a meeting in Sophiatown in April 1954 to resist removals (South African History Online n.d. j.). Protest meetings were held across the country in February 1955, and Albert Lutuli urged "Non-Europeans and Europeans in every part of South Africa" to "join in this struggle of the people of the Western Areas, not only to save their homes, but to end...apartheid" (Lutuli 1955).

The Natives' Resettlement Board on January 7, 1955 issued the first

---

79. But liberals were divided on broader issues: some wanted to retain the status quo; others, to widen the Cape franchise and add more land (Hirson n.d).

removal notices that would eventually end Saint Francis' history as an African mission. On 10 February a police force of 2,000 began removing the first 110 families of blacks at gunpoint to the black city of Soweto, mostly to Meadowlands, but also to Orlando, Diepkloof, Dube and Rockville. At the opening of the Catholic parish building in Meadowlands later, a former Saint Francis parishioner who had been removed said: " 'We will never recapture what we had at Martindale, ' " recalled Haynet Alves (Alves 1993). She had been a parishioner at Saint Francis since 1945 and had attended the Meadowlands function. When the slow and painful process of removals were completed in 1961, Sophiatown was bulldozed and subdivided. The major part was renamed Triomf (Afrikaans for "triumph").

The removals began while Father Delajod was parish priest, and was completed while Father Leo Muldoon O.M.I. (1902-1982) ran the parish (1955 to 1961). Black participation at Saint Francis came to an end, although the four black marriages there after 1961 (the last in 1976) implied that a few black parishioners continued to attend. The areas immediately surrounding the parish building were declared white neighbourhoods. Saint Francis Xavier School had to close its doors in 1959, although the Sisters of Notre Dame de Namur continued to serve the parish until 1965. Some Sisters went to teach their relocated pupils at a school begun in 1959 by the Marist brothers in Orlando West. The secondary school envisaged for Martindale was instead now built on the farm of the bishop at Venterspost-West in 1952, as a boarding school for black girls. But the Venterspost-West school was not out of reach of the Group Areas Act, and in 1958 also had to close. Ironically, the financial obligations associated with building the school meant that it had to continue as a school for white girls until 1969 (Sisters of Notre Dame de Namur n.d.).

Under the Act, Coloureds were also forced out, some to just across the major street (Main Road) that separated the newly white suburb of Martindale from the now coloured Western Township. Some coloureds were moved more than once, at first from Newclare and Sophiatown to Albertsville, where they could not own property. Next they were shifted from Albertsville to Western Township, or to the coloured suburb of Bosmont. Possibly because of such events, "One coloured family pretended to be white, and did not mix with the rest of us coloured or black parishioners" (Alves 1993).

In response to the coloured removals Father Jan Molenaar O.M.I. (b.

1912), parish priest from 1961 to 1972, had a church built in the nearby coloured suburb of Bosmont. While the building was under way, Saint Francis bussed in coloured parishioners from their new residences to Mass (Alves 1993). Although the racial mix at Saint Francis during the 1960s was largely white with some coloureds, Chinese and Portuguese ethnic groups also came to Mass. The Chinese were still evident in Saint Francis by 1976 as indicated by an entry in the marriage-register, but subsequently had left.

Numbers at Mass declined until the mid-1970s, when the diocese considered closing the parish. Father Vic Kotze's appointment in 1978 marked a turning point in numbers and ethnic mix, pulling in some and repelling others. A parishioner said that Kotze "makes people feel wanted." By now so many of the parishioners were Portuguese that a Portuguese priest successfully requested permission to conduct Mass in their vernacular at Easter, Christmas and special Portuguese holy days. In the 1980s the first Indian parishioner since the 1940s arrived, later bringing his cousin, too. The Indian parishioner was attracted to Saint Francis by the warm welcome he experienced, but also by the singing of " 'Nkosi Sikelel' iAfrika" during Mass. Alves (1993) recalled that "Vic's political views also drew a lot of people." By 1982 about 80% of parishioners were whites (McGregor 1992). Overall attendance at Mass steadily increased, but not all found Saint Francis under Kotze to their liking. Kotze calculated that as many as half of the politically more conservative Portuguese left because of his political views. In 1992 people of Portuguese descent made up an estimated 3-4% of the parishioners as a whole (McGregor 1992).

Kotze's tenure also signalled the introduction of more overt symbols of resistance to apartheid, such as a Sunday liturgy in 1988 that included a dramatic presentation of detention without trial. The state had in April 1987 prohibited calls for the release of detainees, a decree ignored by Catholic Archbishop Stephen Naidoo, who subsequently called for prayers for the release of detainees (Villa-Vicencio 1988:95). Naidoo in turn was upholding a tradition in the South African Catholic Bishops Conference, who spoke out in the 1972 document *A Call to Conscience* "for the detained, banned and restricted" (Mukuka 1997).

For the dramatic presentation, members of the parish's Justice and Peace group occupied the sanctuary, said a prayer for detainees, and lit a candle with barbed wire around it. Some of them were chained and had blindfolds on. The altar[80] was decorated with prison bars cut from paper. Afterwards someone reported Kotze to the Special Branch of the police, prompting an "angry sermon about traitors," related a parishioner. Kotze remembered that he had discovered later that it had in fact been a visitor and not a parishioner that reported him. A parishioner interpreted the event as a clash between Kotze and the people on justice and peace issues. Other responses suggested that parishioners objected more to the medium than the message. "They felt that the spoken word conveys enough; the priest can talk about these issues. I do not believe that Mass is a drama—it is a time to lift up hearts and minds to God," a parishioner said. In his opinion, "other parishes call Martindale a circus." Another agreed that "people feel that the liturgy is not a place to put a point across so heavily." Some approached the liturgy group and asked them to tone down such events. Perhaps people were repulsed not just by the emotionally charged symbols, but by the invasion of "sacred" space by a "profane" (political) issue.

Some parishioners had also reacted negatively to a 1991 Mass during which someone had knocked loudly at the church building door, to represent those who were locked out of society. At another Mass, members of the Justice and Peace group read out letters from detainees. These events, along with Kotze's preaching, led to a raised political awareness at Saint Francis. The state's unbanning of the liberation movement in February 1990 were "a major event for the parish; something that was prayed for and seen as God at work" (Te Riele 1992). In an August 1992 Kotze declared in a sermon that the Holy Spirit was seen in those who are born-again, but also in released political prisoner Nelson Mandela "reaching out a hand of reconciliation." He referred to then-State President F.W. de Klerk's 1990 unbanning of organisations as another example. Although people often did not think that the Spirit lives in them, "God in us" helped us to be tolerant "where we had been intolerant before...God's Spirit helps us survive, breathes in us an ability for justice...everything that makes us human."

No doubt due to the historical ties between neighbourhood and parish, parishioners expressed a strong awareness of spatial identity. The church building was restructured in 1989 around a particular emphasis

---

80. 'Altar' refers to the table on which bread and wine is prepared for communion as well as the raised area on which it stands. The latter is also called the sanctuary (Fenn 1992).

on liturgy,[81] "a deepening eucharistic community," and a "sense of common priesthood" (Saint Francis Xavier 1989:2). Before the remodelling, the church building had the long and narrow east-west shape typical of Catholic churches, with the altar at the eastern end faced by rows of wooden pews. The present layout turned the seating north-south, with the altar on a raised stage in the southern part and upholstered chairs facing it in a semi-circle. The present arrangement expressed the essence of "Christianity: embracing around the altar," suggested a parishioner (Taylor 1992). The table, made from the old pews, was to be "as simple as it would have been in the early church" (Taylor 1992). Another reflected that the remodelling was "answering a need arising in the parish for a greater sense of community" (Hyam 1992).

Interior space was used in a highly symbolic manner inside the church building—particularly through the stage at the front, which suggested sacredness by being raised above the level where parishioners sat. This sense that some space was more associated with sacredness was heightened by the specialised liturgical functions performed by those allowed to occupy the stage during Mass. A flat, round baked bread was used instead of the usual round wafers that were the norm at Mass for Catholic and Anglican churches. Parish priest Kotze broke the bread facing the people. Every eligible person took wine, slightly unusual for the Catholic Church, where communion either takes the form of bread, or the form of wine. Due to their awareness of sacred space, parishioners often longed for a church hall, as they found it "difficult to have a purely non-spiritual event when the sacrament and altar is there."

Other visual references on the stage included the table (the Altar of Sacrifice, where the communion bread is broken), candles, and a transparent perspex cross with a wooden Christ-figure. In keeping with the idea of a common priesthood, barriers (altar rails[82]) between priest and parish were deliberately omitted, as were those between parishioners themselves. The usual rows of church pews were replaced by chairs arranged in a semi-circle. Parishioners demonstrated their awareness of the significance of space by the way that specific groups habitually occupied the same section of seats every Sunday or Saturday. In inter-

---

81. By a "simplicity within spaces (including the furnishings)," according to parish member Mike Hyam, who designed the interior (Saint Francis Xavier 1989:3).

82. This is unusual but not totally unique; altar rails are also absent in the Bosmont parish building (Fothergill 1992).

views parishioners could easily recall where different groups or families sat.

A plaque inside the church building commemorated the suffering of forced removals that began in 1955, linking the present to the past.[83] Continuity with the past—painful for the most part—is important, given that the old building was retained and reshaped, rather than completely demolished. Demolition would probably have been too painful to contemplate here, given experiences of forced removal and the destruction of homes that followed. Some old benches were recycled as wooden furniture, used in constructing the Tables of the Word and Eucharist, for instance (Saint Francis Xavier 1989:3). In this way the new building and furniture recalled and transformed the past. Parish priest Kotze, who is also a qualified psychologist, motivated that "this great sadness and injustice must be understood and assimilated...if our present growth is to be graced by God." The focus is neither to "take on the guilt" nor "rest on the glory of the past," but to assimilate and acknowledge both. This would help people at Saint Francis to "become fully alive in the present in order to create our future" (Saint Francis Xavier 1989:1).

The past was also unintentionally recalled in other spatial ways. Generally, the darker people's skin colour, the further away from the altar they sat. Looking towards the altar, a visitor could observe that the left back and right front seats were particularly favoured by people of darker hue. Differentiated seating strongly linked the political past with the churched present. Black parishioners who sat towards the back provided a visual link with Saint Francis's pre-1989 internally segregated history, particularly with 1955. The habit of some to sit in the same place in a group with others of the same race served as a reminder of an era when coloured and black parishioners occupied the back pews.

TOWARDS A POST-APARTHEID CONGREGATION (1990-94)

Ironically, given the forced removals of the past, blacks, Indians and coloureds had recently begun buying houses in Martindale. By 1994, relatively few white parishioners lived in the suburbs immediately surrounding the church building, most travelling quite some distance to

---

83. The plaque reads: "This marble plaque was part of the original altar of this church. It is placed here to commemorate all those who suffered so much when the Group Areas Act scattered the people of the community then known as Sophiatown. He will send out His angels and gather His chosen from the four winds – Mark 13.27."

attend Mass (Kelly 1992). Parishioners at a small-group meeting that I attended recognised that Saint Francis was "not strictly a suburban church." Most parishioners usually came from afar, from suburbs—such as Florida, Bosmont, and Victory Park—that fell within the geographical boundaries of other parishes. At the time, such freedom of movement was still relatively unusual among Catholics, who tended to remain within parish boundaries. Fothergill estimated that about one-fifth of the parishioners come from within the boundaries of the Florida and Coronationville parishes, which at the time were predominantly white and coloured, respectively. By 1993 the single largest number of parishioners came from Florida, part of Roodepoort municipality at the time.

While Saint Francis was very obviously racially-mixed and multi-cultural by 1993, some parishioners recognised that the ethos included not only "a clear non-racial stance" but one that was also more widely inclusive. A parishioner said, "There is a commitment and liveliness [here] that you do not get in a lot of parishes...I have been around, but everyone finds here what is lacking elsewhere—what other [parishes] avoid or skirt" (Hyam 1992).The lay leadership was intent on promoting inclusive language in the parish. At a Pastoral Council meeting the opening prayer referred to "our Mother and Father God," and at a Mass similar terms were used. At a liturgy meeting the need to "de-sex" the popular songs sung by the congregation was accepted. In general, the gender inclusiveness of the leadership appeared not to have filtered through to the rest of the congregation, some who still used traditional male terminology for God in their prayers. The choir was singled out at the liturgy meeting as still singing the "old" (sexist) words.

A parishioner remarked that Saint Francis' was "set-up" for the emerging new South Africa. Another said Saint Francis was the only parish that met her need for a "non-racial parish...I would rather not go if that need is not met: I need a place where I can be different from the norm." She said the "liturgy and ethos [is] based in the current situation" (McGregor 1992). While about four Indian couples and 10 blacks were among the 230 people in total who typically attended Mass on Saturday or Sunday, most parishioners were either coloured or white. Whites still formed the majority grouping. The cultural mix included Lebanese, Portuguese, white and coloured English-speakers, and Afrikaans-speakers. Saint Francis' official estimates show that about 600 Catholics live within the parish's boundaries.

By 1994 Saint Francis appeared to be in transition to becoming a congregation in which coloureds formed the majority of parishioners. In part this was due to coloured parishioners residing closest to the parish buildings. An estimated 80% of all youth attending catechism classes was coloured. By contrast, in 1992 only one of the six eligible coloured families sent their children to catechism, according to parish notices. About 80% of all baptisms were of coloured infants, according to parish priest Kotze. Half of the parish youth group were white, and the other half, coloured.

Due to the continued effects of apartheid, parishioners at Saint Francis differed in racial and cultural terms, as well as in income and education. While most white parishioners were from middle to upper income and education brackets, most coloureds were workers from lower income groups. Some coloureds fell into the middle income and a few in the higher income brackets. A white parishioner estimated that most parishioners found it very difficult to make ends meet. About 20% were unemployed, and about 30% lived at subsistence level. Another parishioner suggested that the parish is mainly financed by "a very few" people (Kelly 1992). The largest monthly contribution came from a coloured family. Some parishioners suggested that people who resided in Martindale itself earned middle to lower incomes. By contrast to the socio-economic status of local parishioners, the homilies drew white intellectuals from Johannesburg suburbs where residents earn relative higher incomes, such as Bryanston and Yeoville (Fenn 1992).

Parishioners evinced a strong sense of Saint Francis' identity, often describing the parish as unique in the Johannesburg diocese. Parish priest Vic Kotze was partly responsible for creating this sense of uniqueness. He based his strong vision for the parish's role within the wider South African Catholic Church on the belief that lay involvement at Saint Francis pointed "to the future of parish life and the service of humanity" (Saint Francis Xavier 1989:2). Parishioners concluded that "Our parish is an example of what Vatican II had in mind: the church is the people, not a building." Parish co-ordinator Gordon Fothergill explained that Pope Pius XI had spoken of Catholic action "in the marketplace," which by definition meant the laity (Fothergill 1992).

Despite the racially-mixed Masses, few informal interracial contacts occurred among parishioners. Interracial contact usually took place in formalised interactional spaces dominated by white representatives, including Mass, Catechism classes, and Saint Vincent de Paul Society activities. Interracial contact tended to be initiated by whites. Small group faith-sharing meetings like Renew provided an informal space for mixing, but most took place in segregated all-white and all-coloured groups. Tea-time after Mass presented another informal space, described as "an important part of our Sunday liturgy here at Martindale" (Saint Francis Xavier 1994:12). Spontaneous conversations across colour lines did seem to occur here, but a parishioner thought that these remained superficial, without deepening relationships. Several parishioners said their lives were too busy when asked to explain why there was so little interaction.

In the rare instances that interracial interaction did happen, a coloured family was usually invited for a visit by a white family; the opposite happened more rarely. A white parishioner said that the initiative lay with whites. She experienced her visits to black and coloured friends as making them "embarrassed and humiliated." She explained that coloured families felt that their homes were not suitable to receive (white) guests. One of her black friends lived with nine others in Soweto; another in a small servant's room behind a white person's home nearby. Another white parishioner said that his family used to visit a coloured family, but that this fizzled out because "of the differences...there wasn't enough in it for us." Some contact did occur, and some parishioners did have interracial friendships outside the parish, even in those adjoining Martindale. "My own coloured friends go to Bosmont [Catholic Church]," explained a white parishioner.

Several possible reasons may explain this lack of contact. First, the informal relating which happens in Renew small groups was then a fairly recent and developing structure at Saint Francis. Second, the gaps in income and education between parishioners were perceived as too high a hurdle to cross. "The interracial aspect is now overlaid by education and the standards of living of whites...people will find it easier to accept one another once there is equal education," opined a parishioner. Third, because neither racism nor the multi-cultural nature of the congregation had ever explicitly been addressed by Saint Francis' parishioners, the dominance of cultural values associated with whites remained unexplored in liturgical and other structures.

EXPLAINING SAINT FRANCIS' RACIALLY-MIXED COMPOSITION

The evidence showed that the major contributions to the racial mix at Saint Francis included historical factors, such as the original mix of the area and the proximity of nearby coloured Western Township. Symbols that fulfilled an integrative function included the building and the past it represented, as well as the racial mix itself. The priest's role in creating a climate of inclusion for everyone was particularly important in helping to integrate the congregation.

Despite the unusual disregard that parishioners at Saint Francis had for the geographic boundaries that usually mark a Catholic parish, some measure of racial mix did derive from the presence of coloured people who lived within walking distance. The limited socio-economic circumstances of coloured parishioners must have prevented them from attending Mass in alternate parishes. Yet these reasons did not explain why some passed by other parishes that were even closer in order to attend Saint Francis. For example, a Charismatic parish in the coloured area where most parishioners lived presented a strong and obvious alternative to Saint Francis. Proximity did not explain why many whites came by car, most travelling for more than 6 kilometres and ignoring other parishes en route.

The racial and class mix at Saint Francis were among the symbols that attracted people who could be classified as representing various racial groups. A parishioner explained that "probably the main factor I go is the multi-racial mix...It is also wonderful to discover the class mix—poor whites as well. This mixture of people is [what makes the parish] alive." He continued, "parishioners who come [here] display, by coming, an acceptance of one another" (Te Riele 1992). White parishioners offered various reasons why some blacks and coloureds come. According to one they come because "some [of their] hurt is officially recognised and articulated from the pulpit...in the presence of whites." Because of the non-racial stance of the parish, "they are not primarily seen as a member of a different race group in contrast to white Roman Catholics." Another white parishioner opined that some come "just for the hand-outs."

The priest himself attracted parishioners regardless of racial classification. A parishioner estimated that about 80% of the present congregation started coming because of Father Vic Kotze. "Most parishioners have been there ten years or less," he said. My survey of the parish revealed that the second most prominent reason people gave for attending services at Saint Francis experience was feeling accepted, which they attributed to Kotze. As people were accepted without having to perform a role, participation served to enhance their social status. A white parishioner opined that "coloureds experience a real conflict of identity," and that some may come because "they want acceptance from whites." I would suggest that the opposite may also have been true.

Saint Francis is more a by-product of a general inclusivity than an overt attempt to attract different racial groups. Gay people as well as those married outside the Catholic church were made to feel welcome. Parishioners could point to non-Catholics who regularly attended Mass and received communion, which is not generally accepted Catholic practice. Race did not feature as a conscious category within parish discourse. Instead, a "clear non-racial stance" was embedded within a broader "inclusive" approach, as a parishioner remarked. Despite the inclusiveness, strong boundaries were drawn by parishioners between Saint Francis and other Catholic parishes, and between the ideological orientation of those attending Saint Francis and others who resided in the vicinity. Referring to the predominantly low-income Afrikaans-speaking residents then living in nearby Triomf, some parishioners remarked laconically that "what they [would] hear and see at Martindale would not suit them."

I would argue that integration happened at Saint Francis as the result of the construction of a symbolic universe which drew people who shared similar convictions. Similarly the decline in Portuguese, Chinese, and even coloured parishioners could be ascribed to the loss of the network of ideas and artefacts that supported their presence. These included a changed building, disappearance of ethnic forms of celebration (e.g. Portuguese holy days), the type of language used in sermons, and the altered liturgy.

The shared conceptual universe was constructed from a number of centripetally functioning symbolic resources, including the accepting attitude of the priest. Other building blocks included Catholic tradition, public opposition to apartheid by key denominational figures the theological orientations of parishioners, their ideological political positions, and their prior experiences with people of colour. As a Catholic parish Saint Francis had access to—and used—tradition as resource for binding people together. Tradition was often used in discussions and sermons to underline a point; for example, by referring to a letter of Pope Leo XIII written 130 years ago. The awareness of the denominational stance on racial issues is reflected in the comment of one parishioner who said:

> The Roman Catholic Church has always been non-racial...I feel Martindale accurately represents what society should be—not separate development...if there is a language problem then an

interpreter is needed, not separation.

The language used in sermons and on posters in the church building raised awareness among parishioners about linkages between faith and socio-political realities. Many whites who come to Saint Francis were open to the interracial contact that participation presupposed. Some had existing interracial friendships outside the parish. Other issues which attracted this subgroup included a desire to promote human rights, work against poverty, create employment, reverse the defects of traditional forms of charity which enchained people by creating dependence on hand-outs, and the then-looming 1994 elections.[84] A parishioner who remembered her parents as committed to fighting against apartheid, her mother participating in the Black Sash, can serve as an example. "We always had black people in our home, and I was brought up to believe that people were equal," she said. In other words, a symbolic universe of shared concepts attracted white people in particular, whose own ideological frameworks and prior experiences were in this way validated.

Despite the inclusivity and a strong sense of differentiation from others in the neighbourhood, sub-group identities were clearly evident within the parish. Parishioners could easily distinguish between non- and Charismatics among them; between non- and traditionalists (referring to liturgy); and between politically conservatives and non-conservatives. The strong sense of place observable among parishioners in Saint Francis also helped to mark out different sub-groups.

A self-ascribed conservative could point out other political conservatives (many long-standing parishioners) of whom nine, in his opinion, were also liturgical traditionalists. He said that in Saint Francis, as in the wider Catholic church, "there is not enough concern for conservative Catholics: it should be fifty-fifty" with progressive Catholics. Another thought that parishioners who attended Saint Francis at that time spanned parties as diverse as the African National Congress, the National Party, and the Federal Party. Such perceptions cast doubt on the conclusion of a Parish Council member who said: "I do not think there are any politically conservative people in the parish; they would have left after that [pro-detainee] Mass." A political conservative parishioner thought that parishioners were mostly "democratic, with a slight CP/NP presence;" referring in the first instance to the whites-only Conservative

---

84. Two posters issued by the South African Catholic Bishop's Conference were displayed in the church, urging people to get identity documents to be able to vote.

Party. Yet, he suggested, even the conservatives were relatively open-minded, as he himself accepted the African National Congress' Freedom Charter. He did object, though, to the South African Communist Party's presence within the African National Congress. Although he identified with the conservative Catholic movement Tradition, Family, Property that considered the Catholic church to be subverted by liberation theology (Bate 2001), he also thought they were "fanatics." He spoke approvingly of Kotze, "who does well; he speaks against injustices, but does not attack the [then National Party] Government."

The inclusive culture nurtured at Saint Francis functioned to marginalise—to varying degrees—liturgical or political conservatives, who nevertheless continued to be drawn to the personal acceptance extended to parishioners as individuals. Several parishioners recalled friends who had left Saint Francis for one reason or another. The general political climate and the informal leadership style (revealed in decision-making by unspoken consensus rather than through open vote) worked against the continued participation of politically conservative parishioners. The resultant tension emerged in a white female parishioner's description of the liturgy committee as "the Inner Circle." The more recently introduced vernacular liturgy was subtly subverted by the parishioner who still said the rosary during Mass—recalling one of the few functions open to the laity when Mass was still conducted in Latin. The discomfort of traditionalists at Saint Francis related to tensions evident across the wider Catholic church.

The changed physical environment (removal of most statues, permanent crucifix) and ritual (no robes worn by altar servers, change of place and size of altar) must have alienated liturgical conservatives. But simultaneously these factors attracted those who felt at home in this environment. An example of a more liberal liturgical viewpoint was expressed by a woman who said, "The Feast of the Assumption of Our Lady was sucked out of the [Catholic] church's thumb...I agree with the Protestants on idolatry—I do not pray to or through her."

Yet some who disagreed with their priest continued to come. A parishioner said, "There is far more to him [Vic] than that [politics]: he takes a strong position, but is also a man of immense understanding of sin, sexuality in all forms...People have disagreed, but come despite that." Vic was credited with not favouring a specific political party, but speaking of gospel values instead (Fothergill 1992)—a phrase that parishioners often repeated. A contrasting view is that Vic used the

African National Congress' name, but "only insofar as protesting against injustice." He had "castigated the A.N.C. when it was seen not to operate on Christian values." The political tension between the political conservatives and progressives clearly surfaced in the infamous Mass for detainees, and afterwards, when Kotze was reported to the Special Branch.

Various groups used race and physical environment to reveal the nature of social relations in the parish. Different sub-groups usually sat in the same area every Sunday (Coloureds, religious, elderly, those with children, leaders). Coloured parishioners tended to sit at the left back and "immediately to the right of the main door, especially on Saturdays," a parishioner said. The seating habits also showed how symbols functioned differently for different races and cultures. Coloureds, Indians, and blacks sit further away from the altar while blacks used to sit near the plaque. The enclosure of the plaque in a newly constructed room at the back of the church signalled, at the time, the loss of "their place" and an end of black presence altogether. Symbols may be more important to people with less formal education, while also appealing to better-educated contemplatives. Appropriate enough for the post-apartheid context in which the neighbourhood was again integrating, the plaque is today more prominently displayed "near the votive candle stand" (Kotze 2005).

Distinctions were also drawn between those who embraced a Charismatic style of Christianity and those who did not. A politically and liturgically conservative parishioner referred to the Charismatic parishioners as "happy-clappies." If they clap hands in the recessional hymns I walk out," he said, "it could be disturbing." Parishioners place Kotze in the non-Charismatic (expressively more conservative) sub-group. His sister, who also attended Saint Francis, were identified as part of the Charismatic groupings: "They are two sides of a coin: the intellectual versus the born-again—very different, strong Christians." Mainly composed of women, the Charismatic group became visible during a healing service that parishioners afterwards described as "very exuberant." The group included the newly appointed deacon, a self-described Charismatic.

The discussion so far reintroduces a theme I noted in the Introduction, namely the overlapping of contrary ideals of integrationism and personal prejudice alongside each other in an integrating congregation. The state of affairs clearly concerned the priest and some parishioners. Some white and coloured parishioners at Saint Francis continued to express themselves in relation to black Africans in terms that at best were paternalistic. Leadership structures and processes tended to exclude people of colour, who were under-represented in the Pastoral Council and the liturgy committee, for example. On the other hand, coloured and black parishioners played a dormant, passive role within the congregation as a whole, particularly in those leadership structures where they were represented. The situation recalled that at Central, where black congregants showed little involvement in congregational programs, and demonstrated little interest in indigenising worship styles. At Saint Francis an attempt was made to use African languages and rhythms in the so-called 'organ choir.' While some interviewees thought that these expressions of cultural diversity ceased after conflict with the liturgical committee,[85] Kotze pointed to the occasional use of African musical instruments to the present (Kotze 2005).

One way of reconciling these contrary indications is to recognise that while Saint Francis served as an example of the institutionalisation of integrationism within South African society, non-racialism still had to be internalised within the parish itself. In this way one can reconcile exclusionary phenomena with the immense personal suffering endured by many at Saint Francis under apartheid, and the obvious courage of those who attempted to integrate in a context that clearly mandated against such rapprochement. The varying economic circumstances may also have contributed to the status quo. A white parishioner explained that some black and coloured parishioners "come just for sustenance," that they where as involved as they could be, given the "time, energy, or finances" that they possessed.

---

85. The conflict was about differences of interpretation about appropriateness of songs to elements of the liturgy (Kotze 2005).

4

Erasing Boundaries of the Black City: Johweto Family Vineyard, Soweto

INTRODUCTION

The Johweto Family Vineyard was a small independent Evangelical-Charismatic congregation that met in a rented hall in Mofolo, Soweto on Sunday mornings. The name embodied the founders' vision of creating a racially-mixed community that would erase the racial and economic lines drawn by the apartheid state between (white) **Joh**annesburg and (black) So**weto**. The combined name indicated the interdependence of these two cities and all its races, a notion foreign to apartheid, under which the cities were administered separately. The founding vision of the congregation anticipated by 15 years the first steps towards formally unifying the two municipalities into a common system of service delivery. Similarly, the strong emphasis on interracial personal contact developed by the congregation anticipated the normalisation of social relations that South Africa still strives towards today.

As the case study of Johweto varies in some respects from the previous two, so do the contents and structure of Chapter Four. A comparison brings out not only a static view of historical, denominational, and geographical differences between the three congregations, but also a dynamic sense of political change. Central Methodist got under way in 1887 on the eve of the Transvaal becoming a British colony, while Saint Francis was founded in 1929 during the Union period. By contrast, Johweto started out in 1985 as an independent congregation during one of the most repressive periods induced by the apartheid regime. Johweto's recent founding date prevented me from dividing the material according to three major historical periods as I did for the other congregations. Where I do use historical subdivisions, the time span is far shorter, and they only partly overlap with those used for the other case studies. Unlike Central Methodist and Saint Francis, Johweto had no denominational pre-history prior to its own founding. While Johweto's location in Soweto was very significant, the congregation was far less directly linked to its context than either of the other two congregations. In the historical section below, I first briefly overview the broader independent Charismatic movement, and refer to race relations where possible. As the history of the South Africa's most recent Charismatic movement has not yet received adequate academic attention, except for some work by Irving Hexham and Carla Poewe (1988) and a brief summary in Ezekiel Mathole (2005:189-195), my reflections are necessarily incomplete. The history of Soweto is covered briefly as background to the story of Johweto that follows in the next section. Finally, due to the process by which Johweto was founded and the small size of the congregation, the pivotal role of the founding figures are also covered in more personal detail than for the other case studies. The small size of the congregation and the compressed time span results in a far more detailed and intimate portrait than was the case for Central Methodist and Saint Francis.

THE INDEPENDENT CHARISMATIC MOVEMENT AND RACE RELATIONS

The Charismatic movement in modern guise swept through South Africa from the mid-1960s to mid-1970s, touching most denominations. The Anglican, Methodist, and Catholic churches alike were affected, as were isolated Dutch Reformed congregations in Pretoria and Stellenbosch. While some denominations contained the movement by creating organisations or allowing particular congregations to specialise, others experienced schism due to internal conflict between leaders who welcomed and those who opposed the movement. As a result, some Charismatic congregations separated from pre-existing denominations. Others were planted directly from abroad, mainly by representatives of churches in the United States.

Earlier waves of ecstatic worship and associated phenomena (such as healing and glossolalia) were reported in South Africa from about 1860, leading to the emergence of local Pentecostalism. In anticipation of the more recent wave, the earlier movement was associated initially with a mainline denomination, in particular with the Dutch Reformed Church and two of its representatives, Rev. Andrew Murray (1828-1917) and missionary Pieter le Roux (1865-1943). From the interaction between Le Roux and the healing movement emanating from the Christian Catholic Church at Zion City, Illinois, grew first black and later white Pentecostalism, and eventually the African Independent Church movement.

In South Africa the movement overall had mainline as well as Pentecostal roots, with initiatives undertaken by local and global actors who sometimes worked in conjunction. In this regard both earlier and later movements represented the forms of transnational organisation that so clearly marked South African events. The more recent manifestations of Charismatic worship differed from the earlier independent churches historically and liturgically. Charismatics generally embraced a quieter type of service than those associated with Pentecostalism, and emphasised healing and intimate worship more than other spiritual manifestations such as glossolalia.

From a political perspective both Charismatic and Pentecostal churches were accused of promoting loyalty to the Nationalist state through a so-called a-political stance which often merely thinly disguised overt support for apartheid (Villa-Vicencio 1988:39; Anderson 2000, Horn 2005). In some cases, such as the black independent churches, this stance probably resulted from a faith perspective that eschewed any political involvement (Ntlha e.a. 1999). But other Pentecostals courted the state more explicitly, as illustrated by an Apostolic Faith Mission pastor who was elected a National Party senator in 1955 (Anderson 2000; Horn 1991). The pentecostal Apostolic Faith Mission, for example, declared in 1944 that " 'The Mission stands for segregation. The fact that an Indian, native or coloured is saved does not render him European' " (Horn 2005:12). Pentecostal-Evangelical leaders "frequently participated in government commissions," such as the one that shut down the Christian Institute in 1977. They also opposed the work of the South African Council of Churches against apartheid (Ntlha e.a. 1999).

A study of Pentecostal churches along the east coast of South Africa described them as promoting faith-as-withdrawal (Morran and Schlemmer 1984). Towards the mid-1980s a gradual shift towards a more critical stance regarding state policies developed among Pentecostal-Charismatics and Evangelicals, with critical groups like Concerned Evangelicals emerging in 1985 (compare Villa-Vicencio 1988:39; Ntlha e.a. 1999, Ntlha and Mosupi 1999). The major networks of independent Pentecostal-Charismatic churches during the early 1990s comprised the International Federation of Christian Churches and the Associated Christian Ministries. Both were white-dominated, although the Associated Christian Ministries had strong Indian support and the original International Federation of Christian Churches congregations had been racially-mixed. In 1995 the Apostolic Faith Mission, the Assemblies of God, and twenty-nine other denominations merged to form the multitiracial Evangelical Alliance of South Africa under black leadership (Ntlha e.a. 1999).

The exact total of those who belong to the Charismatic groupings today are not known, although the although the 2001 census mooted 3.7 million for 'Pentecostal-Charismatics.' This figure excludes other groupings that may be pentecostal, such as the Apostolic Faith Mission (246,193), Other Apostolic churches (5.6 million) and all African Independent churches (9.2 million affiliates) (Statistics South Africa 2001).

The Evangelical churches in South Africa were generally just as racially divided as the Pentecostal and mainline denominations during the apartheid era. The line between Pentecostal and Evangelical churches is often a fine one. Pentecostals are generally speaking Evangelical, although not all Evangelicals are Pentecostals. White Evangelical leaders supported apartheid, just as white Pentecostal leaders did. Pentecostals participated in Evangelical associations. For example, F. P. Moller, leader of the both the Apostolic Faith Mission of South Africa and the Fellowship of Pentecostal Churches in South Africa, publicly denounced the anti-apartheid stance of Archbishop Desmond Tutu at the 1987 National Association of Evangelicals in the United States (Edwords and McCabe 1987). Black pastors "who stood for justice and human rights were often defrocked and victimised by their own churches" (Ntlha e.a 1999). By 1999 white independent Charismatic-Evangelical churches such as Hatfield Christian Church still had separate black services and black leadership sections, even though all races could attend their services.

Among the exceptions was Concerned Evangelicals (1985-95), who published *The Evangelical Witness* (1987) as a counter to the general Evangelical support for apartheid. Some Pentecostals followed suit with *The Relevant Pentecostal Witness* (1988). And the evangelistic group African Enterprise not only was racially integrated itself, but actively pursued racial reconciliation through events such as the South African Leadership Assembly (1979). In 1995 the Evangelical Alliance of South Africa was formed out of 31 denominations, including the Alliance Church in South Africa, the Apostolic Faith Mission, the Assemblies of God, the Baptist Convention of South Africa, the Baptist Union of South Africa, and the Vineyard. The constitution of the Evangelical Alliance recognises the complicity of some Evangelical churches in apartheid and racism (Ntlha e.a. 1999).

Johweto's leaders straddled Pentecostal, Evangelical, and Charismatic worlds, but were closer to the black progressive than to the white conservative evangelical positions. Alexander Venter, for example, is described as both a Charismatic and an Evangelical, and was a pastor in the pentecostal Assembly of God church (Ntlha 2004; A. Venter 2004:33). As Vineyard congregations spread across South Africa, they initially became part of Cape Fellowship Ministries under Derek Morphew, until the national Association of Vineyard Churches in South Africa was formed in April 1997 (Association of Vineyard Churches n.d.). By 2004 there were 32 Vineyard congregations, half of which were predominantly white (A. Venter 2004:113-14). The Association joined The Evangelical Alliance of South Africa Association of Vineyard Churches in South Africa. The Vineyard only formally started dealing with racism in its own churches in 2001, after being challenged by Trevor Ntlhola, formerly a Johweto pastor, now leader of the Pimville Zone 3 Vineyard. Venter was asked in 2002 to produce a position paper in a consultative manner that could be worked through in all Vineyard congregations. The result was *Doing Reconciliation*, intended to help the Vineyard to turn "our congregations into safe places for people of different races." In September 2002 Pentecostal, Charismatic and Evangelical churches held a Reconciliation Summit to seek meaningful responses to South Africa's racial past (A. Venter 2004:12, 116, 120).

A BRIEF HISTORY OF SOWETO

Soweto was founded as temporary accommodation for the black labour needs of the white city. The white civic leaders of British-controlled Johannesburg established Klipspruit in 1904 as the first black settlement outside the city. In 1918 two further "native" townships were developed to the east and west of Johannesburg. The 1923 Natives Urban Areas Act held councils responsible for providing housing for black Africans living within their areas. A clinic was built at Orlando in 1932, and in 1935 Orlando Township was established (see Figure 3, next page). A portion of Klipspruit was renamed Pimville in 1934. Today Pimville and Orlando form suburbs of Soweto. In 1941 the Imperial Military Hospital (now Chris Hani-Baragwanath Hospital) was built in what today is Diepkloof for British soldiers recuperating during the Second World War. Jan Smuts indicated at the opening of the hospital that it was intended for future use by the black population of the Witwatersrand (City of Johannesburg n.d.).

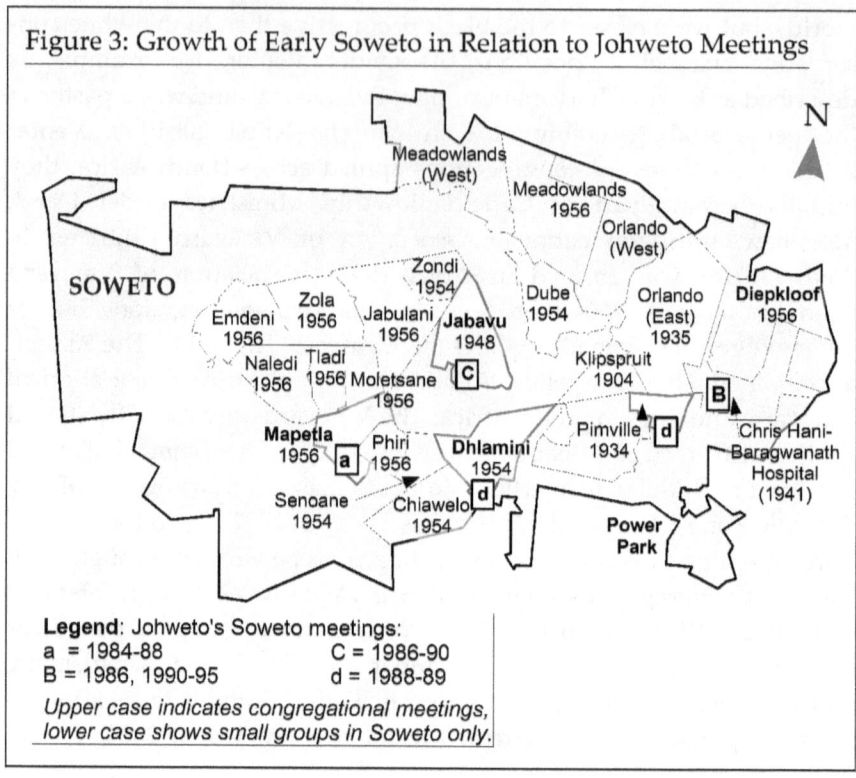

Figure 3: Growth of Early Soweto in Relation to Johweto Meetings

Legend: Johweto's Soweto meetings:
a = 1984-88   C = 1986-90
B = 1986, 1990-95   d = 1988-89
Upper case indicates congregational meetings, lower case shows small groups in Soweto only.

The increased urbanisation of black Africans that accompanied the industrialisation of South Africa during the Second World War fuelled the growth of informal settlements in the area. In response, the Johannesburg city council in 1944 created emergency camps next to Orlando, followed in 1946 by the Moroka Emergency Camp and Central Western Jabavu. More people were moved from the city's freehold areas in 1953 as a result of the Group Areas Act (1950) to the townships which would later form Soweto. Tladi, Zondi, Dhlamini, Chiawelo, and Senaoane townships were created as serviced sites in 1954. Dube was established in the same year for the black middle class, who built their own houses. Because of the eviction of migrant workers from the inner city in 1955, Dube hostel was constructed. During the same year a soccer field in Kliptown became the venue for thousands of delegates from across South Africa, who gathered as The Congress of the People to adopt the Freedom Charter. Meadowlands and Diepkloof was built in 1956 for people displaced by the continued forced removals (City of Johannesburg n.d.).

Propelled by a R6-million donation to the state in 1956 by Sir Ernest Oppenheimer, ethnically-designated townships were established. IsiZulu- and isiXhosa-speakers were accommodated in Dhlamini, Senaoane, Zola, Zondi, Jabulani, Emdeni and White City, while xiTsonga and tshiVenda-speakers were housed in Chiawelo. Sesotho and Setswana-speakers were allocated to Naledi, Mapetla, Tladi, Moletsane and Phiri (City of Johannesburg n.d.).

In 1963 the name Soweto was officially adopted as the collective name for the townships southwest of Johannesburg. Few houses were added between the 1960s and 1980s, when the private sector became involved. Formal and informal systems of transport represented the only relatively developed infrastructure well into the 1990s. Residents could not own property, nor engage in commercial activity. Roads were not paved, and houses not electrified until the late 1970s. By 2003, some 349 kilometres of Soweto's roads still had gravel or sand surfaces, a situation that the City of Johannesburg corrected by 2005. Whites were legally prohibited from entering without permission until the 1980s, and few enter it afterwards. Residents were barred from running businesses in Soweto.

Protests against the compulsory use of Afrikaans as medium of instruction in high schools erupted in 1976 in Soweto, sparking successive education boycotts across the country for over a decade. The state unleashed its security forces against township protesters, initially using the police, but later resorting to the defence force. Various organisations were formed in Soweto to further black demands, including the Soweto Students Representative Committee (1976), the Committee of Ten (1976), the Congress of South African Students (1979), and the Soweto Youth Congress (1982).

In 1983 Soweto was given municipal status after controversial local elections in line with the tricameral constitution. During the 1980s, the rising middle-class was accommodated in extensions to Diepkloof, Dobsonville, and Selection Park. A wave of violence against township councillors, widely regarded as collaborators with the state, affected Soweto residents in 1984. The African National Congress issued a call at its 1985 congress in Kabwe, Zambia, to make the country ungovernable. Like other black South Africans, Soweto residents embarked on consumer boycotts, followed by rent boycotts the next year that lasted until 1992. During president P. W. Botha's second state of emergency in

1986, isiZulu-speaking hostel dwellers attacked Soweto communities. Reprisals between African National Congress-aligned residents and Inkatha continued to cycle into the post-apartheid period. In response to political violence and state suppression, Soweto residents organised armed self-defence units and street committees, as happened in other townships. The violence against town councillors intensified; some were killed, and many fled the townships (City of Johannesburg n.d.).

The euphoria among township residents following the unbanning of black political organisations and the release of Nelson Mandela and other prisoners in 1990 were soon weighed down by violent attacks from hostel residents.

About a 30-minute drive from downtown Johannesburg, Soweto accommodated an estimated 896 995 people in 2001 (unofficially estimated at 3,5 million) from more than five black African ethnic groups. The township was incorporated into the city of Johannesburg in 2000. Soweto's poorer residents are aggregated in the south-eastern and north-western townships, while higher income residents live in the southwest.

FROM CHALLENGE TO COMMITMENT (1985-89)

Johweto was born out of a challenge issued by Moekete Mpete, a young black man from Soweto, to Alexander Venter, a white pastor from Johannesburg, to come and experience life in Soweto. Mpete and Venter met in a student/lecturer context at the Christ for Africa Institute for Bible Study, a bible college in November 1983 (A. Venter 2004:38). When Venter showed interest in the black context, Mpete challenged the depth of his perspective by inviting him to come and experience township life. They had regular interaction in 1984, but from 1985 met weekly (A. Venter 2004:39).

At the time of Mpete's challenge, Venter was a leader in the Johannesburg Vineyard, an independent Evangelical congregation emphasising Charismatic worship with links to the California-based Vineyard Ministries, founded by John Wimber.

Initially, Venter had been a pastor in the pentecostal Assemblies of God denomination. His discovery of the racism and economic injustices that underpinned South African society received impetus from exposure to black and coloured Assemblies of God pastors, first in Rhodesia (between 1975 and 1977), then in Cape Town (1978) (A. Venter 2004:33-35). From 1980 to 1981 he pastored a congregation in Northcliff, Johannesburg. Venter introduced more spontaneous and expressive worship at Northcliff that used choruses instead of hymns, and that encouraged dancing, clapping, laying of hands (A. Venter 1994c). Differences arose between Venter and denominational leadership about these changes. Venter left the Assemblies of God in January 1982 for the United States, where he trained under Wimber.

Meanwhile, the Johannesburg Vineyard was started as a home-group by Costa Mitchell and Dave Owen. Mitchell had resigned from the Krugersdorp Assemblies of God in solidarity over the way in which Venter was treated, as did James Johnson, Venter's friend and a member at Northcliff. Owen had trained under Wimber between 1981 and 1982. Previously he led The Invisible Church, an independent Charismatic congregation that first met in the Johannesburg inner city suburb of Hillbrow before moving to Waverley, a northern suburb. Owen asked Mitchell and Venter to help bring Wimber to South Africa in 1981 for a series of seminars on church growth. The three South Africans became involved in "an intense dialogue about working together" (A. Venter 1994b).

At the end of 1982 Wimber and a team of about 70 people returned with Venter to Johannesburg to help establish the Vineyard further. Meetings were held at the German School in Parktown, Johannesburg. Regular services started in 1983 in a rented cinema in the Parkview suburb, before moving to the Parkview Primary School's hall.

Meanwhile, about ten of Venter and Mpete's friends started meeting during the week towards the end of 1984 at Mapetla, a Soweto suburb. Mpete had started a small Christian group here in the house of Mama Marks, a middle-aged woman with whom he lodged.

From 1985 the Mapetla group started a second meeting on Saturday mornings at Central Methodist Mission in Johannesburg to discuss apartheid, its effects, and possible solutions. Participants felt that they "wanted to break racial barriers," recalled one, both as an expression of solidarity with black experience and as a form of repentance. Others wanted whites to experience the conditions under which blacks lived. The first year was "very emotional, very confrontational." On visits to Soweto, Venter often had to pass through roadblocks set up by the security forces.

The group included Johnson, who as a chartered accountant would become the financial driving force behind many Johweto projects. Others included Assemblies pastor Nick Mosupi (participated from 1985 to

1988); and businessman Raymond Schultz (from 1986 to 1987). Schultz started employing some of the unemployed black participants, but the experiment failed when labour relations soured. Schulz eventually left because of personal reasons. Mosupi also left as he wanted to remain within the Assemblies of God, an option about which he had been confronted by the group. No doubt there was some pressure from within the Assemblies as well, given the ill-feeling from denominational officials surrounding Venter's departure.

The Mapetla meeting grew to about 60 by June 1985. A dozen or so people from that group started attending Vineyard meetings in Parkview on Sunday evenings.

The Johweto concept and name was born towards the end of 1985 out of an intense dialogue about political issues, lifestyle discrepancies between black and white, and violence (A. Venter 1994a). An extensive debate raged for two years about whether to become a discussion group, a para-church organisation, or a church. During a prayer meeting, Mpete confessed that blacks were not worshipping the God of the Bible but of Soweto: the god of revenge, of black ideology. In turn, Venter confessed that whites were worshipping the god of Johannesburg: the god of arrogance, of gold and wealth. Out of this repentance "was heard the call of the God of justice, and to reconciliation, unity, and forgiveness" (A. Venter 1994a; 2004:42). People became aware that the group was already symbolising a unity across various differences. Venter suggested Johweto as a name which reflected the vision of the group "not to recognize two separate cities, separate churches, different worlds of experience, but to bridge the gap, make peace, seek justice, heal the broken, release the oppressed and [letting] 'the two become one' in Christ" (A. Venter 1989b:1). With the decision came the slow growth of self-understanding that they wanted to be a "church" (congregation). The desire of the three Soweto fellowship groups to come together in one meeting contributed to this decision.

In 1985 Venter went to live on a farm near Grasmere, 30 kilometres southwest of Johannesburg and nearer to Soweto. The farm, renamed the Johweto Kehillah (Hebrew for community), had since 1981 belonged to Ron and Sandy Gold, a couple Venter had met through the Vineyard which they had attended since 1983. The Golds joined Johweto in 1985 (A. Venter 2004:48). The Saturday group's evolving desire to minister to the poor was soon met here in what became the Sweetwaters informal settlement. About 80 shacks (without infrastructure or services) sprung up on the border of the farm that year, as they did at ThulaMntwana and Weiler's Farm elsewhere in the vicinity. An unprecedented flood of people came to live in such shack settlements around this time, driven by a shortage of formal housing and long distances from places of work. Johweto members occasionally taught in the settlement's school (Johweto Private Primary School). Some spent a weekend living in the settlement (A. Venter 2004:49).

In 1986 the Parkview and Soweto meetings came to be regarded as two local congregations that met together occasionally for celebrations, after the Vineyard model. The differentiation of the Parkview and Soweto congregations came partly through a variety of means. Venter wanted to pursue the formation of a congregation with Mpete. Mitchell and Owen agreed to release him from Parkview, and funding from that congregation for Venter was gradually phased out by 1989. But tensions had also meanwhile arisen between white Vineyard members and the Mapetla group, who was frequently late for meetings at Parkview, due to lack of public transport.[86] Parkview Vineyard members also became increasingly uncomfortable with Venter, whose sermons they now criticised as "too political." Mpete's group eventually concluded that travelling from Soweto to Parkview merely repeated in microcosm the history of blacks having to go from the black city to the white one and back again. As in other multi-racial church meetings which then were becoming fashionable, meetings mostly happened on white 'turf.' The Soweto group decided to stop attending the Parkview Vineyard. By 1988 the Parkview congregation had relocated to the Bryanston suburb, while the Mpete-Venter group met in Soweto. As Mpete now also wanted to become a Vineyard pastor, he accompanied Venter to the United States in 1985 where they met Vineyard leaders and explored various church models.

The group at Central divided into three smaller groups in 1986 that met on Tuesdays in Soweto homes, as well as on Saturdays at the Funda Centre near Baragwanath Hospital. Initially, the Soweto groups had unstructured meetings that concentrated on informal fellowship and sharing personal stories. People were learning about one another, often through sharing meals together, remembered Sandy Johnson, a white participant. Among other things whites were learning about the limited living space available for Soweto people, as they had to sit on a bed in a single back room in Soweto, for example. Johnson described

---

86. The habit of not turning up on time continued to characterise Johweto meetings, and were mentioned occasionally in minutes (e.g. Johweto 1989a:1).

this period as very intimate. Whites were "trying to get to know people, to eat their food. There were times when we were very disillusioned: nothing seemed to work, we were so many miles apart" (Johnson 1992). From January 1986 the group worked on the Gold's farm together on weekends, removing rubble, planting trees, erecting fences, and converting the existing property into a community centre. A shed was constructed, a garage converted into a dwelling, a vegetable garden planted, and a borehole sunk.

From 1986 the newly-named Johweto met on Sunday mornings at the Funda Education Centre (established 1984) in Diepkloof, Soweto. The Diepkloof location at the edge of Soweto adjoining a major road was chosen mainly to improve access to the black city for whites. A white woman reflected that the meetings at Funda were "very informal, we were about 10-15 people who sat in a circle, worshipped and prayed. Compared to the [Johannesburg] Vineyard it was very relevant." Some of the group attended a seminar on African Literature held at the Funda Centre by well-known black South African authors Es'kia Mphahlele and Don Mattera. In similar fashion some went to hear economist Eugene Nyati speak in 1988. After six months the meetings at Funda came to an end when the new Centre management no longer wanted to host religious groups (Moroa 1993; A. Venter 1994a).

From the start the leadership strenuously resisted the notion that one could become a "member" of Johweto. Those in the congregation similarly spoke of "belonging" rather than of "being a member." Consequently, no official membership assimilation process existed. One became a member through "being there over a long period of time," a Johwetan explained. One "belonged" by participating for an undefined but extended period in Johweto activities, and by expressing commitment privately to the leaders. Over the following eight years Venter occasionally expressed anxiety about the lack of numerical growth, but he recognised that the high levels of interaction within Johweto would have been unlikely if the group was larger.

From September 1986 Johweto rented a room in the Ipelegeng Community Centre of Saint Paul's Anglican Church in White City (colloquial name for Jabavu, a Soweto suburb) for Sunday meetings. Meetings at Ipelegeng lasted until 1990, and was later recalled as a frustrating, unhappy time. The room was small and several other groups met in neighbouring rooms at the same time, so that ambient noise were high. A white woman just returned from a year's travel overseas with her husband remembered that "everyone seemed very burnt-out." A team led worship, and popular Christian songs were projected onto a wall. The new meeting place reversed the decision to have a site more accessible to whites, as Ipelegeng lay in Soweto's heartland, so-called 'Deep Soweto.'

The political context was marked by escalating state repression and counter-violence. Violence flared up in 1984 in townships across the country, sparked partly by P. W. Botha's 1983 referendum that introduced a tripartite Parliament in which coloureds and Indians were included, but not blacks. Black town councils were instituted by the Black Local Authorities Act (1982), ostensibly providing limited democratic elections to townships. Councillors were widely regarded as having been co-opted into structures that served to legitimise racially segregated polities and the associated unequal distribution of resources (Van der Merwe 1999). Consequently, few residents participated in council elections. Civic organisations emerged from 1979 to organise township residents at street level against local councils (Royston 1998). African National Congress-aligned activists intimidated and assassinated councillors, mayors, police, and others regarded as collaborating with the new system. Activists, including the civics, in turn came under attack by state forces. South African Defence Force units were deployed in the townships from 1984 on. The African National Congress launched a campaign to render the townships ungovernable, supported by rental, school, and consumer boycotts. The house of one Johweto's members was burned down, whose father was a councillor (A. Venter 2004:43).

The response of P.W. Botha's government was to use the Public Safety Act (1953) to declare a State of Emergency in July 1985 over 36 magisterial areas. The South African Defence Force were deployed to supplement the police, and were granted powers of detention. Detainees could not see any visitors, even lawyers. To reveal the identity of a detainee before the Minister of Law and Order had done so became a criminal offence. The Minister was given powers to ban any individual, organisation, or publication thought to endanger the security of the state. Despite being briefly lifted on March 7, 1986, the state of emergency was expanded to cover all of South Africa on June 12, 1986. Political violence erupted in Natal at about this time, between supporters of the African National Congress and Inkatha (a political organisation comprising primarily isiZulu-speakers, led by Chief Mangosuthu

Buthelezi). The conflict spread to other provinces and lasted well into 1994. State agents abetted such events and ruthlessly eliminated political opponents, while sporadic actions by the white right wing escalated public violence.

During that year Venter and Mpete were stopped and their car searched at a security force check point, with Mpete especially receiving a torrent of abusive language and aggressive questioning. Two people had been murdered nearby 20 minutes before by the so-called necklace method. The 'necklace' referred to petrol-soaked tyres that were placed around the necks of suspected collaborators who were then burnt to death. Such incidents may first have appeared in 1985, when a town council member was executed in this fashion (Ball 1994 includes alternative dates and explanations). About 300 such executions occurred between 1984 and 1987; with a further twenty-nine between October 1989 and February 1990 (Ball 1994). In 1986 the state banned the possession of tyres or similar material and inflammable liquid where their use implied the commitment of an offence.

Soweto residents were not always happy about Johweto's racial mix. Black church leader Ceasar Molebatsi, well-known in Soweto, opposed the idea of a white-black church starting there. Some were angry with black Johwetans for mixing with whites. Such reactions may have been prompted by Black Consciousness, or merely by the fear that whites may be security operatives. Negative black reactions created the feeling among whites that "we are not really wanted in Soweto" (Johnson 1992). But not all Sowetans opposed the group. Edgar Molefe spoke of the friendly curiosity of Soweto neighbours when whites visited the Molefe home—they, too, wanted to have white friends, they said.

Venter and Mosupi attended an international Vineyard's pastors' conference in the United States in 1987. The pair established contacts with the Church of the Savior in Washington D.C. And Reba Place Church, a Mennonite congregation in Evanston, that would endure over time.

At the end of 1987[87] the Golds made their 16 hectare Grasmere farm available to Johweto as a reconciliation kibbutz—"the place where our struggle for community work and ministry will be worked out," and "retreats and seminars" offered (A. Venter 1989b:2). The farm was renamed Kehillah, Hebrew for congregation or community (A. Venter 1994a). A development program was drawn up and a management team co-opted (A. Venter, Gold and Johnson 1986:11; 1987:9). The plan was to

---

87. A conflicting date of 1986 appears in *The Johweto Vision* (A. Venter 1987:5).

develop the Kehillah so that black and white, rich and poor believers could live and work together. As a community they intended to minister to the poor while developing "a viable independent business project" and financial self-sufficiency (A. Venter 1989a:2; 1989b:2; Johweto 1987:1). Some wanted the Kehillah to be an education and training centre, others a primary health care centre, or a creative arts outlet (Venter and Johnson 1987:4). Others wanted to build six three-bedroomed units for community living, and two units for labourers (Johweto 1988 d:4). By and large, these plans remained unrealised by 1994, possibly due to a shift in focus after the purchase of a communal farm elsewhere. Yet, for a while, about ten people did live there in about 1988.

Johweto's activities attracted Security Branch attention by the end of that same year. Venter received a call from a white man who ostensibly wanted to talk about developments on the farm. At a subsequent appointment the man revealed that he was a captain in the Security Branch. He wanted Venter to supply him with information about alternative structures formed to undermine the government, but Venter refused.

"I realized they [the Security Branch] had information about me, and was watching me, because he [the captain] referred to a meeting I had with [Afrikaner anti-apartheid opponent] Beyers Naudé at the S.A.C.C. [South African Council of Churches]. I suspected that my post [mail] was interfered with...three banned books sent to me from the States never arrived," recalled Venter. The books included *Biko* by Donald Woods and *Kaffir Boy* by Mark Mothiabane. "One Sunday during 1988, plain-clothes policemen, probably also Security Branch, burst into the meeting at Ipelegeng, demanding to know 'what's happening here.' I said I would speak to them outside, and told them to contact the security branch captain if they wanted any information." The incident was repeated some time later (compare A. Venter 2004:71).

Lawyer Carien Engelbrecht was asked in April 1988 to summarise security legislation and its possible effects on Johweto. The resulting document was sixteen pages long. She briefed Johwetans one Saturday on how they should react when arrested, what their rights were, and which books were banned. In May Venter submitted a list of his books to her; only one was undesirable in terms of the appropriate Act.

By July there were six home groups, including one at the Kehillah and one in Alexandra township, northeast of Johannesburg, at David Marobe's house in Eighth Street (Johweto 1988 a:1). Each group contained about eight people, and functioned with various degrees of success. Meetings were marked by an "an eagerness to know each other which [now] has possibly died down...We were willing to go into Soweto five times a week," recalled Johnson (Johnson 1992). Groups of eight to twelve worked on the Kehillah on weekends, including some from the Johannesburg Vineyard. Venter and the Golds were soon drawn into contact with the nearby informal settlement through having to mediate in weekend fights that often involved stabbings. One weekend Venter was asked to bury an old man who had died two days previously. He invited Johwetans along, and so Johweto's involvement there began. But the funeral also impacted Venter's vision of his own ministry profoundly: "Blood from the decomposing body [in the coffin] flowed over my hands...I felt God was saying to me that unless I get my hands dirty with the blood of the poor, I cannot talk about, or judge them" (A. Venter 1994a).

The proximity of informal settlements led to a number of initiatives by individual Johwetans during 1988-89, while drawing more people to Johweto. Such settlements arose all over South Africa, fuelled by a shortage of housing, among other factors (Stevens and Rule 1999). Some people begun visiting the settlement, taking blankets, and praying for others. Kellam Beard started a ministry to the children; a Vineyard woman began a school; and a feeding scheme was initiated for children that attended the school. Through the activities of the leaders outside of Johweto, others were drawn to the Kehillah. Physician Steve Carpenter joined Johweto in 1988 after attending Venter's seminars on healing at the Benoni Methodist Church. Carpenter relocated to the Kehillah, and operated a medical clinic among the squatters (Johweto 1989 a:2). Similarly, through a visit to the evangelistic organisation African Enterprise by Mpete, Euan and Lynn Ross-Taylor came to hear of the Kehillah. They arrived in 1988 with a two-fold vision of working among the poor and establishing community.

During 1988 the congregation debated whether the gospel was compromised by an individual who participated in military operations, whether those of the South African Defence Force, or of the African National Congress's military wing, *Umkhonto We Sizwe* ("spear of the nation," created in 1961). A group of about 30 met over a weekend to decide the issue and drew up a response. The final decision was left to individuals, who were urged to "dialogue diligently" with other Johwetans (Johweto 1988 b:1). Some white men in Johweto had refused compulsory military service in the South African Defence Force before joining Johweto; one completed community work in Alexandra, instead.

Between 1988 and 1989 a more structured process was introduced to Johweto's home groups, similar to Koinonia's home meetings. A new programme was started every eight weeks, followed by two weeks of social time—a silent picnic, a joint meal, watching a film together. But outreach or growth lay beyond their capacities, with four groups declining to follow the leadership's suggestions in this regard. The exceptions included groups that met at Mpete's and at the Kehillah (Johweto 1988 a:1).

The eight people living together on the Kehillah were by 1989 neighbours to an estimated 12,000 people in the huge informal settlement[88] next door (Johweto 1988c:2; A. Venter 1989a:2). Mpete started a Thursday night meeting at the Kehillah which grew to about 80 people before inexplicably tapering off. A Kehillah tap on the border with the settlement provided the only supply of clean water for its residents. Many in the settlement were later moved to more formal sites planned for them by the provincial authorities at Weiler's Farm and Orange Farm further south. Others soon took their place.

A nurse, Mary-Ann Lutzky, joined Johweto during that year and went to live in the Vlakfontein settlement nearby (A. Venter 1989a:2). Carpenter started a medical clinic in the nearby Sweetwaters settlement and helped Lutzky with the one that she started in Vlakfontein. Carpenter also founded a medical clinic at the Weiler's farm settlement, for which R20,000 was raised through Johweto's contacts with Church of the Saviour in the United States and the Besom Foundation in the United Kingdom (A. Venter 1989a:2). Lutzky later married Carpenter, and in 1991 they left for the Winterveld settlement after having lived in Orange Farm. Another nurse who had helped the Carpenters, Zandra Murray, now took over the clinic and drew in other non-Johwetans. Murray had worked with heroine addicts in Hong Kong, as had the founder of the Besom Foundation, James Odgers. Mama Marks brought numerous children from Mapetla to the Sunday meeting, and with Beard started programmes for them. They began to bring the children

---

88. Inhabitants of informal settlements were commonly referred to as 'squatters,' a term that implied the illegal occupation of land owned either privately or by authorities. Some saw the term as pejorative, given that previous apartheid governments failed to provide adequate housing and infrastructure for black Africans.

out to the Kehillah on Saturdays, while also gathering others from the settlement. The children received spiritual input with a meal of high-protein soup and bread. Special events were arranged for them, such as a teddy bear Christmas party.

In May 1988 Johweto became an incorporated association not for gain, with property held in trust that included the Kehillah and a house bought for Mpete in 1989 in Pimville, Soweto (A. Venter 1989b:2). An account was opened for foreign donations (Johweto 1988 c:3). Mpete's house was intended to be "a focal point for ministry and community" (A. Venter 1989a:2). About R75,000 was spent between 1985 and mid-1988 on Johweto infrastructure and projects (Johweto 1988 c:5). Meanwhile the leaders again initiated a search for a more suitable and larger meeting place. After a fruitless eight month quest the option of buying property and building such a place was mooted, but not realised (Johweto 1988 c:5, A. Venter 1998:1). In 1989 the possibility of meeting in a supermarket near the Pimville house was aired, but this did not happen (Johweto 1989 b:1).

In 1989 the movement towards becoming a congregation was structurally formalised for the approximately fifty people who met as Johweto. Owen and Mitchell now recognised Johweto as a Vineyard congregation, with Venter as its full-time pastor. There were now three Vineyard congregations in Johannesburg: Parkview (under Owen), Bryanston (under Mitchell), and Johweto (under Venter). A mini-congregation consisting of young people had also emerged, called Doves (Minutes 1989a:2). The separation was cordial, with amicable relations continuing between Johweto and the local and international Vineyards.[89] The new arrangements ended the financial support that Venter had received from the other two Vineyards, which he had in turn shared with Mpete. The financial burden for Johweto was now shouldered primarily by Johnson, who had increasingly assumed financial responsibility for Venter and Mpete since 1986, with additional support from about six of the employed whites.

In the same year collective activities and emotions started spiralling downwards, marked by a number of conflicts and a slow attrition of participants. Beard voiced "highly judgemental and condemnatory prophecies" of Johweto's socio-political focus during Sunday meetings.

---

89. Letters written in 1989 with the Johweto letterhead had the statement "Johweto —in association with the Vineyard Christian Fellowship" at the bottom.

He urged the congregation to worship " 'in the Spirit' " rather than fall prey to " 'defeatist talk of politics' " (A. Venter 1994a). Venter and Mpete confronted him on his "highly spiritual, gnostic[90] ethos," and forbade further 'prophecies.' During Beard's absences between 1988 and 1989, Mama Marks and three others (including a visitor from the United Kingdom) shouldered responsibility for the children's ministry. Beard and Mama Marks moved the children's programme from the Kehillah back to Soweto in 1989. By the end of that year Beard no longer attended regularly. Clashes also occurred between the Ross-Taylors and the Golds regarding rules of community living, and both couples left. Concerns surfaced about Johweto's mostly Western worship style, with Steve Carpenter calling for more Black influences at a leadership meeting. The minuted response was cautiously favourable, although "we should be selective in doing this" (Johweto 1989 b:2).

The home groups experienced a similar contraction. Of six home groups that met in 1988, three remained the next year: one each in Dlamini and Power Park, Soweto, and one in Alexandra (Johweto 1989 b:1). The Mapetla home-group closed "at the landlord's request because of fear of election militancy" during the coming white general elections. Another group stopped meeting due to a number of reasons, ranging from a marriage crisis, lack of an alternate venue and transport (Johweto 1988 a:1; Johweto 1989 b:1). As most blacks were young and single, they did not have homes to offer as venues for the groups (Johweto 1989 b:1). Few blacks had drivers' licences, and only three had cars, a situation that affected their home-group and congregation attendance into 1992.

Events in the wider society contributed to Johweto's malaise, as political violence between Inkatha and the African National Congress escalated (A. Venter 1994a). Initially contained to Natal, the violence spread to the Witwatersrand and so into Soweto. Inkatha- and African National Congress-aligned sections of townships turned against one another, hostel dwellers and squatters attacked one another, and passengers using public transport were killed. Johwetan Victor Shabalala was attacked on a train by members of Inkatha, part of a trend in which about 438 commuters were killed between 1990 and 1992 (Dixon 1992). Inkatha mobilised squads from among the 200,000 amaZulu migrant workers housed in 120 single sex hostels in thirty-one townships along

---

90. Venter defined 'gnostic' as an extreme "spirit/matter division," in which the spirit is judged the more important, with earthly matters (e.g. socio-political action) regarded as not falling within the scope of the Gospel (A. Venter 1994c).

the Reef (Human Rights Watch 1991). Supporters in African National Congress-controlled areas organised self-defense units against attacks from Inkatha cadres, who in turn formed "self-protection" units. Johwetan Gideon Sennelo saw people hacked and shot to death. At least one black Johwetan joined a local African National Congress Self-Defence Unit to guard against attacks in Pimville, and later helped to form the Pimville Youth Association. But defense was not the sole function of self-defense units' some killed twenty-three residents of an Inkatha-controlled hostel in Tokoza, for example (Jeffrey n.d.).

About 50% of black Johwetans were unemployed, prompting discussion on how to meet their needs through education and job-creation. A Child Sponsorship and Johweto Education Fund was set up for black Johwetans in 1989 (A. Venter 1989a:2). Johwetans also experienced psychological exhaustion from the intense interpersonal contact, and physical and financial fatigue from travelling over 40 kilometres three times a week. By 1990 Beard stopped coming altogether, and three others followed suit (A. Venter 1994a). In a small group like Johweto the loss of even such small numbers were significant. The conflict around Beard continued to affect some Johwetans, saddened by the affair. No doubt prompted by internal dissension and external change, the dominant underlying issues in most Johweto meetings from 1988 to 1991 were questions of identity, values, vision, and sustainability.

TOWARDS A POST-APARTHEID CONGREGATION (1990-94)

The greater political freedom following the unbanning of the liberation movements in 1990 was a positive experience for the Johweto congregation, just as it had been for many at Saint Francis. Some in Johweto understood "God is behind that [political changes]" (Sennelo 1992). Prayers in the congregation had pleaded with God for the downfall of the apartheid government during the 1980s. The South African Council of Churches had issued a call for such prayers in 1987-88 (A. Venter 2004:108). Such sentiments were in line with secular arguments about the illegitimacy of the apartheid regime, and with the theological expressions of the influential *The Kairos Document*. *Kairos* was a 35-page document published in 1985 that justified the mobilisation of democratic forces to overthrow the government (Bate 2001).

In November 1990, Venter participated in the Rustenburg Conference of over 80 denominations and 40 para-church organisations, a watershed event that produced the Rustenburg Declaration (n.a. 1990).

Attended by over 230 representatives from Christian churches, the Rustenburg gathering was the largest since 1960. White church leaders were at last able to bring themselves to publicly repent of apartheid, and receive the equally publicly offered forgiveness from their black counterparts.

National changes were paralleled by an internal shift in Johweto's congregation, from a strong emphasis "on the racial divide to more of an established feeling...with no particular battle to fight" (Johnson 1992). Black Johwetan Lizzie John interpreted the transition as "first we wanted to know who we were; but now we are becoming a church" (John 1992). As part of formalising its nature as church, the following structures were envisioned: a Sunday gathering, fellowship groups, a core group course, and mission groups. Sunday meetings would alternate between formal and informal styles, and all who attended had to participate in small groups of four each for two-and-a-half weeks.

The congregation decided after group discussion to move to rented classrooms in the Soweto Careers Centre, next to the Funda Centre. The congregation by now consisted of about thirty-one people, eleven of whom were white. The Careers Centre was established after the 1976 student uprising in Soweto's Diepkloof suburb. Its immediate neighbours were two clinics (Koos Beukes Community Health Centre, Laneledi), a home for the mentally handicapped (Takelani), an educational centre (Funda), and the Diepmeadow Traffic Department. The nearest suburban houses were about 500-600 metres away, although it appeared further, because of intervening tracts of open land. The entrance to the biggest hospital in Africa, the Baragwanath Hospital, was within a kilometre of the meeting place, and situated opposite it was a large mini-bus taxi rank. Changes also took place at the Kehillah. In 1990 John Mothiane, a successful farmer in the Qua-Qua "homeland," agreed to Mpete's request to come and manage the Kehillah as a vegetable farm, and as a means to create employment for others. Despite the farm being in a dry area, Mothiane grew and sold a lot of *dhanya* (leafy plant used in cooking) to Indian buyers. New Zealander Mike McCullough started a fibreglass factory in a tin shed on the Kehillah, and later erected a factory building there.

Although Johweto did not make formal contact with the houses or institutions in the immediate vicinity of the Careers Centre, the leaders did connect with a wide range of ecumenical and secular conferences, institutions, groups and individuals locally and internationally. Venter,

Mpete and trainee pastor Trevor Ntlhola attended meetings with church groups and pastors in Soweto and Johannesburg. Venter and Mpete regularly ran courses for parachurch organisations such as Youth for Christ and Youth with a Mission. Other ecumenical interaction in the greater Johannesburg metropolitan area happened through participation in ministers' fraternals, such as the Yeoville-Berea fraternal and the Rand Initiative for Christian Conciliation. The leadership also participated in the Soweto's Ministers United for Christian Co-Responsibility, an organisation related to the Black Consciousness movement and the Permanent Black Priests Solidarity Group, as I described in Chapter One. Other linkages occurred through the Association of Christian Ministries, the national network of independent Charismatic churches in which Johweto participated before the formation of the Vineyard South Africa. Venter and Mpete also attended the annual conferences for Vineyard leaders in the United States.

The weak links to Soweto concerned some black Johwetans, who thought that Johweto should be more involved with the civic organisations, for instance. A white Johwetan agreed that "There is not enough penetration into the black community—if this does not happen, Johweto will die" (Laverty 1992). In late 1992 Nlthola and others made contact with their immediate neighbours from the house where they lived in Soweto's Dlamini suburb.

Trevor Ntlhola, a member since 1988, became trainee pastor after finishing high school and some college. He had attended the John Wimber conference in 1988, and afterwards attended the follow-up mini-conference at the Ipelegeng Centre, where he met Mpete and Venter.

Ntlhola trained at the pentecostal Full Gospel Bible College in White City (Jabavu) in Soweto, between 1987-1988. He was expelled from the college after boycotting class as part of a campaign to reinstate a lecturer, Mogashudi Ngoetjana. Ngoetjana had been dismissed in September 1988 on the grounds that he taught liberation theology (A. Venter 2004:67). Similar events took place elsewhere in the country, both in secular and religious organisations. At Saint Joseph's (Catholic) Theological Institute, Cedara, a lecturer was expelled from the country in 1986, for instance (Denis and Mbaya 1997).

The students at the Full Gospel Bible College were also unhappy with the anti-sanctions stance of their denomination, about which the leadership had not consulted the black majority of the church. The students held a press conference denouncing the pro-apartheid stance of their denomination at the office of anti-apartheid Afrikaner cleric Beyers Naudè. Ntlhola thought that their actions contributed to their expulsion (A. Venter 2004:68). The students' actions were labelled "politics" by church authorities. When the college called in police, Ntlhola and other protesters were taken by Moss Ntlha to a hiding place in Pimville Zone 1 (A. Venter 2004:68). At the time Ntlhola was a member of a multi-racial Full Gospel congregation in Dinwiddie, Germiston, which he joined in 1986 after a visit by a team to his school, Ponego High School, Katlehong (Ntlhola 1994).

Johweto members expressed concern for Ntlhola, as during this time many activists disappeared due to the activities of state death squads. He found their care confusing in contrast with his experience with the college's white principal. Ntlhola was attracted to the mix of politics, faith and the Bible he found in Johweto. He went into hiding for four months. He turned down a chance of attending the University of Natal because he felt that university life would compromise his faith. Mpete and Venter asked him to come and work with them, and he agreed on condition that he be allowed to complete his studies through distance-education at the University of South Africa. He was given the task of preparing the venues for the Sunday meetings (Ntlhola 1994).

Johweto leadership always emphasised the provision of employment as a ministry goal, and the Kehillah in 1990 became the springboard for this purpose. Vegetable farming supplied employment for eight people from the nearby squatter camp, and the M & M fibre-glass factory on the property provided work for four people. Attempts to involve unemployed black Johwetans in either the farm or the factory were unsuccessful—possibly because under apartheid, manual labour had largely been reserved for blacks. Personality clashes between the fibreglass factory manager and prospective employees played an inhibitory role, too. Johweto's leaders and others also helped individuals with finances for academic and business ventures. During that year some were aided in pursing theological studies, a secretarial course, and public relations training. The farm, a fibre-glass factory, a taxi whose purchase was funded by Johnson, and pottery-decoration enterprise were other examples of Johweto-funded small businesses. Money was extended as a loan, with only the interest payable until the business could generate a salary. Only then were any profits to be divided between the business and Johweto.

In 1991 Johweto leaders initiated a six-month group discussion of what

Johweto was, and where it was going. Motivated by a continued sense of dwindling congregational energy, the exercise was called Commitment Process, intended "to sort out where people were" (A. Venter 1994a). The Process included exercises in the classic spiritual disciplines, like meditation, and discussions regarding various forms of community. Later the same year a seminar for singles, held at Mpete's house in Pimville, addressed sex and how to avoid single parenthood.[91] In September Venter spent three weeks in the United States, participating in the Vineyard Pastors' Conference in Denver, and visiting Reba Place Church (Evanston) and Church of the Savior (Washington D.C.). In a newsletter that month, Venter noted that his return coincided with the violent deaths of 127 people in the greater Johannesburg area (A. Venter 1991:1).

Following long-term discussions about the desirability of living in geographic community among seven married couples, five couples (four white, one black) bought a farm that included four houses and a cottage in 1991. The farm, located about 10 kilometre south of Soweto, was at first popularly referred to as NewFarm, and in 1993 named Southfield.

Conflict flared up in the congregation about the decision, with some arguing that the decision should have been discussed communally. A Sunday service was suspended to give people the opportunity to openly express their opinions. The families were adamant that their decision was of a private nature. Some argued that if the congregation as a whole was moving towards community, then decision-making should increasingly be communal. Another concern was that the distance of the farm to both Johannesburg and Soweto—and so from many in the congregation—would create an isolated elite that contradicted Johweto's communal ideal. If home ownership was the criterion for participating in communal experiments, some pointed out, Johwetans who could not contribute financially would be excluded. Others interpreted the exchange as an opportunity to think through the practical implications of living in community. Johwetan Chris Murray said that

---

91. A number of single black mothers attended Johweto. Unsubstantiated colloquial evidence indicates that single parenthood in Soweto may result from the financial inability (or unwillingness) of men to pay the traditionally-required bride price. Consequently, unmarried couples live together for a while, with the male typically abandoning the woman after a child is born. The same sources suggest that some male-dominated black ethnic groups believe that a woman has to prove her fertility by bearing a child before marriage.

the exchange was "not conflict, but an issue which was well talked through" (Murray 1992). In 1993 the issue was partially resolved, with the families deciding that the property would become Johweto premises. The farm would be open to anyone who wanted to come, but the four houses would remain private property.

The dissension revealed tensions between an emerging ideal of community and continuing notions of private property. Class, as affected by the unequal racial distribution of resources under apartheid, was exposed as a fault line within Johweto as within many racially-mixed congregations. Questions of power about who could control decision-making remained unexplored at this time.

The decision to establish a communal farm highlighted that living in geographic proximity had become a particularly pertinent problem for Johweto. Most members lived about 20 kilometres away from their Sunday meeting place. Security soon proved a major problem on the farm, with the house of George and Gonsie Moroa repeatedly broken into. The Moroas' dwelling was separated by some distance from the other three, and was demolished by vandals when the family temporarily moved back to Soweto for their own safety. Later a large abandoned shed on the farm was converted into a home for the Moroas. The Southfield families regularly held community meetings, and later formed a fellowship group. Various uses were discussed for the new property, with suggestions ranging from an art centre, vegetable farming, tea garden, hospitality cottage, home for single mothers, to a retreat centre —none which had materialised by 1994. The formation of community brought about new relational structures, with the Southfield families meeting every two weeks to discuss events on the farm, with social get-togethers held once a month.

In December 1991 Mpete and his family left for a one year stay at Reba Place Church in Evanston, Illinois. Mpete cited mental and emotional fatigue as reasons for this sojourn. By default, Venter became the controlling partner in leadership, although declining to make major decisions in Mpete's absence. Mpete's departure created space for new worship leaders to emerge, a challenge first taken up by whites, before a worship team slowly formed that was led by blacks. A commune consisting of three people was established in the Moroas's vacated house in Dlamini Extension 2 that included Ntlhola and Curtis Chang, a Chinese-American visitor. Catherine Wirth, a member of Reba Place Church, was now stationed at the Kehillah, helping the elderly in the nearby settlement with their pensions, and the children with a feeding scheme. The settlement now contained an estimated 1,000 dwellings and 5,000 people, and was blamed by farmers for theft in the area.

The phrase "core" emerged in the congregation between 1991 and 1992 as a term to identify those who had belonged to Johweto nearly as long as the pastors. For some this meant "mainly" those who lived on the communal farm Southfield. Others argued that "the core is Johweto," or "everyone who is there on Sunday mornings" (Murray 1992; Laverty 1992).

Visitors who occasionally came to meetings in the Careers Centre served to remind the congregation of their linkages within South Africa as well as beyond its borders. Baptist minister Michael Eaton, formerly from Alexandra township, visited from Kenya. Eaton commented on various types of racially-mixed congregations and stressed the need to found a church that was truly African. The congregation's embeddedness in the wider South African independent Charismatic movement was symbolised by a visit from Derek Morphew, head of the Associated Christian Ministries network to which Johweto belonged. Links with the United States were emphasised by a visit from Sally Schriener of Reba Place Church. In April 1992 Johweto held Sunday services in the Centre's newly completed hall. Although the small size of the congregation was emphasised by the large space, Johwetans perceived the occupation of the hall in a positive light.

A communal house was bought in 1992 in the mixed-race Johannesburg suburb of Yeoville. The Yeoville house fulfilled dual roles, serving as a communal home for a white and a black Johwetan, and as a meeting point for Venter and an advisory team that was instituted in 1992. By 1994 three groups of Johwetans lived in Yeoville, holding out hope for establishing an urban outreach program there.

By March 1992 the congregation had grown to 39 adults (15 black), and 13 children; towards August the number stood at 45[92] (22 black), with about 30 children (10 toddlers). The majority of whites in the congregation were married in their mid-30s, with children younger than four. Most had university degrees, earned middle to higher-middle incomes and had two cars; some fell in the upper income bracket. Most blacks were single, in their 20s, and some had children. Some blacks had college diplomas, some were high school students, and some were unemployed. The blacks who did work held lower-income occupations

---

92. An address list compiled for the congregation in 1992 contained 49 adult names.

or entrance-level white-collar middle-income occupations. Only two black Johwetans had a car. Although three blacks were attending university, only Mpete had a university degree. The whites were "very competent, struggling with spiritual life and God, [but] the majority is well-educated," while the blacks were "a very mixed group—struggling at a more basic level" (Murray 1992).

The safety situation deteriorated on the Kehillah in 1992. Gates, fencing and vegetables were repeatedly stolen, and armed robberies occurred on nearby farms. Most of the surrounding areas were now occupied by squatters, such as the Orange Farm settlement. The Kehillah's farming project ran at a loss of R4,500 per month by August 1991, mostly through lack of stable outlets. In May 1992a drought destroyed more than 70% of the crops. During the same year the Erbach-Adams couple came from Kastellaun, Germany, to work on the Kehillah. Pia Erbach-Adams helped Wirth, while husband Jurgen did carpentry, a skill he tried to impart to some of Johweto's unemployed. Meanwhile Ntlhola started a fellowship group at Dlamini on Tuesday evenings that attracted a number of blacks and five whites who travelled in to attend. The Dlamini commune actively tried to reach out to their neighbours, and a well-attended block party was held.

Mpete's return from the United States at the end of 1992 had an unexpected impact on Johweto, as he decided to revert to his African name, Moekete. Previously, like most black South Africans, he had used his middle "Christian" name, Paul. Blacks used their "European" names to facilitate interaction with whites, who apparently could not learn to pronounce African names. A chain reaction followed, with a number of blacks reclaiming their names. Even Venter started using his full name instead of the childhood nickname by which he had been known. But a few blacks said that as they were known by their European name even among family, they would continue to use it. In another language-related change around the same time, Johweto's all-male leadership began to make a more noticeable effort to use gender-inclusive language. This was partly due to pressure from white women in the congregation, who challenged the use of non-racial phrases alongside the retention of stereotypical terms for women.

Up to mid-1992 leadership comprised pastors Mpete and Venter, white financial resourcer James Johnson, and black trainee pastor Trevor Ntlhola. Ntlhola and Lizzie John occasionally were given opportunity to lead services. There was no overt process by which to become a leader, although it was commonly understood that one became a leader through: (a) people recognising how you served the group, (b) people finding help in what you did, (c) accepting responsibility, and (d) long-term involvement. Informal training in aspects of ministry (e.g. praying for the sick) took place through the leaders modelling it for others—a practice that was highly regarded. Apart from this primary threesome, secondary leaders could be identified only through their prominence in various meetings. Close friends of Venter, this group acted informally as his advisors, without any executive power. Venter also from time to time convened more formal groups with specialised functions, such as an administrative team in 1988-89. Between the end of 1992 and the beginning of 1993, Venter brought together a more formalised group to help plan services. Relative to the size of the congregation and the limited programmes, a great deal of planning happened among the three leaders. Formal records were kept of all meetings between March 1987 and June 1989. A large number of documents were generated, testifying to numerous meetings with topics ranging from budgets and schedules for farming (1991) to vision statements (1993). In 1993 Mpete withdraw from leadership shortly after his return from the United States due to personal reasons.

In terms of decision-making, Johweto struggled towards consensus, while straddling a leadership that wavered between theocracy and democracy, according to Mpete. No formal process of decision-making existed, although discussions—sometimes in the time allocated to Sunday services—were used to generate decisions. This protocol was regarded as making it easier to assess and engage people. Decisions which influenced all Johwetans sometimes occurred through discussion, such as moving the congregation from Ipelegeng to Diepkloof. Other decisions affecting everyone were sometimes taken by Johnson and Venter with little or no overt input from others. An example of a decision taken solely by the leaders is the selection of the advisory team in 1992, concerning which there was no wider consultation. In 1992 many Johwetans were concerned to open up all aspects of congregational life to allow everyone to participate.

By January 1993, half of Johweto lived in some form of geographic community, whether in one house (Yeoville, Dlamini, Kehillah) or on one property (Southfield, Kehillah). The communes were widely dispersed between Johannesburg, Soweto and the two farms south of Johannesburg. The composition of the house in Yeoville changed in

1993, with the white marrying and leaving to pursue studies. Two other blacks moved in—one from the Dlamini house—so that three blacks then lived there. When the Dlamini property was reclaimed by its original owners, the Moroas (who had left Southfield and Johweto), the Soweto commune moved to Pimville. Occasional services and social events continued to be held at the Kehillah, such as a baptism service in late 1993 at which Ntlhola officiated. The McCulloughs left the Kehillah in 1993. Long-standing relational tensions between McCullough, his workers, some black Johwetans, and the Mothianes could not be resolved, despite arbitration by Johweto's leadership. The blacks took exception to some of McCullough's actions and attitudes, but instead of confronting him voiced their concerns to Mpete. McCullough felt that the leadership sided against him, and this, added to his own unhappiness with Johweto's model of being church, led him to withdraw (A. Venter 1994c).

By late 1993 one white and the black family withdrew from the community project at Southfield. The white family decided against continuing in the commune, but persisted in meeting with the rest of the congregation. The black family told Venter that they needed to return to Soweto due to family and cultural issues. In an interview, the black family reported that they had experienced increasing financial pressure to keep up with the lifestyles of their white neighbours at Southfield, which they felt had continued to project an implicit inequality. The combination of financial and cultural pressure extended to the nursery school their daughter attended with other Southfield children in Johannesburg. While they had difficulty meeting travelling expenses to work, their daughter experienced pressure to value things white above things black. For example, she expressed the desire to have long blond hair. This family chose to sever their bonds with Johweto. In 1993 farm manager Mothiane moved from the Kehillah to Southfield, and another white couple did so in August 1994. Three groups of Johwetans lived in Yeoville, holding out hope for establishing an urban outreach program there.

A simmering conflict about leadership style led to two white couples withdrawing from Johweto. Meanwhile, key Johweto figures agreed with Venter that Ntlhola should become the primary team leader for Johweto. Venter remained to assist with the transition. The unresolved conflict worsened in 1995. After attempts at third-party arbitration, six critics were expelled from the congregation. Venter left in September

1995 to pastor Valley Vineyard in Bryanston.

Johweto was now primarily a black congregation. Briefly known as the Johweto Society, it was formally reconstituted as the Zone 3 Vineyard under leadership of Ntlhola in Pimville. The shift in name reflected Ntlhola's desire for the congregation to be more rooted in its immediate context. In 2001 the Zone 3 Vineyard initiated *Emthonjeni* (isiZulu for Fountain of Life), an HIV/AIDS community-based care facility at the ehillah (A. Venter 2004: 50, 75).

EXPLAINING JOHWETO'S RACIALLY-MIXED COMPOSITION

Johweto was an example of an intentional,[93] integrative, and non-transitional type of racially-mixed congregation. Most members did not live in the neighbourhood where they met, nor in a mixed neighbourhood; neither was ethnic transition happening in the surrounding context. Johweto was a commuter congregation, with little or no ministry links to its Soweto context. Members were uninvolved in their immediate contexts, apart from secondary support to a squatter camp outreach near one of its farms. Links did exist on a structural level (ministers' fraternals), and individual members were involved in educational and health projects. According to the classification system of congregations' mission orientations developed by David Roozen and others (1984), this confirms Johweto as a civic congregation; to which the lack of collective action also bore witness. Johweto's civic mission orientation meant her beliefs would not be translated into corporate programmes of action.

Johweto became integrated through the actions of its two founding leaders, and through the resulting vision. A significant portion of those who made up Johweto initially participated either because they were invited by friends or knew Venter or Mpete. By 1992 most had known them for more than a decade. A membership recruitment strategy document spoke of "growing from friendship groups." Their bondedness led some to believe that their "relationships will last beyond Johweto." The theological base of the founding vision derived from an interpretation shared by the congregation that the gospel required a crossing of racial and economic barriers. The mixed leadership and congregation drew others who held similar beliefs. So the mechanisms that aided the initial unity were not particularly radical, except for including those from dif-

---

93. The intentional nature of the congregation was often stated in Johweto documents (e.g. Venter and Johnson 1987:4).

ferent racial groups who grew closer by living and working together on the Kehillah. Despite the disparate social positions of Johwetans, a high level of social interaction occurred. Johweto presented a rare congregation which had attempted to reinvent its structures in line with its vision, in the process moving from a church-type of religious organisation to that approximating a sect-type.

Clearly the founding vision of a community crossing racial boundaries drew in others who identified with all or part of this theological and political identity. The emphasis on relationship with God, with one another, and on a strong socio-political awareness[94] attracted others who felt similar. The vision arose from the socio-economic and political bottom of South African society represented by Mpete's initiative. Events in South Africa were often at the centre of Johweto's Sunday services, taking the form of a sermon on the massacre of forty-five inhabitants of the Boipatong informal settlement in 1992, for example. A whole communion service was planned to help people express feelings about this violent event. On such occasions the black hymn "Nkosi Sikelel' iAfrika" was sung as a cry to God to end the violence, sometimes accompanied by weeping among those in the congregation. The family of some Johwetans were killed during the political conflict that swept through the Reef townships, and also during civil unrest, such as the 1992 hospital strike. On one Sunday the sermon was suspended for a discussion of whether the National Peace Accord—brokered in September 1991 to set codes of conduct for some twenty-seven political organisations (Byrnes 1997)—was working.

The majority of Johwetans surveyed said they attended Johweto because of the racial mix. Sandy Johnson spoke for many Johwetans when she said, "I will never join a white church...Because we have been separated in the past we have to work at getting together" (Johnson 1992). In 1991 the Lavertys left their Yeoville apartment because the landlord would not allow black friends to visit them and stay overnight. White Johwetan Chris Murray said it was important that the church was in Soweto. He was looking for a church which "married the spiritual with the social and the political...The major part is the black and white mix, but if it does not draw me deeper into God I could not stay" (Murray 1992).

Johwetans felt that their congregation held out an unique microcos-

---

94. The politicisation of Charismatics in the United States has been noted in Robbins (1988:206). albeit in a right-wing direction, contrary to Johwetans' orientation.

mic solution for South Africa. In their view, Johweto served as a representative model for the South African church and society as a whole—a common theme in the other case studies, too. A white Johwetan said her husband would have immigrated had it not been for Johweto, while another white Johwetan said that "Johweto is what the church should be in South Africa—multi-racial. I never felt comfortable elsewhere" (Von Veh 1992).

Almost all Johwetans had left other churches, and some regarded their experiences in their previous congregations negatively. A number felt that they could never go back to an all-white church, that "church should be representative of [the racial mix in] the country" (Von Veh 1992). Murray distinguished between older participants who had joined Johweto because they had been disillusioned by previous church experiences, and those who had come more recently "because it is a more whole expression of what church should be in South Africa" (Murray 1992).

But a black member felt uncomfortable with the implicit assumption that Johweto "is first in the race, with others following behind...others have met as non-Christians [before] while we hid [from meeting] behind the mantle of Christianity. Black and white hobos [homeless people] have better relationships than we [at Johweto] have."

Despite the vertical economic and educational differences between Johwetans, horisontally many members came to occupy similar socio-political margins in their respective black and white societies. Their social dislocation was caused by their positive attitudes towards blacks or whites. On the other hand, they shared negative attitudes towards nationalist policies, as well as towards the racial exclusiveness that dominated the wider white church and society.

In contrast with their social peers in 1985, people "wanted to break racial barriers." Both positions were in line with an ideology of non-racialism. Blacks chose to ideologically distance themselves from those opposed to ethnic mixing—the latter stance encouraged in some Black Consciousness quarters.

Prior to attending Johweto, some whites had refused conscription into the defence force (e.g. Mike Laverty), or had opted for non-combatant status (e.g. Chris Murray). At the time military conscription was compulsory for all males over eighteen, and refusal resulted in prison sentences or considerably extended non-combatant service. Conscientious objection had steadily gained pertinence since the South African Council of Churches had resolved in 1974 that members should challenge their affiliates to debate it. Many white Johwetans had prior relations with other blacks before Johweto through various projects. The Lavertys and Poppletons, for example, had considered moving into Alexandria and Tembisa townships, respectively. George Moroa remembered suggesting to black youth groups that they meet with whites (Moroa 1993). Four single black people had moved into a mixed suburb in 1993 —still a somewhat unusual experience at the time, as white landlords in the area resisted renting residences to blacks.

In other words, participants in Johweto drew on resources for integration that existed in the conflicting ideologies of society. Many Johwetans were opposed to government policy (racial or otherwise) and affirmed black/white interaction prior to joining Johweto. But they lacked a spiritual institution in which to base their convictions. Johweto's theologically-based vision was linked to a required and replicable experience of racial interaction. The vision pulled individuals across the boundaries of their societies into a single institution that could satisfy their political, social and theological needs. Moroa choose to become part of Johweto because he explicitly identified with the apostle Paul's writing that the boundaries between Jew and Gentile had been obliterated in Christ (Moroa 1993).

Although Johweto represented a symbolic redrawing of boundaries between the white city of Johannesburg and the black city of Soweto, all the tensions associated with socio-economic differences could not be resolved. With regards to the relationship between the informal settlement and the Kehillah, farm manager Mothiane mused that the squatters "should have been drawn in" (Mothiane 1993a), a sentiment also offered by former Johwetan Euan Ross-Taylor, who believes that the fences between the farm and the settlement, added to the habit of "us" going out to "them," contributed to friction and a siege mentality. Mothiane recognised that attempts were made to link with the informal settlement, but noted that perhaps more time should have been expended on these efforts (Mothiane 1993b).

Internal tensions between cultural assimilation and expressions of cultural difference gradually emerged within Johweto. The constant debates between Johwetans about which elements of whose culture was relevant meant that cultural assimilation was resisted to a degree. Cultural resistance was strengthened by the use of different languages in worship songs. Solutions to differences in cultural interpretation were not always found. Some whites were unwilling to attend funerals of the distant relatives of black Johwetans, as is required practice among black South Africans. This remained a sore point throughout Johweto's history. Yet a pull towards assimilation was evident in the dominance of English as common language. "There is still a language barrier which we have to cross," said a black Johwetan. He pointed out that in meetings whites would often distort what a black person said, even though this happened in the guise of a rephrasing, such as "If I understand so-and-so correctly..." The example and strength of Mpete as a black leader, and occasional challenges by Ntlhola, John, and Edgar Molefe, helped to keep the cultural imprint of whites from dominating completely.

Johwetans expanded a great deal of energy on increasing mutual understanding, whether through informal interactions or addressed formally in meetings. A large number and variety of joint social events were arranged. Some Johwetans attended a Black Consciousness seminar together at Soweto's Funda Centre in 1986, and in 1992 attended a play about Malcolm X together. In some small group meetings people talked about the differences between white and black, sometimes accompanied by quarrels. So, for example, whites asked blacks to make more of an effort to initiate social interaction with them, to avoid all the initiative being taken by whites. The openness of dialogue helped shift Johweto's orientation from a focus on the racial divide to a more unified feeling.

A second internal fracture ran along class lines, evident in obvious differences between white and black lifestyles. Economic disparity was the direct systemic result of apartheid policies that built white prosperity at the expense of blacks, and could not easily be overcome. Black Johwetans would occasionally confront their white counterparts about differences in relation to means of transport, housing, and entertainment. While most whites in Johweto owned two vehicles, most blacks had to use poorly developed public transport systems. All whites lived in housing visibly more luxurious and larger than the single rooms inhabited by many black Johwetans. Because many black Johwetans were unemployed or part-time employees, expressions of community that involved buying property (as at Southfield) implied financial commitments well beyond their means. Participating in such prospects would increase their embarrassing and ongoing dependency on white largesse. A black remarked of participants in the Southfield project that "people were chosen because they were liked, or had the finances." Although many whites regularly attended cinemas, many blacks lived on or below the poverty-datum line. Interclass differences were accompanied by intraclass contradictions. While some blacks had to support large extended families on meagre incomes, they insisted on wearing name-brand quality clothing.

The tensions that arose from material differences manifested in a certain defensiveness among some whites, although others admitted that they had to re-examine both their lifestyles and ambition. Economic differences corresponded to social variance, as most blacks were single in contrast to most whites, although the average ages of whites (mid-30s) and blacks (mid-20s) probably were more significant in this regard.

Ironically, the use of the language of community and the counter-culture ethos that bound Johweto together so effectively, were commonly understood to imply greater equality than had actually been attained.

A second important driver of Johweto's racial integration was the strong counter-culture identity of the congregation that erected strong boundaries. This identity was expressed in a sense of uniqueness similar to that found at Saint Francis. The boundaries were negatively enforced by the feeling for many that Johweto was a last-chance option. If the glorious experiment failed, there was nowhere else to go. The number of overseas visitors that participated in Johweto from time to time also affirmed the congregation's sense of its own significance. In 1992, for example, a German couple, a Chinese-American, and an American woman participated in Johweto activities for extended periods.

The congregation's boundaries were concretely enforced by the actual distances that whites had to travel to get to Soweto. The geographic location simultaneously aided and discouraged new membership. Whites had to travel at least 35 minutes by car, demonstrating their choice to identify with blacks. By 1992 sixteen Johwetans came from two communal farms to the south; eight from Johannesburg to the north-east, and four from the coloured suburb of Eldorado Park to the south. The dozen or so who lived in Soweto were also separated by several suburbs from one another.

Participants erased some boundaries while maintaining others. In order to erase the boundaries of the apartheid city, Johweto had to invent alternate boundaries that embraced race and class. Boundaries between Johweto and the wider (white and black) society had to be ignored. Those between Johweto and white society, other congregations, and the larger South African church had to be maintained. The initial opposition by a well-known black church leader, like the infrequent anger of Soweto residents towards black Johwetans, drew lines between the congregation and its immediate context. Some whites felt unwanted in Soweto. The negative experiences of Johweto's participants in Soweto may have contributed to the lack of commitment to this local context. By participating in a mixed congregation, black and white Johwetans alike crossed cultural boundaries. A striking example of the resulting conflict for black participants was provided by Gideon Sennelo, who decided not to participate in any event in the township at which an *izinyanga* (isiZulu, "indigenous spiritualist") officiated—the usual practice at almost all major stages in a black person's life cycle.

Congregational boundaries were also enforced by informal covert contracts into which one entered upon joining Johweto. For example, one was expected to replicate the founding experience of forming friendships across colour lines, and of experiencing life on the other side of the racial divide. Johwetans were expected to become friends who have meals and conversations during the week, not just to sit next to one another on Sundays. The implicit political stance, the financial cost implied by the distance, and the theological orientation tested commitment to the founding vision and sifted out actual from potential participants. Not all managed to negotiate the contract: one person who had come for eight months confessed that he did not "really know any black well."

Johweto's interracial identity provided important affirmations for the political orientations of participants. Blacks could feel that they belonged to an institution that would not betray their political cause. Whites were offered the opportunity to work through collective guilt without compromise. For most blacks, racial interaction at the time still primarily took the form of employee-employer relations. In Johweto such social roles were inverted, just as they had been in Central Methodist's People Centre.

In an odd way the economic differences between whites in higher income-education brackets and blacks at the lower end of the scale also acted to draw Johwetans together. The lop-sided distribution of skills and resources created a measure of dependency of some blacks on some whites. This issue came to be viewed negatively, and was raised as such in meetings. Viewed positively, a person who belonged to Johweto long enough to establish friendships could count on others for material support, such as food or money. But the unequal distribution of social and economic resources affected Johweto's organisational structure. A white Johwetan suggested that blacks often felt that they could not take on a leading role, or that they did not possess the skills for such a task. Such perceptions would inevitably result in white domination of congregational processes. Nevertheless, a high level of concern existed among Johwetans to open up all aspects of congregational life to all participants.

Some blacks may have viewed friendship with whites as a means to gain resources. Johweto's leaders detected a pattern of money-less blacks befriending whites, who then acted as patrons on their behalf, sharing finances and skills (e.g. driving). Sometimes this produced positive results, such as a young black woman who was helped through high school and college by a white couple, and eventually held her own in a high-powered advertising firm. Sometimes the results were negative, as when a person used the same reason to borrow money from different white Johwetans. A white placed such interactions in the early phases of Johweto's history, saying that at first blacks had "a 'gimme' feel," but "now things are balanced out." A black Johwetan agreed that "some blacks think the whites will help them." Immediate need was prompted by high levels of unemployment in South Africa, which did not fall below 31% of the labour force between 1993 and 2002 (peaking at 41.8% in 2002; Kingdon and Knight 2001, 2005). But economic dependence was also driven by a general desire among blacks for the rightful redistribution of resources from which they had legally been excluded. By contrast, Johweto's leaders felt that friendship should precede resource-sharing, and should not demean either person involved.

Some participants in the Johweto story maintain that gradually an implicit contradiction emerged between Johweto's values and practices, which ultimately undid the hard work of establishing a non-racial community in a hostile environment. From this perspective, Johweto imploded under the weight of failed expectation and ideals.

5

Inverting Segregationist Norms

INTRODUCTION

In this chapter I expand on how the formation of racially-mixed congregations relates to the historically competing social norms of integration versus segregation in South Africa. Using the same approach I can explain the apparent contradictions within such congregations, such as continued individual resistance to integration, or organisational bias towards cultural assimilation. The preceding four chapters linked congregational segregation to urban organisation through references to the development of an increasingly segregationist state. I now widen my focus by looking at how congregations, urban settlements, and national policies related to global institutions.

To recap my arguments about racially-mixed congregations as inversions of segregation the first section of this chapter reprises the historical evidence for the institutionalisation of segregation and integration as *contested* national norms. As a prerequisite step, I first return to the meanings of 'institutionalisation,' 'norm,' and 'national.' The operationalisation of the major terms will help me demonstrate the degree to which these norms were institutionalised and contested by state and civil actors during various periods in South Africa's history. The review allows me to stress the historical continuity of general strategies of resistance or accommodation to national norms that were embodied in racially-mixed congregations and political organisations alike. The second subsection describes the extent to which the institutionalisation of integrationism and segregationism in South Africa depended on global political developments. A dialectical interplay between local and transnational norms, individual and collective actors, all contributed to establish such norms in South Africa. As befits my emphasis on mixed congregations, I stress those forces that promoted integration. The third subsection assesses how integrated congregations inverted global, national, and urban norms of segregation and inequality by creating a space in which actors could attempt to re-normalise racial interaction.

The second part of this chapter shows how the case studies can be used to construct a tentative typology based on the inversion of segregation in congregational structures, neighbourhoods, and social interaction. To demonstrate the potential generalisability of my arguments, I include additional data about similar congregations in the United States. In a concluding section I construct a tentative theory about the formation of racially-mixed congregations under apartheid by integrating the historical overview (Chapter One) with the case studies (Chapters Two to Four) and my overall argument about competing social norms.

MIXED CONGREGATIONS AS INVERSIONS OF SEGREGATIONIST NORMS

The small number of South African Christians who between 1948 and 1994 insisted on attending church together participated in small-scale demonstrations of alternates to the racial segregation that was the hallmark of apartheid. The South African state had achieved almost complete segregation of institutions and of geographic space by 1980 in line with robust state ideologies that promoted separateness. By contrast, racially-mixed congregations participated in the institutionalisation of an alternate norm that promoted integrationism.

Chapter One showed that segregation and integration were both institutionalised as norms by competing class and ideological formations in South African society. The state's formal deployment of segregation as national policy in the 20th century was countered by civil society organisations who worked towards integration. The emergence of the first wave of racially-mixed congregations during the 1960s signalled an incipient shift towards integration among political sectors of the general populace. The direction of the shift was in line with the multi-racialism embodied in the Freedom Charter (1955) and embraced by a number of organisations across the social spectrum. On the other hand, racially-integrated congregations that existed from the colonial era to the present show continuity with an older ideal of integration.

Segregation and integration co-existed as contested national norms because their institutionalisation were more or less complete at different times, in various organisations, and across society as a whole. The institutionalisation of these norms can broadly be conceived in terms of incipient (informal), intermediate (formal), and completed stages. The stages do not necessarily follow one another in teleological fashion. Instead, intertwined spirals of integration and segregation rose, expanded, and contracted over time. An informal strand of integration was ascendant between 1665 and 1852. From 1870 to about 1912 informal segregation was ascendant, intersecting the declining arc of integrationism. Segregation was formalised into grand apartheid between 1913 and 1948. Apartheid's declining arc was intersected by informal integration around 1985. Informal integration was ascendant from about 1928 to 1994, solidifying into formal integration, as Figure 4 on the next page illustrates.

The above distinction between a general increase or decrease in degrees of convergence around a norm can be further extended to distinguish levels of normalisation:

- an *informal (incipient) stage* signals the emergence of a pattern of practices and ideas among members of a social group that affects the organisation of some individuals, without formal legislative support;
- an *intermediate formal stage* comprises formally expressed ideas associated with certain social structures, policies, or legislation in support of particular practices, but lacks a comprehensive mechanism that applies to all social institutions;
- during the *complete formal stage,* the norm affects all institutions of a society, regulating most aspects of the lives of a majority of individuals.

We can trace the historical process through which national norms were institutionalised so as to view changes in roles, expectations, and behaviours over time. An obvious strategy for doing so is to contrast the state's organisation of society at the height of the apartheid period (about 1980) with colonial efforts to do the same.

Segregation became increasingly institutionalised between the middle and end of the 19th century in churches, hospitals, schools, urban planning, and constitutions of the Boer republics. During the Union period (1910-48) the creation of a unified state enabled segregation to be incorporated into national legislation during the 1920s. Under apartheid, the formal restriction of racial interaction advanced rapidly after 1948. For most of the 1950s and 1960s, religious institutions remained one of the

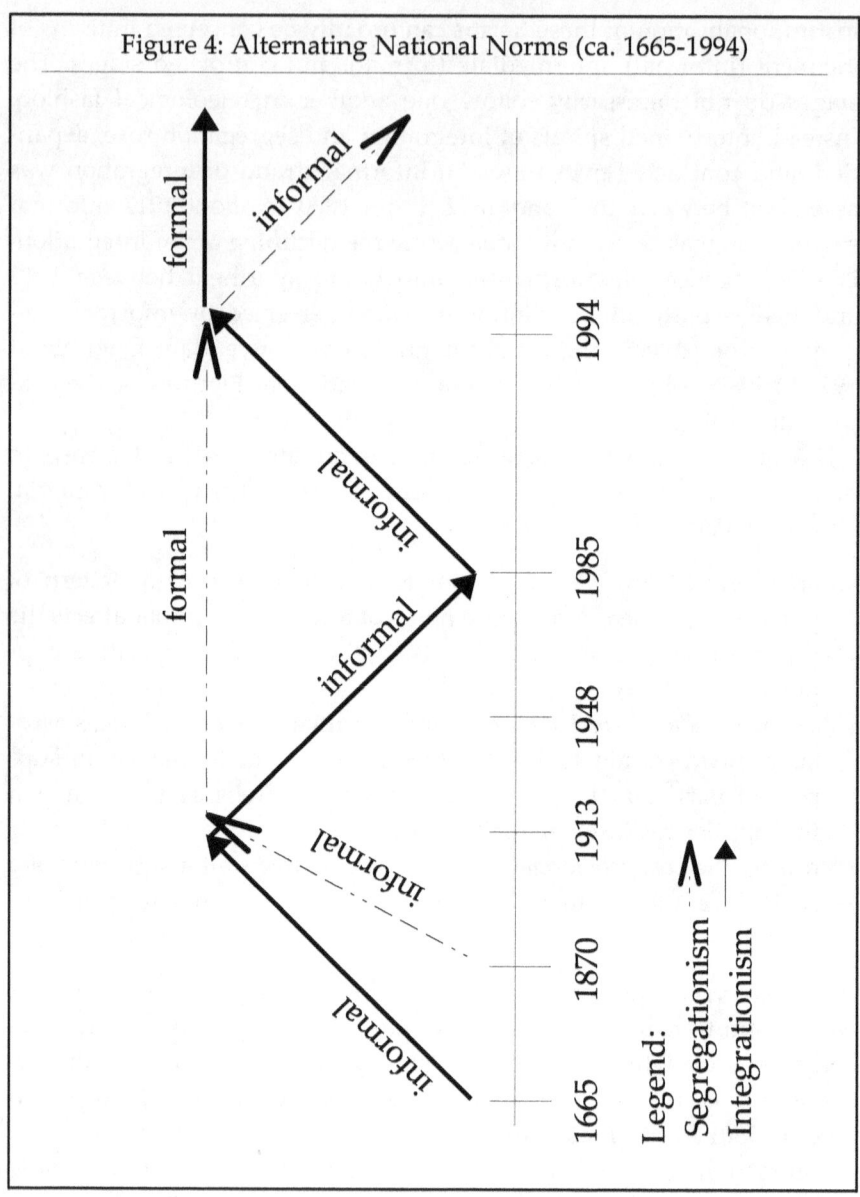

Figure 4: Alternating National Norms (ca. 1665-1994)

few remaining spheres in which voluntary racial interaction was not legally prohibited. Other notable exceptions occurred within tertiary student organisations, as the National Union of South African Students embraced non-racialism from the 1960s. Meanwhile a few people of colour managed to attend white universities, such as Indian students at the University of the Witwatersrand during the 1970s. Some trade unions remained racially integrated until 1964.

Overall, segregation developed from an optional and informal praxis that affected some institutions in the colonial period to the mandatory legislation of the apartheid regime that affected most institutions. Integration followed similar historical patterns of informal and formal advances and retreats across all institutions, before being embedded in post-apartheid legislation.

The next section shows in more detail how segregation and integration was incorporated into colonial regimes before the state adopted apartheid as national policy. Readers should not allow my use of the rather anaemic heuristic term "segregation" to obscure the full historical horrors of forced removals, violent security actions, and daily humiliations that people of colour endured under apartheid. Racial prejudice and racism, prodded by economic imperatives, supplied the rationale by which the state adopted racial segregation. Segregation was not a voluntary option for the majority of South Africans who bore the brunt of apartheid. The state enforced segregation through an insidious and inherently violent bureaucratic and securocratic state apparatus, driven by the ideology of apartheid.

REDUX: SEGREGATED INSTITUTIONS, CONTESTED NATIONAL NORMS

We now examine when integration and segregation were institutionalised, and the extent to which they were contested. Integrated institutions have been much neglected in histories of South Africa, implied only in the work of the few who traced the emergence of non-racialism (e.g. Julie Frederikse 1990, Robin Petersen 2000) or the history of non-racial trade unions.

The institutionalisation of racial segregation began with the development of terminology which defined indigenous actors and their roles in increasingly prejudicial terms. Initially, officials of the Verenigde Oostindische Compagnie during the mid-17th century used relatively neutral terms for indigenous bands that they encountered at the Cape. Names included "dese lants natie" (people of this land), "Strandloper" (beach ranger, for the *Goringaikonas*), or "Kaapmans" (Cape people, for *Goringgaikwas*) (Liebenberg n.d.:37). Larger groupings were later defined as "Hottentoos" (Hottentots), first in a diary entry by Jan van Riebeeck in 1658, and more formally in a 1677 peace treaty. "Hottentot" originally had ethnic rather than racial undertones. Indigenous peoples like the Hottentoos were then further subdivided according to their general location and leadership. By 1701 overtones of prejudice appear, associated with hostile groups such as the "Bosjesmen Hottentots" (Bushmen, for San). The names "Hottentoten" and "Kaffer" [sic] both appear on Isaac Tirion's 1730 map of the Cape Colony (Tirion 1730). "Kaffir" was coined in the 16th century as a borrowing from the Arab religious distinction *qafir*, "unbelievers." The term was applied from 1589 by Europeans to the inhabitants of sub-Saharan Africa, pre-dated by earlier references to African indigenes as "Negro" (ca. 1555; Harper 2001).

By the end of the 19th century, these descriptive terms were incorporated into an emerging operational racial construct among settlers inside and outside the Cape Colony. An early formal deployment of racial terms in conjunction with technology occurred in 1865 in Cape Town's first census, which distinguished between "Hottentot" and "Kaffir." "Coloured" by the 1870s usually referred to all those who were "other than white," but were sometimes used about those who were not black Africans (Bickford-Smith 1995:30). A report on the 1875 census defined "Kafir" as excluding the "Fingo" (Mfengu) and "Bechuana" (Batswana) groupings (i.e. including the amaXhosa, amaZulu, and others). In 1885 the Zuid-Afrikaansche Republiek introduced legal distinctions between whites and "Coolies, Arabs, and other Asiatics."

Racial terms were eventually used to organise social space—first *ad hoc*, then with increasingly systematicity, as signalled by the constitutions of the Orange Free State (1854) and the Zuid-Afrikaansche Republiek (1858). Initially, segregation proceeded along class lines that overlapped with—and obscured—the underlying racial thinking. One of the earliest instances of residential segregation dates to 1679, when company slaves were housed separately from early colonists. Slaves differed in race, class, and status from their owners. Some commentators have argued that racial segregation was developed by the English during their colonisation of Ireland in the 15th century (Wilkinson 2004) —although in contemporary terms, this would be more a matter of ethnic prejudice than racism.

The various formal and informal attempts to implement racial integration and segregation in parallel in various colonies across the southernmost part of Africa map the fortunes of both processes. Arguments among ordained denominational officials of the mid-19th century about whether to integrate indigenes into worship services alongside colonists show that neither integration nor segregation had yet achieved hegemony. Related disagreements continued between some clergy and laity, anticipating a similar trend during apartheid. Saunders argues that by the mid-19th century, racism (exemplified by some 1820 settlers and the Cape's British governors) paradoxically co-existed alongside a critical opposition to racism that was bolstered by legislation that downplayed race. He suggests that during the 1840s "harsher racial thinking" was "introduced from Britain" (Saunders 2002).

Note that while I describe the institutionalisation of segregation and integration in the following two sections separately in order to more clearly contrast their development, I do not intend to abandon my arguments for their simultaneous implementation.

The Emergence of Segregation as Norm

The progress of the institutionalisation of segregation in South Africa can be traced across stages that yield increasing scales of analysis across a variety of institutions. Yet, rather than developing in a linear manner, segregation was implemented in an undulating way through processes that were not always related. Colonists along the eastern frontiers as well as politicians in metropolitan Cape Town contributed to the diffusion of segregation, as did Boer *Voortrekkers* in the interior. Some colonial and denominational officials, settlers and indigenous groups, resisted segregation, while others encouraged or acquiesced to it. Historically, segregation emerged as norm first in residences (company slave lodge, 1679), congregations (slave sections, 1834), regions (Kaffraria, 1848), urban settlements (East London, 1849), states (Orange Free State, 1854), and denominations (Nederduitsch Hervormde Kerk, 1855).

The institutionalisation of segregation unfolded from informal to formal stages during the development of the South African state as it did in urban areas and churches.

The **informal stages** of the colonial and union periods were marked by *ad hoc* actions by settlers, administrators, and other agencies. Initially, most social, financial, and educational institutions were shared by people who were already being considered racially distinct. Gradually, earlier attempts by colonial authorities to introduce equality gave way to policies that inclined towards segregation. While legislated equality remained mostly intact in the Cape Colony, segregative practices increased. Settler congregants in the Cape Colony assigned slaves to segregated seating before 1834. In line with the organisation of urban space, the general division of seating in terms of class determined by pew ownership tended to coincide with racial differences. Yet racial euphemisms were also employed to reserve seating for the "heathen" and the "Malays."

From the mid-19th century colonists, colonial representatives, mining companies, and later town councils implemented a range of racialised organisational options across the colonies. In the Cape and Natal Colonies some Dutch Reformed churches had by 1850 segregated liturgical and sacramental events, such as confirmation and baptism. During the Dutch colonial period the secular authorities at first resisted such efforts by congregations, as did some denominational leaders during the British period. After 1850 the usage of racial designations increased in colonial society as a whole, particularly "coloured," for everyone considered to be not "white."

The institutionalisation of segregation proceeded along similar stages for urban settlements as for churches. At Cape Town partial residential segregation between black Africans, coloureds, and whites was introduced between 1875 and 1902, during a prosperous economic period spanning the mid-1870s to 1880s. The arrival of 7,100 black Africans, brought from the eastern frontier and Mozambique as labour for farms and the expanding harbour, spurred the process (Bickford-Smith 1995:44). Upper class residents of Cape Town gradually began to reside in more racially-homogeneous areas than did the lower classes, for whom income and colour still overlapped. Segregation remained incomplete, due in part to the dominance of local merchants, who had little interest in the racial separation of its labour force. Cape Town was not the first urban settlement to be segregated, as we shall see. Segregation was more extensively adopted by some religious institutions at the Cape than by their secular counterparts. Mission schools were segregated already by the 1890s, to help resolve white poverty that had arisen (Bickford-Smith 1995:211). By contrast, hospitals and prisons were segregated only by 1902.

Inevitably, segregation at the Cape elicited political and social mobilisation from those most affected by it. Rent boycotts were organised at Ndabeni location in 1901. The African People's Organisation was founded as a political organisation in 1902 with aims that included promotion of coloured education and unity. Similar organisations had already formed on the colony's eastern frontier. In Port Elizabeth, for instance, in 1882 *Imbumba yamaNyama* (isiXhosa for "Unity is Strength") was founded by Isaac Wauchope, among others (Masilela n.d.). The African Methodist Episcopal Church journal expressed an incipient anti-settler Africanism (Bickford-Smith 1995:212) that anticipated similar views from the Pan Africanist Congress later. The effectiveness of such reactions from below was dampened by government responses that divided subordinated groups. In 1926 prime minister Barry Hertzog, for instance, contained the reaction of the African People's Organisation to segregation by tabling legislation to extend the coloured franchise over the rest of the country (Bickford-Smith 1995:212).

By the close of the 19th century, segregation was ascendant across South Africa's colonies, with integrationism playing a decreasing counterpoint. In urban areas residential segregation was introduced at East London in 1848, Port Elizabeth in 1855, and Durban in 1871. Mining companies constructed segregated labour compounds in Kimberley in 1886, setting a precedent for other towns. City councils excluded "Asiatics" from title deeds, as Pietermaritzburg's did in 1898. Segregation was extended over regions as colonial authorities introduced racially separated residential spaces in Kaffraria from 1848. In Natal a system was implemented that segregated white areas (farms, urban settlements) from black locations that were ruled, in turn, by hereditary black leaders supervised by whites. The Orange Free State in 1891 excluded Indians completely from residential rights in that territory.

The informal and intermediate stages of institutionalisation overlapped greatly, partly due to differences in governance systems of the various British and Boer colonies across South Africa. At the end of the 19th century segregation in Johannesburg proceeded from regional formal racial distinctions that were implemented by the city council in 1885 in an uncoordinated fashion. The lack of a formal city-wide policy rendered the council's actions informal, even though they were based on formal, legal distinctions between whites and others introduced three decades earlier by the Zuid-Afrikaansche Republiek. Further segregation only became possible after the Group Areas Act was applied from 1955 onwards.

The **intermediate stages** of the institutionalisation of segregation lasted roughly from the mid-19th to mid-20th centuries, with segregation now more formally institutionalised, but not yet applied systemically across all institutions. Laws and policies were formulated, and administrative departments were formed to regulate and enforce their implementation. Formalisation was necessitated by the desire to apply racial prejudice to larger scales of organisation, from congregations to denominations, towns to territories.

Segregation at a denominational scale was introduced by the Nederduitsch Hervormde Kerk (established 1855), a breakaway from the Dutch Reformed Church after the Great Trek. The Dutch Reformed Church allowed its congregations to segregate from 1857 on, and by 1881 had started creating separate sub-denominations. Other denominations publicly espoused an acceptance of all races, but in practice resisted implementing these pronouncements in their congregations. This double-sided reality continued through much of the 20th century. Rob Robertson's struggle from 1961 to 1968 with the Presbyterian Church of Southern Africa to establish the North End congregation serves as a good example. The continued use of segregated seating in Catholic parishes represents another.

After 1910, the Union government started devising policies of segregation centrally, decreasing the ability of councils to influence local residential patterns markedly. Some municipalities had in 1922 actively encouraged the central government to enact greater segregation in the proposed Natives (Urban Areas) Act of 1923 (Rich 1996:23). The Act held municipalities responsible to the national government for implementing Group Areas within their boundaries. Yet urban councils were only able to implement complete residential segregation after the apartheid state's segregation policy was embodied in the Group Areas Act of 1950.

Racial exclusion from political institutions was encoded in the constitutions of the Boer republics between 1837-1858, as it effectively was in Natal, too. The Zuid-Afrikaansche Republiek's Regulations for Towns (1899) introduced a larger scale of racial organisation, by segregating usage of some public space (sidewalks). The Regulations demonstrate that segregation had achieved an ideological status that was to some degree independent of the material interests that initially drove it. The same relative independence emerges in the racial discrimination in matters of church and state built into the constitutions of the Orange Free State (1854) and the Zuid-Afrikaansche Republiek (1858). In both instances there is little—if any—connection between legislation and economic arrangements. Yet racial discrimination did fit in with widespread notions of black inferiority that supported the increasingly racial division of labour against the intention of earlier proclamations such as Ordinance 50 (1828). The economic shifts following the mineral revolution that encouraged employers to pay workers less also helped public opinion to gradually tilt towards segregation. Other institutions in the Zuid-Afrikaansche Republiek soon also became segregated: Indians were legally prohibited in 1897 from marrying white women, for instance. By 1907 segregated schools were proclaimed in the Transvaal by the Education Act. Yet church schools — as we saw at Saint Francis — remained integrated until 1959. Earlier pieces of legislation laid the groundwork for later ones, with the Cape Colony's Native Reserve Location Act (1902) preceding the Natives (Urban Areas) Act (1923) as the foundation for urban segregation

The institutionalisation of segregation required that state structures be transformed to more effectively implement segregationist policies. The Union government began to introduce segregation as a term in legislation during the 1920s. The Native Affairs Department was restructured in 1927 away from a liberal paternalism to a more inflexible segregationism, in line with the proposals of the Stallard Commission (Dubow 1989). Until then, the Department operated in an assimilationist mode in line with the Cape franchise system. The relative weakness of the Department earlier on is demonstrated by the differences between the larger portion of land allocated to blacks in the initial Land Bill (1912) compared to the smaller ratio bestowed by the final Natives Land Act (1913). Native Affairs Minister Hertzog's intentions for a more generously proportioned allocation for the Orange Free State was severely undermined by white agriculturalists via their Members of Parliament during the passage of the Bill. In 1914 Lovedale's *The Christian Express* remarked that opposition to the Act was " 'the first thing that has united the Natives throughout the length and breadth of South Africa' " (Rich 1996:182, footnote 21). But the Act did not bestow complete control over blacks on the Native Affairs Department (Rich 1996:17), which had to wrestle for it with the Department of Justice.

The **complete** (or formal) **stages** of the institutionalisation of segregation were marked by the development of a centrally co-ordinated national policy and of the bureaucratic mechanisms with which to implement it. After 1948 the apartheid state formalised segregation in urban areas, superseding pre-existing legislation that allowed municipalities to do so voluntarily. The remaining history of the complete adoption of segregation under apartheid is well known enough to avoid recounting too much detail here. Further urban segregation was made possible when local authorities were able to force racially-defined groups into separate residential areas according to formal policies encoded in municipal ordinances, backed up by legislation proclaimed by central government. The apartheid state's legislative framework disembowelled Cape Town municipality's resistance to the Group Areas removals of some 60,000 people from District Six between 1968 and 1982.

In Christian institutions the final stages of the adoption of segregation arrived when individual affiliates accepted the separation of believers in their denomination into racially-specific meetings as "natural." Denominations which adopted a formal policy of segregating congregations from 1855 on and those which rejected the theological and political bases for apartheid had over a century later all accepted this arrangement. Racially separate congregations had become a norm in all denominations long before the state enforced residential apartheid. The few congregations that choose to be integrated were the exceptions that proved the rule.

The discussion so far demonstrates that the institutionalisation of segregation did not unfold in completely distinct phases, but through various stages that overlapped with one another. The overhang between intermediary and formal stages, for instance, can be illustrated in the history of East London on the eastern boundary of the Cape Colony. Special Commissioner John MacLean in 1849 horded "natives" (amaXhosa) into a single location adjacent to the white village of East London. A different set of regulations applied to the location than to East London (Tankard 2004). The implementation of urban racial segregation by officials represents a step beyond the informal stage. Here the segregated areas, racialised criteria for defining them, and separate sets of regulations already anticipated the final stages of institutionalisation. But the uncoordinated implementation confers an intermediary status on proceedings. Without a formally constituted municipality, segregation could not be implemented across the whole settlement. With the establishment of a municipality that took control of locations, East London entered this formal phase only in 1876. But by 1884 the East London council had failed to remove all black residents from "white" East London, as "civilised" blacks could then still legally live within its boundaries (especially in North End) (Tankard 2004). Even as late as the 1960s, after the formal introduction of apartheid, East London's local authorities had not yet achieved complete segregation, as North End Presbyterian Church demonstrated. The inability of the council here to completely segregate residents demonstrates a contestation between proponents and opponents of segregation.

Despite similarities between the institutionalisation of segregation by urban and central governments, and by church polities, there are also significant differences which are not just a matter of scale. First, the apartheid state could control city councils through legislation far more than it could restrain denominations. As voluntary institutions that were funded privately, churches remained outside direct state control. Yet denominational property located in urban areas that could be racially rezoned, like individual affiliates who could be forcibly removed, could not escape the state's influence. A second difference is that denominations like the Nederduitsch Hervormde and Dutch Reformed Churches could implement a more complete segregation of affiliates by the mid-19th century than urban authorities or colonial states could. Colonial states during the 19th century lacked the coercive power to enforce segregation, which was instead advanced by non-state organs (city councils, mining companies) with whom state interests often overlapped. In general, prior to 1948 urban and state authorities were unwilling and unable to consistently implement segregation. In historical perspective, segregation gained momentum as option of choice among settler institutions. Slaves were affected from the start, followed by converts to religious institutions, then urban residents, ethnic groups, and finally, whole colonies.

Yet contrary to appearances, there was no straightforward progression in the scale (small to large) and scope (partial to complete) of segregation. Segregation of indigenous peoples occurred at larger, regional scales (Kaffraria, 1848) before affecting smaller scales of organisation, such as denominations (1855) and then congregations (1857). Large-scale segregation did not necessarily indicate complete segregation. Even where progression in scale is noticeable, in the Dutch Reformed Church for example, complete segregation did not follow immediately. Despite the apparent progression from separate seating for slaves (ca. 1834), to segregated liturgical and sacramental events (ca. 1850), to segregated congregations (1857), and to racially-based subdenominations (1881), some Reformed congregations chose not to implement segregation. The Stockenström congregation remained mixed until 1862. Saint Stephen's in Cape Town not only remained coloured but also part of the white Dutch Reformed Church. Nor did all institutions become segregated at the same rate. While Cape Town's mission schools were segregated already by the 1890s, hospitals and prisons, among other institutions, only became so by 1902. The Zuid-Afrikaansche Republiek represents a good example of the lack of correlation between scale and scope. Despite the racial discrimination entrenched across all of the Transvaal by the Zuid-Afrikaansche Republiek's constitution (1858), and the proclamation of segregation in education (1907), some church schools there remained mixed until 1959.

The Emergence of Integration as Norm

The institutionalisation of integration in South Africa was a more complex process than for segregation, although informal and formal stages can also be discerned. Both segregation and integration occurred in different waves that peaked at particular periods. The first informal wave of integration occurred during the colonial era, and the second during the apartheid period. The current formal emphasis on integration of post-apartheid societal institutions represents a third wave of integration. The few congregations that managed to remain integrated throughout all periods represents a thread of continuity, to borrow an image from Julie Frederikse (1990).

During the British colonial period the **informal racial integration** of some institutions rested on formal attempts by authorities to introduce equality of all races before the law. Limited equality was extended to all who could assimilate the central tenets of European civilisation via nominal affiliation with Christianity and education. Informal practices racially integrated towns, churches, schools, and prisons.

From the colonial to the post-apartheid periods the ideal of racial integration was kept alive by ideological movements that operated below and above urban and state agencies. Clergy, political activists, students, and political organisations attempted to organise space in which racial interaction could occur formally and informally.

The visit by the 1921 Phelps-Stokes Commission of Enquiry into education in Africa provided a special impetus. The Commission (comprising clergy from the United States, Africa, and Europe) was nominally multi-racial through the inclusion of James Aggrey, a Ghanian educated in and—at the time—residing in the United States. Aggrey addressed mixed audiences on such topics as racial co-operation and black self-sufficiency (Walls 1998, Brody 1998). Subsequently, South Africans established twenty-six Joint Councils of Europeans and Natives to foster racial interaction and to promote black interests. The Joint Councils, in turn, created the South African Institute of Race Relations in 1929 as co-ordinating and research body (Dubow 1989). Parachurch organisations like African Enterprise organised racially-mixed events in 1973 and during the mid-1980s.

After the 1960s the reversal of segregation inside the country was accomplished largely by South African and other actors who worked to establish racial equality as norm in transnational organisations and social movements. Racial discrimination was confirmed as an aberrant norm by the same external sources, supported inside South Africa by organisations like the Black Sash. Other groups, like the Liberal Party, succeeded in keeping a version of the ideal of integration alive from 1953 to 1968, when the state forbade racially-mixed political organisations. The extent to which integration as global norm was adapted by domestic structures can be measured by changes in the organisation and behaviour of groups. Accordingly, religious and educational institutions preceded the state in implementing the second wave of integration, but not without internal conflict. State organs were in fact among the last institutions to comply with the newer norm. But other institutions had not completely changed yet, either, as the post-1990 struggle to integrate churches demonstrates.

The apartheid state used a mix of formal and informal means to gradually and selectively desegregate residential areas as well as selected social and political institutions without eliminating apartheid completely. Racial integration was completely absent from national policies by the mid-1940s, only to re-emerge after 1985. Formal measures included the creation of a tricameral parliament and the abolition of the Prohibition of Mixed Marriages Act in 1985. The state's increasing reluctance from 1982 onwards to prosecute Group Areas Act transgressions permitted informal integration in Johannesburg's inner city. The cumulative effect of such informal practices, added to formal arrangements—such as allowing city councils to apply for zoning of racially-mixed business districts—integrated the inner cities of Durban (ca. 1976) and Johannesburg (ca. 1985). Through the Free Settlement Areas Act (1988) the state appeared to "allow" so-called "grey areas" to develop in formally designated white areas. In reality, the state's action merely acknowledged an unresolved existing phenomenon.

Formal state measures followed informal initiatives by blacks to racially integrate urban areas during apartheid. Practices ranged from erecting informal structures, to squatting in empty buildings, to subletting residential units. The acute shortage of housing in the townships motivated such largely successful movements into previously white areas. After 1985 the state's retreat from centrally co-ordinated policies was abetted by continued pressure from political and civil agencies at home and abroad. The result was a climate in which the informal integration of residential areas was harder to prevent. Meanwhile, integrated religious communes had emerged by the late 1970s in East London, as secular racially-mixed communes of students did by 1986 in cities like Pietermaritzburg.

In retrospect, South African congregations actually inverted two norms during different periods, as the title of this book implies. The majority of congregations inverted the incipient norm of voluntary integration that emerged during the Dutch and early British colonial periods, opting instead for segregation. By contrast, a minority of congregations inverted the voluntary segregationism of the late colonial and Union periods, as well as the involuntary segregation of apartheid. During the latter era, South African institutions were obviously dominated by a norm of segregation, given the formal codification of apartheid in national legislation.

CONTESTING SEGREGATION AND INTEGRATION

The historical overview summarised in the preceding sections point to the emergence of incipient (informal) integrationism followed by nascent segregationism during the colonial period. Incipient integrationism was more the consequence of a *laissez faire* attitude on the part of colonial authorities and colonists than of deliberate action. Segregation, on the other hand, preceded from a more conscious application of 'otherness' to the organisation of physical and social space.

Initially, integrationism was 'incipient' in the sense that racial interaction—albeit based on participation in a shared British 'civilisation'—occurred in some institutions, but not others. The limited admission criteria for non-settlers, added to an uneven institutionalisation of equality, led to a disjunction between institutions that were integrated and others that were not. For example, some workplaces continued to be integrated until 1947. The initial support by colonial authorities for the informal integration of institutions was reversed by self-governing British and Boer colonies.

Once both integration and segregation were accepted as external realities, public preference for either of these organisational strategies over the other alternated historically, geographically, and from one official to another. Material and ideological factors contributed to related contradictory actions and opinions exhibited by colonial officials, settlers and missionaries towards colonised populations. Those involved were motivated by a range of intentions, varying from the protective to the exploitative. Liberal whites accepted the selective incorporation of indigenes with settlers into local institutions, while others argued for separate institutions and settlements. Proponents of protective practices towards indigenes were inclined to favour integrated institutions in urban settlements alongside segregated protective reserves in rural areas, as Bishop Robert Gray of the Anglican Church did. Those propelled by an exploitative imperative argued for general segregation, as Cecil John Rhodes did, and in particular for separate urban locations in which to house labour. Indigenes were not passive in this regard, as similar differences of opinion also emerged among them about the desirability of integrating with settlers. As a result of these contradictory forces, segregated and integrated institutions were established simultaneously. The paradox is illustrated by colonial urban settlements that contained both racially-mixed and segregated suburbs at the same time, such as East London and Johannesburg.

The alternation between segregationism and integrationism proceeded from the dual nature of the British colonial project itself. On the one hand, colonialism was founded on a widespread belief in the superiority of British civilisation, including its religious institutions. Colonialisation was perceived as a civilising mission to indigenous peoples in the colonies. Conversion to Christianity was a primary condition through which colonised people could, in principle, attain social equality with colonisers. Anti-slavery activists argued that freeing slaves would prove the superiority of British civilisation. Later they proposed that all subjects of empire should be equal before the law. But other colonisers and colonists were primarily interested in exploiting material resources through control of indigenous labour. For them, colonialism incorporated norms of prejudice and inequality that justified the exploitation of indigenes for the extraction of material resources that were exported to the homeland.

Incipient integrationism in South Africa arguably reached its height between the 1830s and 1870s. Like those who proposed integrated institutions, individuals in racially-mixed congregations probably drew on (and generated) alternate ideas that circulated within South Africa and across the British empire. Humanitarianism, anti-slavery activism, and socially-concerned religious movements contributed to the integrationism of the early colonial era. In Britain, anti-slavery activists influenced colonial policies through organisations such as the Select Committee on Aborigines (1835) and the Aborigines' Protection Society (1837). Individuals with first-hand experience of the colonies (such as John Philip) and those who would later exercise administrative oversight (such as George Grey) supported these groups. Yet during the late 19th century, integrationism lost ground in South Africa.

The contested nature of both norms up to the mid-1930s also depended on divisions that arose among blacks in response to state policies of segregation. Some divisions were driven by ideological opposition between supporters and opponents of communism (e.g. Josiah Gumede versus Pixley ka Seme), leading to a split between the Communist Party and the African National Congress in 1930 (Simons and Simons 1968). Other tensions arose due to the ambiguous potential that blacks saw in segregation to develop their own institutions independent of white control. For this reason, John Dube and A.W.G. Champion from Natal supported segregation (Rich 1996:162). Some feared that active opposition to the state would lead to loss of existing rights and greater repression. These differences led to divisions and leadership struggles within organisations, such as the Industrial and Commercial Union and the African National Congress. At times there were violent confrontations: James Thaele's supporters clashed with participants in the communist party-driven Anti-Pass Campaign of 1931, for instance (Simons and Simons 1968).

Broadly-speaking, some blacks—like D.D.T. Jabavu—supported the assimilationist incorporation of Cape liberalism. Hertzog tried to exploit this position in 1935. Support for limited integration arose from the rapidly-fading hope that Cape liberalism would be extended across South Africa. Similar anticipation later drove other blacks to adopt the more egalitarian promises of non-racialism, whether understood in passive form (assuming that racial equality already exists), or in an active sense (seeking to confront and overcome racism; compare Lazerson 1994:264-65). But by the post-Second World War years some black activists, spurred by the expectation of domestic change, started to shake off liberal solutions and to embrace national liberation as goal. Their quest was to undermine the legitimacy of the state in favour of a new government founded on a popular base (Rich 1996:167-8).

During the 1950s the state tried to prevent opposition to segregation from unifying around black nationalism by increasing the authority of chiefs in line with principles of indirect rule embodied in the 1927 Native Administration Act. The state sought to divide black activists through a similar strategy of appearing to devote less attention to Africanist organisations that favoured segregation (Rich 1996:164).

Some black agitation in the period between the two world wars contributed to the popular acceptance of segregation among whites. Black activism was fuelled by "the declining productivity of the reserves, the development of capitalist agriculture and the quickening pace of proletarianisation" (Dubow 1989:40). By 1948 segregation was well established as national norm. In a dialectic irony, congregations of the 20th century were now segregated according to an increasingly hegemonic notion first introduced by the Nederduitsch Hervormde and Dutch Reformed denominations in the 19th century. By contrast, colonial authorities prior to this time had formally opposed racial discrimination in line with Ordinance 50 (1828).

Prior to the Nederduitsch Hervormde Kerk in 1855, no denomination seems to have adopted a formal segregation policy for all its congregations. Particular Dutch Reformed congregations were segregated prior to this, apparently due to individual or local prejudice. Even after the Dutch Reformed Church also adopted internal segregation of its congregations (1857) and its mission branches (1881), some of its congregations remained integrated for some time. Saint Stephen's Church in Cape Town (founded 1839) was a coloured congregation that stayed within the white Dutch Reformed Church. The Dutch Reformed Church's actions were incongruous in the context of the limited racial integration based on class that marked political institutions at the time. Free Black and coloured members of the Dutch Reformed Church could at this time vote, but not attend church with whites.

To understand the role of religious institutions in establishing segregation as normative in South Africa, we have to compare the mission policies and actions of various denominations to practices in other institutions. Given its theological support for apartheid, the actions of the Dutch Reformed Church towards its own affiliates should receive particular concern. Does the comparison allow us to draw conclusions about whether similar effects appear simultaneously in other institutions as in religious ones? If so, then incipient segregation drew on ideas that existed beyond the churches; if not, then churches themselves were the sources. The history of segregation inside and outside South African churches provide some answers. The diffusion of proto-segregation was probably aided by the limited number of individual actors who played different roles in various institutions in South Africa's early colonies. Sirs George Grey and Theophilus Shepstone serve as good examples, as I detail later on.

RELATING NATIONAL NORMS TO GLOBAL INSTITUTIONS, IDEOLOGIES

Segregationism and integrationism in South Africa had transnational, national and subnational (geographic) sources. The local competing norms for racial interaction can be linked to historical global ideologies of racial segregation and integration. My emphasis on the agency of the South African state does not ignore the wider theoretical discourse on globalisation which claims that the power of states are diminished by global forces. The history of the apartheid state actually illustrates the process by which domestic policies were undermined by the degree to which anti-apartheid agents could generate global pressure. Both the apartheid state and its opponents attempted to legitimise their actions by appealing to global norms. And so attention to the local struggle reveals which norms had become institutionalised in the world polity by the mid-1980s.

The segregationist strategies of interaction that became normative by the late colonial period were embedded in world-wide flows of historically-developed racist ideologies. The globalisation of racial prejudice was largely a consequence of the Western colonial project, but also depended on exploitative interactions that pre-dated it (e.g. slavery). White politics in South Africa aligned with global racial norms that were circulating in the world system of the 19th and early 20th centuries. The opposite is true of black political aspirations across South Africa: by the early 20th century their demands for political inclusion and civil rights corresponded to norms established in Britain as well as in transnational organisations.

By contrast to white segregationism in South Africa, an alternate ideological stream emerged among those colonised indigenes who from the late 19th century onwards insisted on establishing segregated parallel institutions. They were partly inspired by Pan-Africanism (first as Ethiopianism, later as Africanism) and partly by contemporary African-American efforts. During the 1920s Garveyism contributed to the idea of trans-ethnic solidarity and African self-reliance within this movement. From 1968 the same transnational sources fed the Black Consciousness movement's espousal of institutional segregation as interim measure. By contrast, norms that favoured racial segregation enforced by whites were becoming anachronistic in global fora by the 1960s. Segregation as a domestic policy built on racial domination came in direct conflict with opposing ideologies of racial equality.

Political and social actors in South Africa generated a counter-ideology of integration with concomitant strategies which competed with white and black segregationist ideologies for normative stature.

As described in Chapter One, incipient non-racialism was promoted by the International Socialist League (founded 1915) and the South African Communist Party (1921) (Frederikse 1990). The term surfaced in the title of the Non-Racial Franchise Association, founded by Cape liberals in 1929 to promote universal franchise on the basis of "civilisation" rather than race (Dubow 1989:159). The Non-European Unity Movement (founded 1943) took non-racialism up more explicitly (Petersen 2000), as noted in Chapter One. Transnational influences and universal franchise were linked in the first resolution of the (white) South African Congress of Democrats in 1953. Informed by the internationalist perspective of Communism, the Congress of Democrats framed South Africa's racial oppression in the context of the Universal Declaration of Human Rights and the Cold War (Lazerson 1994:73). Their predecessor was a committee of black A.N.C. intellectuals that studied the Atlantic Charter in 1943 (Atlantic Charter Committee 1943). By 1955 the African National Congress moved towards embracing non-racialism, as the Freedom Charter revealed that year.

In addition, transnational activists working with political exiles from South Africa led the United Nations and the organisation of African Unity to condemn racial subjugation. The United Nations declared apartheid a crime against humanity in 1976 (A. Venter 2004:116).

During the apartheid era, racially-mixed congregations were self-conscious, collective representations to apartheid society of a different South Africa. As such, they unknowingly aligned themselves with the incipient integrationism of early colonial institutions. More consciously, congregations allied with the non-racialism that emerged during the union period and that marked anti-apartheid organising much later. Participation by whites in events where they encountered other racial groupings served to hum anise 'others.' At the same time, whites often drew positive energy from the acceptance that they experienced in such encounters, which served to affirm their oppositional roles in wider society in ways that mixing with other whites could not. Racial interaction provided a sense of "building something positive, a future for whites" (Lazerson 1994:263). This was true regardless of whether congregations espoused an active or passive non-racialism (compare Lazerson 1994:264-65).

Racially-mixed congregations participated alongside a range of collective and individual actors in the effort to change those shared understanding of racial roles and expectations that were associated with apartheid. As a symbolic confrontation of segregation in South African society, the congregations were drawn to deal with an institutional paradox of their own. As pioneers of racial integration, mixed congregations ultimately had to invert the effects of segregative norms on their denominational institutions and their own internal structures.

The discussion so far illustrates how national norms were interrelated with transnational political developments. Through a dialectical interplay between local and transnational norms, individual and collective actors, racial integration was eventually established as norm in South Africa. Work by Audie Klotz (1995) and by Elizabeth Elbourne (2003) provide insights into the mechanics of the process. Transnational institutions influenced some South African activists, who in turn participated in transnational political and religious networks, that again affected global institutions.

Audie Klotz's work offers additional insights into the process by which racial equality became entrenched in transnational institutions which exerted pressure on other institutions and nation-states. Klotz makes helpful suggestions regarding the genesis, institutionalisation, maintenance, enforcement, and alteration of global norms and their influence on South African policies.

She suggests that norms tend to derive from previously existing sets, and that their implementation do not require a blanket acceptance by all units under analysis. While norms tend to be viewed in terms of coercion (e.g. sanctions), they can also be part of a unit's identity. Opposition to apartheid within the Commonwealth, for example, led to changes in that organisation's collective identity and organisational form. Norms play a constitutive role in the composite identity of states, which includes international, transnational and domestic dimensions (Klotz 1995:171). A state's compliance with norms need not necessarily coincide with its material interests. As norms fulfil social roles, a state may choose to adopt a norm in order to preserve its reputation in relation to other states. Compliance need not stem from coercion, whether of a military, economic, or diplomatic type. There is no state whose policies comply completely with international norms (Klotz 1995:5). South Africa's disregard under apartheid of global norms of racial equality, for instance, did not invalidate their status as norms.

Klotz concludes that norms define an actor (in our case, states and organisations) and prescribe its goals. The adoption of racial equality by member states became a constituting norm for the Commonwealth, as for the Organisation of African Unity. Klotz's insight regarding how norms build from pre-existing sets helps us to link racial integration to a chain of global norms stretching back to the campaign to free slaves. Her work also provides us with historical benchmarks against which to trace the institutionalisation of integration within South Africa.

Klotz' discussion draws attention to apartheid as not merely a recently constituted domestic agenda but one that initially drew on norms of racial superiority that justified the colonial system. As these norms shifted over time, the state's policies of segregation had to be bolstered by adapting newer norms to their service. The Union state adopted the British system of indirect rule as the mainstay of its policies. Smuts was aware of the need to pad a policy of trusteeship towards blacks sufficiently with liberal features to maintain international approval (Rich 1996:158). The apartheid regime attempted to legitimise the creation of homelands in terms of later norms of self-determination in domestic policy (Klotz 1995:170). Historical precedents existed in the reserves created by the United States for Native Americans, and in the protectorate system created by the British in New Zealand and Australia. South Africa's gradual international isolation resulted from its institutionalisation of segregation "at a time when the international trend was to favour racial equality" (Klotz 1995:4). Another example of a domestic shift in apartheid policy in relation to changing global norms occurs in the state's attempt to defend against the imposition of sanctions by justifying separate development with terms extracted from an emerging global norm of group rights. The state's lack of success in this regard was due to a shift towards an international individual human rights regime (Klotz 1995).

Integration, on the other hand, can be linked to the institutionalisation of racial equality and the associated demand for universal suffrage for individuals. Klotz (1995:18) argues that the norm of racial equality emerged from debates about slavery, and about the role of free and unfree labour in the emerging capitalist system. The so-called Clapham Sect (1790-1830) of abolitionists, that included William Wilberforce, used the motto "Am I not a man and a brother?" on a porcelain medallion—depicting a chained slave—in their anti-slavery campaign. The notion of individual equality was strengthened within the West by liberal philosophies and, later, by demands in the rest of the world for decolonisation. Yet experience in the United States showed that in (former) colonies not all abolitionists promoted racial equality.

The idea of all men as equal before the law was diffusing through the British empire from the 1830s on, having been established in the Cape Colony in principle by Ordinance 50 (1828). Statements by Queen Victoria about equality to the Commissioner of Natal in 1843 reveal that this was still the official position fifteen years later. A key moment in the history of equality was the 1835-36 Report of the House of Commons Select Committee on Aborigines, which linked the anti-slavery movement to the racial politics of the Cape Colony via the philanthropic efforts of missionaries. Abolitionists were active on the Committee, and contributed to drafting its report. John Philip of the London Missionary Society had a hand in the final draft. Philip went to London with coloured and amaXhosa Christians who gave evidence in 1832-33 before the Select Committee. One member of the Committee was Sir George Grey, later governor of the Cape Colony and Imperial High Commissioner (1854-61). The Committee's demand that Australian aborigines be regarded as British subjects who were under the authority of British law (Elbourne 2003) anticipated similar claims in the South African Native National Congress's petition to King George V against the Natives Land Act (1913). The principle of racial equality was supported by the colour blind franchise contained in the constitutions of the Cape's first representative (1853) and, later, of its Responsible government (1872). A shared franchise also encouraged occasional cross-racial alliances in local elections (Bickford-Smith 1995: 26, 77).

Most importantly for my theme, the Report of the Committee on Aborigines called for "the creation of race-blind common societies," so providing an early instance of non-racialism as motivation for racial integration. The Report was followed by the creation of the London-based Aborigines Protection Society. The 1913 delegation of the South African Native National Congress contacted the Protection Society, which mediated with the Colonial Office on its behalf. After the meeting with colonial secretary Lord Lewis Harcourt in 1914, the Protection Society helped the deputation to draft an appeal to the Imperial Parliament and the British public (Elbourne 2003).

While not always applied in practice, legal racial equality provided a platform for colonised peoples in South Africa to demand equal treatment. The outh African Native National Congress's Land Act petition claimed "the full benefits of British rule like all other British subjects." From 1887 local colonial authorities had gradually removed the qualified franchise enjoyed by all free residents of the Cape Colony. Legislation that disenfranchised black voters — such as the Voters' Registration Act (1888) — fuelled black political demands for racially-mixed institutions. The petitioners against the Natives Land Act cautioned that the "segregating and separating of the natives and the Europeans" would lead to racial conflict. Ironically, the same argument would later be used by the National Party to justify the necessity of apartheid.

While self-determination as a norm was formally institutionalised in Europe only with the founding of the League of Nations (1919), black people across Africa, North America, and the Caribbean were rallying around Ethiopianism as an earlier form of the same principle. Emerging in the 18th century, Ethiopianism bolstered racial pride and a desire for independence among black peoples by using Scripture references to an ancient North African empire. Ethiopia was mythologised as invincible after Menelik II defeated invading Italians in 1896 (Homiak n.d.).

As an expression of an emergent black bourgeoisie in South Africa, Ethiopianism flourished under the slogan "Equality for Africans" from the 1890s to the 1920s—especially in the Eastern Cape and the Witwatersrand (Kruss 1985, Venter 2004, Gardner 2004). The emergence of the slogan coincided with the exclusion of a black elite from full participation in the structures of democracy, early capitalism, and Christianity (Kruss 1985). Ethiopian leaders were drawn from a well educated African corps that included wealthy farmers, professionals, and craftsmen who were well connected with the old pre-industrial political structures (Kruss 1985). The leaders accepted the colonial premise that political equality extended to all colonised peoples who assimilated European education, cultural expressions, and religion.

Fed by white intransigence, Ethiopian churches broke away from white-dominated Protestant churches from 1884, whose organisation and doctrines they retained. South African Ethiopianism was supported by religious leaders from the United States, such as Bishop H.M. Turner of the African Methodist Episcopal Church. From 1908 a similar movement occurred among the landless amaZulu underclass who founded Zionist Christian churches. Churches under black leadership corresponded to the Ethiopian emphasis on creating segregated black institutions. Segregated political organisations emerged, first *Imbumba yamaNyama* in 1882, followed thirty years later by the South African Native National Congress (founded in Bloemfontein). The first black newspaper, *Imvo zabaNtsundu* (1884-1998), was founded by J.T. Jabavu in King William's Town, Eastern Cape. Black unions (Industrial and Commercial Workers' Union of Africa, 1917-30), black schools (John Dube's industrial school at Inyanga, 1904), came later.

The institutionalisation of racial equality as a global norm in the 20th century advanced when the South African question was placed on the agenda of transnational organisations by domestic and international actors. Since 1907, India had raised the question of the equality of its nationals who had emigrated to South Africa. Both Britain and India insisted on citizenship rights for South Africa's Indian population, even as successive Union governments under Barry Hertzog and Jan Smuts tried to undermine their claims (Klotz 1995:41). India brought the issue of citizenship rights to the United Nations in 1947. In 1952 India drew the General Assembly's attention to apartheid in order to try to obtain equal rights for Indian emigrants. India and the United Nations framed the issue in terms of individual rights, while South Africa defended its treatment of Indians in terms of non-interference (self-determination) and group rights (Klotz 1995:42,43). Perhaps this defense shifted anti-apartheid activists towards emphasising *racial* equality, thus also embracing a group identity. In any case, the emphasis on group rights remained a defensive state strategy through the 1993 negotiations about interim government.

The plethora of discriminatory laws passed by the apartheid state between 1950 and 1953, and repressive legislation enacted between 1962 and 1976, increased international opposition (Klotz 1995:43). The South African state attempted from the 1930s to consolidate segregation by creating native reserves that were ruled indirectly by territorial chiefs. The state's strategy lost legitimacy because Britain was during the same period moving its colonies towards direct rule. In Basutoland (contemporary Lesotho), for example, the Colonial Office introduced a system of native administration by 1912. By the 1930s it had introduced more democratic local rule in Nigeria (Rich 1996:17,35).

An additional defensive strategy offered by the apartheid state was to present its struggle against anti-apartheid organisation as part of the global Cold War. During the Treason Trail in 1956, for instance, the state claimed to be defending South Africa as a bastion of Western civilisation against communist encroachment, represented by the defendants (Rich 1996:14, 168).

Up to the 1960s the international political linkages established by black African leaders with the outside world were relatively ineffective in influencing South African domestic policy and internal opposition to segregation (Rich 1996:161). Deputations to Britain were cut off by the 1931 Statute of Westminster, which recognised South Africa as an independent dominion (Rich 1996:170; Halsall n.d.). Given the increasing significance of international linkages for sanctions after the 1960s, the strength of the South African state related inversely to the efficacy of international linkages. The less effect international linkages had on domestic policy, the stronger the state's coercive power (1930s-60); more effective external linkages decreased the state's power (1960s-90). Viewed differently, transnational organising became more effective to the extent that it was matched by mobilisation of a broad base of domestic support (Rich 1996:161).

By 1960 opposition in the United Nations had converged around racial equality as norm. After the Sharpeville massacre that year, apartheid itself was declared reprehensible in U.N. Resolution 1598 (Klotz 1995:44). Consequently, even to appear to support South Africa's domestic policies became difficult to sustain, as revealed by an increase in the number of abstentions whenever a vote on South Africa was called for (lotz 1995:45).

By 1963 commitments to racial equality and decolonisation dominated the formations of the organisation of African Unity and of the Commonwealth (Klotz 1995:75). Commitment to racial equality was accepted as a formal requirement for membership in the Commonwealth in 1961, and was formalised in the Declaration of Commonwealth Principles in 1971 (Klotz 1995:56, 60). Commonwealth member nations had by 1965 translated their commitment to racial equality into arguments for majority rule in the two Rhodesias (today Zambia and Zimbabwe), Nyassaland (Malawi), and South Africa (Klotz 1995:61, 62). Consequently "a wide range of diplomatic, economic, and military sanctions" against South Africa were adopted between the 1960s and 1980s (Klotz 1995:48). Pressure for internal negotiations and support for the armed struggle to end apartheid were affirmed by the Organisation of African Unity's *Lusaka Manifesto* in 1971 (Klotz 1995:77). Specific criteria were generated by 1985 that defined a transition to universal suffrage which would support the lifting of multilateral sanctions (Klotz 1995:67).

In line with external pressure, the apartheid state sought to represent its policies in universalistic terms by allowing suffrage within the homelands during the 1960s and 1970s. A similar effort supported the establishment of the Tricameral Parliament (1984), framed in terms of group rights in an approximation of consociational democracy. Yet despite apparently moving in a more democratic direction, political control remained authoritarian. The popular and international rejection of both strategies left the state with little political autonomy in the face of increased civil opposition. To defend its remaining autonomy, which depended on the security establishment, the state militarised its administrative apparatus under the centralised control of the State Security Council (Rich 1996:172,170). The passing of the Comprehensive Anti-Apartheid Act by the United States Congress in 1986 signalled the end of any remaining international support for the regime. Increased internal opposition succeeded in destroying the last vestiges of legitimating ideology (Rich 1996:173).

In order to answer whether a particular global norm was incorporated into South Africa's domestic agenda, Klotz suggests that we first specify the criteria implicit in the norm. Next we should examine the extent to which the criteria have sufficiently and systematically been implemented across the range of political, economic, social and individual social structures (Klotz 1995:155). For example, the steps taken by F.W. De Klerk's government (1989-94) to initiate dialogue with the liberation movements show "that sanctions succeeded in diffusing a global norm of racial equality in part through changes in external incentives: sanctions increased costs, and the prospect of their removal induced policy change" (Klotz 1995:158). Sanctions "legitimized opposition to apartheid and...the A.N.C. demand for universal suffrage" (Klotz 1995:161).

One of the consequences of the institutionalisation of global norms was to promote racial equality through socialising South Africans (Klotz 1995:165). Sanctions illustrate an instrumental role for norms as they "constrain states' behaviour through reputation and group membership" (Klotz 1995:166). Accordingly, individuals or organisations that wish to adopt a non-racist identity calculate the social cost of doing so; this cost-benefits analysis is incorporated into the identity (Klotz 1995:168). Similarly, activists who joined mixed congregations calculated the benefits not in material or social terms but by reference to compliance to external norms, such as non-racialism. Sanctions also illustrate a constructivist role in that norms "constitute states' definition of their own identities and interests" (Klotz 1995:166). International sanctions "succeeded in promoting a particular definition of a democratic, non-racial South Africa" (Klotz 1995:170).

Applying Klotz's insights to our theme is not without challenges, as they raise the question whether her conclusions regarding states and transnational organisations apply to individuals.

Yet her arguments regarding the inadequacy of materialist explanations for shifts in collective behaviour (Klotz 1995:8) retains salience with regards to the historical waxing and waning of integration and segregation. The hardening of white racial attitudes is clearly linked to the need for agricultural labour during the early colonial period and for miners after the discovery of minerals. True, the shift to an industrial economy and the consequent accelerating proletarianisation of black Africans could explain opposition to apartheid. But no subsequent material shift occurred to explain why, for some activists, opposition to apartheid should imply active participation in racially-mixed organisations.

In all three case studies, whites, and occasionally blacks, acted against their own social and economic interests to join mixed congregations. Blacks who participated in Johweto's early years travelled long distances to Johannesburg, as whites did later to Soweto. Similar commuter patterns that imposed a financial penalty were observed for white congregants at Central, and for black and white parishioners at Saint Francis. Like states that imposed sanctions, participants in racially-mixed congregations valued non-racist identities and interests above racial segregation. They conformed in group identity and behaviour to alternate norms that prescribed racial equality, and so normalised racial interaction based on roles that levelled statuses among participants. Instead of conforming to state policies, congregants together created alternate institutions that empowered them. By conforming to an alternate set of norms, they were able to act in ways that did not conform to the interests and goals of the state.

Were participants in racially-mixed congregations influenced by the international delegitimisation of the apartheid state, which simultaneously legitimated anti-apartheid activists (Klotz 1995:10)? At the least, their efforts were part of a larger attempt to redefine South African society in non-racial terms. Perhaps participation in mixed congregations enhanced their collective identities and promoted their collective interests, as Klotz suggested for states that supported sanctions (Klotz 1995:10)?

Integrated congregations, in effect, created a space for normalised racial interaction by inverting global, national, and urban norms of segregation and inequality—especially under apartheid. Put differently, to fully invert the national norm of segregation, participants in racially-mixed congregations had to address related norms, including the urban norm of separated residential areas and the denominational norm of segregated congregations. But they also had to invert the racial roles inscribed by apartheid on their structures and programs.

INVERTING THE RACIALISED ORGANISATION OF NEIGHBOURHOODS

The desire within racially-mixed congregations under apartheid to represent an alternative to segregated society inevitably involved congregants in confronting several racial structures. First, integrated congregations transgressed the racialised organisation of urban space achieved by apartheid policies. Congregational activities occurred in areas formally demarcated by the state for exclusive residential and recreational use by other state-define racial groups. Racially-mixed congregations also departed from the race-, class-, and status-defined separate afternoon services held for black workers in white churches. Second, integrated congregations inverted the racial norms of their denominations, which most often passively acquiesced with state prescriptions where they did not actively enforce them. Third, mixed congregations engaged the national political norm that prescribed racial identities and concomitant roles under apartheid. Finally, attempts at integration ultimately led congregations to invert their own internal racialised structures, derived from racist denominational policies.

In what follows I will concentrate on the inversion of racial organisation of urban space as befits the major theme of our discussion. I will only briefly sketch the second and fourth modes of inversion, before incorporating all themes into the final three sections of the book.

The first subsection below discusses the theoretical aspects of the transitional and non-transitional paradigms for identifying the causes for the emergence of mixed congregations. Next I draw together the various possible types of congregations that can be identified from the data so far. As my small sample of South African congregations renders the construction of typologies highly speculative, I occasionally refer to other studies in South African and elsewhere to demonstrate the potential universality of the typology. The validity of the typology must be weighed against such evidence from studies of racially-mixed congregations that date from the 1960s. In order to draw attention to the differences and similarities between the case studies, I then present a typology of racially-mixed congregations built around explicit and implicit strategies of racial integration. I suggest that Saint Francis' case demonstrates an implicit racial strategy of forming a mixed congregation, while those of Central Methodist Mission and of Johweto Vineyard represent an explicit racial strategy. Each strategy had particular consequences, as we shall see.

A discussion of the relation of mixed congregations to their neighbourhoods requires us to deal with the broader dominant transitional paradigm that scholars have evolved to interpret the issue. Even where demographic transition does affect South African congregations, the political mechanisms of segregation have to be accounted for first.

A Transitional Paradigm for Mixed Congregations

As racially-mixed congregations often emerge in neighbourhoods undergoing demographic transition, scholars have developed a transitional paradigm in which ethnic transition is viewed as the major contributing cause to the formation of such congregations. The underlying assumption is that a complete transition in a specific area will occur, inevitably affecting the local congregation. Both neighbourhood and congregation will eventually comprise only members of the incoming ethnic or racial group (see e.g. Wilson and Davis 1966; DesPortes 1973; Davis and White 1980; Yon 1982; Leonard 1983; Kwan 1990).

Older congregational studies in the United States identified a transitional type of racially-mixed congregation that resulted from ethnic demographic shifts in a particular neighbourhood. From this observation, a transitional paradigm was constructed which contained two assumptions. Firstly, a direct causal link existed between the internal racial composition of a transitional congregation and the external demographics of its immediate neighbourhood. Secondly, the racial or ethnic mix was a temporary state that anticipated a complete transition in which one or more incoming population groups would eventually completely replace another that already resided in the area. In sum, the transitional paradigm applied to mixed congregations where a direct causal connection existed between neighbourhood and congregation, where a congregation's geographic boundaries were enforced by denominational officials, and mono-cultural services were the norm.

The historical roots of the transitional paradigm lie in the studies of ethnic urbanisation patterns that changed the segregated nature of urban settlements in the United States. Sociologist Robert E. Park introduced the notion of neighbourhood transition in the 1920s by borrowing from natural ecology. Between the 1950s and 1960s, urbanisation increased the number of African-Americans who resided in cities by over 50% (cf. Wilson and Davis 1966:15; Wilson 1968). The transition paradigm depended on an older institutional model of religious behaviour, when affiliates attended congregations located within particular geographic boundaries as determined by their denomination (compare Ammerman 1993:2). Churchgoers had little, if any, say about where they could attend.

The transition process has been described as occurring in distinct sequences. According to Davis and White (1980:54-58) in pre-transitional neighbourhoods some whites leave, but no visible change occurs. During early transition visible change occurs in the institutions as more, say, black families move in. Late transition is marked by a 'tipping point' which, once passed, leads to flight by the white group. Financial institutions then limit investment. Post-transition is reached when black institutions fill the voids left by their predecessors (cf. Bonner 1982:19-20; Madinger 1989:155-158).

Among the options that congregations in a transitional neighbourhood face were to relocate and sell to a black church. Or, they could stay and accommodate new neighbours. Another alternative is to stay and remain a white middle class institution (Wilson and Davis 1966:35; Porter 1992:51). Faced with these choices, most congregations decide to relocate and sell; or to stay and remain white (Gratton 1989: 2). Those who opt for the latter commonly become commuter congregations (Wilson and Davis 1966:2,13). Those who choose to adjust usually expect to cycle through a full transition from white to black (Gratton 1989:2; Davis and White 1980:70,71). Lyle Schaller outlines different outcomes for congregations who accommodate, or choose to remain white, according to whether they appoint white or black ministers (Schaller 1989:4 1).

Transition remains a functional explanation and accurate description for the genesis of many mixed congregations. Representatives from six of the eight congregations at a 1993 workshop that I conducted at New York Theological Seminary said that neighbourhood transition played a major role in the original integration of their churches. Studies by teams from Emory University showed that ethnic transition played a role in three Atlanta congregations (Foster 1993:10,31,54); as it did in two of four congregations (in Boston and Atlanta) with a white/black membership mix around 70%-30% (Ammerman 1993). After 1986 demographic transition accelerated change at Central Methodist Mission in Johannesburg.

Several difficulties arise when the transitional paradigm is accepted as *sole* explanation for mixed congregations. The paradigm assumes that racially-mixed congregations represent a late stage in the assimilation of different groups into the dominant culture. From this functionalist perspective, all social institutions, including churches, co-operate to divest subordinate ethnic groups of their cultural values and practices, and to socialise them into the dominant group. The implicit connection between integration and assimilation can overshadow theorising about the nature and desirability of racially-integrated congregation-types. The discovery and description of additional types of integrated congregations are obscured. More seriously, the transition paradigm contains an implicit valuation of the homogeneous congregation as normative (Porter 1992:53). Ethnically-mixed congregations are seen as failing to rise above assimilation, and so are deemed politically and ecclesiologically incorrect. Consequently, segregated and non-transitional congregations are viewed as the ideal from which transitional congregations deviate. The transition paradigm fails to recognise that all churches and all neighbourhoods are in some form of transition when viewed over a long period (Porter 1992:53). With no clear time-boundaries, the concept 'transition' has limited application.

Paradoxically, the possibility of a type of non-transitional congregation comes more sharply into focus when we consider the stages of transition, as illustrated in Table 1.

As a model of complete transition, Table 1 can demonstrate the transitional paradigm's assumption that a congregation's population will cycle in teleological fashion from one dominant ethnic or racial grouping (Level 1) to another (Level 3). But if we regard the sequences as reflecting varying degrees to which different congregations can be integrated, then the stages can be viewed from a non-teleological perspective. Then each level or stage can exist independently from those that precede or follow it. And, one level or stage need not follow on another: a congregation can become more integrated, or less so, or retain a stable racial or ethnic mix.

But the various levels and different stages may also represent levels of integration in different types of congregation. The columns in the table then represents six dimensions across which congregations can be integrated, with each row describing their level of integration. Table 1 should not be confused with the complex reality that it reflects only in abstract and reductionist terms. As a heuristic classifying device, this table cannot embrace all possible configurations. Table 1 will be applied in more detail in the discussion of typologies later in our discussion.

The utility and limitations of Table 1 can be demonstrated by applying it to the cases studied. Saint Francis demonstrates Stage II integration across all dimensions measuring integration, apart from the Participation in Programs column, where it is closer to Stage I. Yet, as it matches all other respects of Stage II, the discrepancy does not invalidate Saint Francis' overall classification. Similarly, Johweto differed in one sense from a Stage III level of integration in that blacks outnumbered whites, instead of being balanced, as suggested by column two. Yet it could not be classified as transitional at that stage, as it had none of the other features of transitional congregations. A year after I conducted my study, Johweto did acquire the other features of transitional congregations, yet minus the transitional racial context, as it continued to function in the black city of Soweto. This again illustrates that even empirical studies have limited validity as snapshots that remain generally accurate only for the time at which research was conducted. Even longitudinal studies cannot escape this problem completely, although perhaps offering a more extensible option.

A Non-Transitional Paradigm for Mixed Congregations

Evidence from my detailed case studies, added to studies from the United States, show the need for a non-transitional paradigm to accommodate examples that fall outside the scope of the transitional

Table 1: Stages of Congregational Transition by Levels of Racial Integration

Levels of Integration	Mix of Membership	Mix of Leadership	Orientation of Worship	Participation in Programs	Informal Social Contact
Level 1 **Not Integrated**	Only race *a*	Race *a* only	Culture *a* oriented	Race *a* only	Race *a* only
Level 2 **Integrated** Stage I: Initial	Race *a* larger - race *b* less than 20%	No or little mix & contact	Culture *a* oriented	Race *a* excludes *b*	No or little mix & contact
Stage II: Intermediate	Race *a* larger - race *b* ±20% or more	Some mix & contact	Some aspects of *a* & *b*	Fair mix, some interaction	No or little mix & contact
Stage III: Advanced (equilibrium)	Race *a* about same size as race *b*	Shared	Significant affirmation of all cultures	Highly inclusive	Extensive mixing & contact
Stage IV: Transition	Race *b* larger than race *a*	Race *a* declines	Significant affirmation of all cultures	Race *a* declines	Mix & contact decreases
Level 3: **Not Integrated** (Level 1 Reversed)	Race *b* only	Race *b* only	Culture *b* oriented	Race *b* only	Race *b* only

paradigm. Research shows that integrated congregations also form in non-transitional neighbourhoods. By "non-transitional" I mean "demographically stable": complete ethnic or racial transition is not happening at all in a racially-homogeneous population residing in a particular suburb. Or, ethnic ratios in the neighbourhood appear to have balanced out over the medium term, with minor fluctuations (compare Davis and White 1980:102). Immanent total transition appears unlikely, so that the neighbourhoods, in effect, are neither pre-transitional or transitional. Obviously, neighbourhoods do inevitably undergo change over long periods, as they move through their own life cycles. A neighbourhood like Doornfontein in Johannesburg moved from a haven for upper income residents in the 1890s, to a working class neighbourhood in the early 1900s, to a light industrial zone by mid-20th century. So demographic equilibrium may only be temporary—yet, from a particular viewpoint, a researcher would only discern this stability.

A non-transitional paradigm implies the suspension of the causal linkages between neighbourhood and congregation assumed by the transitional paradigm. The nature of the congregation itself may contribute to this phenomenon: a mixed commuter congregation that draws participants from beyond the immediate neighbourhood. In such a case, the congregation's demographic make-up may retain a racially stable population even in a context of demographic transition. The character of a particular suburb may also undermine an assumption of causal linkages. Mixed congregations may be located in neighbourhoods that are not undergoing transition at a given point in time.

Congregations that fail to manifest a causal link to their immediate neighbourhoods fall outside the conceptual framework of the transition paradigm. Examples have been noted since 1980 (Davis and White 1980:102; Leonard 1983:130; cf. Brightman 1984; Schaller 1989; Porter 1992; Stark 1993). I found three such congregations while conducting a workshop for racially-mixed congregations in 1993 at New York Theological Seminary. In their neighbourhoods, ethnic transition from white to black had been completed between the 1950s and 1960s. Since then other ethnics had poured in to produce the present mixed neighbourhood, which reportedly retained a relatively stable character. Parkchester American Baptist Church's East Bronx neighbourhood was white in the 1940s, became black in the 1960s, and then became multi-racial with the arrival of Hispanic and Caribbean Americans (Gaston 1993:1-2). Following a similar time lapse, Church of the Intercession's 550 West 155th Street neighbourhood changed from white to African-American to an increasingly Hispanic and Caribbean-American area. Along with Philadelphia's University Lutheran Church, these congregations provide further examples of relatively stable mixed neighbourhoods.

Even where causal linkages do operate, the outcome in the congregation need not be transition. A post-transitional outcome is possible where a mixed congregation shares a demographic equilibrium with its neighbourhood. Such a result is implicitly discounted by the transition paradigm. Saint Francis demonstrates an example where the ratio of racial transition in a congregation was not linked to that of Martindale, its neighbourhood. Note that "non-transitional" apply equally to racially-mixed or -homogeneous neighbourhoods.

Types of Racially-Mixed Congregations

The following two sections apply the theoretical insights from the transitional and non-transitional paradigms to the empirical cases in order to demonstrate how the South African cases inverted the spatial organisation of the apartheid city both symbolically and in reality.

The challenge that non-transitional and transitional paradigms brings is to consider the types of congregations that could evolve under either of them. Table 2, below, shows a tentative typology of racially-mixed congregations based on the distinctions non-transitional versus transitional neighbourhoods, explicit versus implicit strategies, and formal versus informal interaction. All three pairs of distinctions emerge from my empirical studies in South Africa and in the United States, as well as other research on such congregations.

The typology distinguishes between types that reflect neighbourhood transition (Types A and B) as well as two non-transitional congregations (Types C and D). Types A and B are further differentiated from one another by the major strategy of integration deployed by its leaders. Both transitional types share common membership origins and limited social interaction beyond Sunday worship. Types C and D share common membership origins with one another, but differ in leadership strategy and degree of social interaction. As no Type D congregation was present among the cases studied, I refer to Rhema Bible Church to substantiate my contention that such a type exists.

The typology can be overlapped with the levels of racial integration in a congregation presented in Table 1 to produce a more detailed classification. Types can be combined with stages, as can be demonstrated with Type A congregation, Saint Francis demonstrated most Stage II characteristics, with the non-dominant group poorly accommodated in programs and leadership. As a Type C congregation, Johweto reflected Stage III features, paying more explicit attention to cultural issues, with high levels of participation from all groups in formal and informal contexts. The types should be seen as fluid rather than static concepts, therefore. A Type B congregation may over time resolve into a Type C. A transitional Type A may become a B-type congregation, should congregants devise a more racially-explicit strategy to maintain the equilibrium of their Stage III mix against a demographic trend of ongoing transition. Similarly, a Type B congregation could move from a Stage I

Table 2: A Typology of Racially-Mixed Congregations

	External sources of integration		Internal sources of integration	
	Context (neighbourhood)	**Membership Origin**	**Leadership Strategy**	**Social Interaction**
Type A St. Francis	*Transitional*: temporary racial heterogeneity	"Neighbours"	*Inclusive*: race is implicit	*Limited*: formal occasions only
Type B Central			*Interventionist*: race is explicit	
Type C Johweto	*Non-transitional*: racially homogeneous *	"Commuters"		*Extensive*: in/formal occasions
Type D Rhema			*Inclusive*: race is implicit	*Limited*: formal occasions only

Note: * Non-transitional (not pre- or post-transitional) means total demographic transition is unlikely in the short term—here, respectively, of Soweto and Randburg (the latter will undergo transition in the long term).

to a Stage II level of integration by introducing a liturgy which expresses aspects of all ethnic groups in the congregation. Possibly some congregations could oscillate between types over time, reflecting the porous nature of the typology's categories.

Interpreted in terms of Table 1, Type A congregations correspond to the first stage of integration. The incoming racial group is not well represented in the leadership, worship, and programmes. This outcome illustrates the difficulty that members of a voluntary organisation face in overcoming the institutional effects of segregation and implicit attitudes towards race.

Type C and D congregations blend race with a political-theological ideology that helps to establish racial-ethnic unity among congregants. Congregants work more explicitly through their racial issues. The ideology, like the racial mix of the congregation and its ministers/pastors, draws like-minded people. Racial-political attitudes in the congregation tend to converge along a narrow spectrum, perhaps more so early in its history than later on. The Type C congregation in the study (Johweto) differed from the Type B (Central) in that in the former all racial groups participated in all congregational programmes to a higher degree. In both types B and C ethnic differences were positively affirmed in the processes. A second difference was that Type C provided evidence of a higher degree of social interaction between participants outside 'official' activities than in all other three types. Johweto was part of an independent church network, while Central Methodist Mission moved beyond its denomination's implicit constrictions on racial interaction. At Central, as at Johweto, people from lower-income and -education groups mixed with people exhibiting a higher- to middle-income and -education profile. Johweto as a Type C congregation recalls others in the United States that attempted to "shift the power dynamics among the congregation's racial and cultural groups from one of hierarchy and dominance to one of interaction and mutuality" (Foster 1993b: 5).

Both Central and Johweto were originally located in unmixed non-transitional neighbourhoods. An example of a mixed congregation in an unmixed neighbourhood in the United States is Lawndale Community Church in west Chicago. Lawndale's composition was directly affected by the expressed intention of being an integrated faith-community, and all white members who join are asked to live in the immediate black neighbourhood. The Church for the Fellowship of All Peoples in San Francisco is regarded as the oldest contemporary example of a congregation formed around the expressed intention of being ethnically-mixed. Founded in 1944, its members included African-Americans, Anglos, Hispanics, and Asians (Thurman 1959; Porter 1992: 2,35-38; The Church for the Fellowship of All Peoples n.d.). For the first five years the Fellowship was led by joint white and black leaders comprising Drs. Alfred Fisk and Howard Thurman. The neighbourhood of the Fellowship played no role in its founding (Porter 1992: 38), and so the primary causation was not transition.

The limitation of using non-transition and transition as central concepts can be overcome by an open-ended typology such as Figure 5 on the next page.

An open-ended perspective would allow a congregation to be described in terms of other combinations of pairs of primary variables. A congregation could be transitional or non-transitional, employ implicit or explicit strategies of integration, and organise high or low levels of

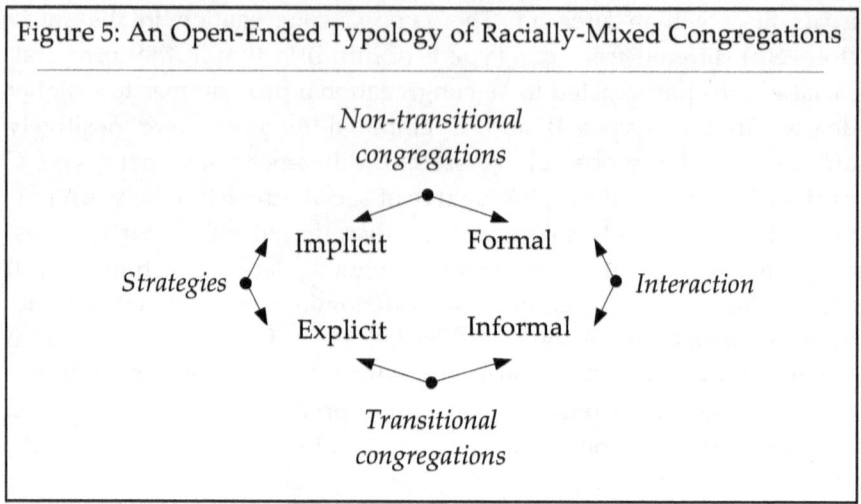

Figure 5: An Open-Ended Typology of Racially-Mixed Congregations

social interaction in either formal or informal settings. Also, such a model would allow researchers to describe variation over time in the same congregation, which could exchange an earlier more racially implicit integration strategy later for one that is more implicit, for example.

Typologies such as these are useful in generating further hypotheses regarding the functioning of mixed congregations. For example, one could hypothesise that the integrative strategy pursued by leaders (explicit or implicit) directly affects a congregation's internal structure and dynamics. Another possibility is that the context (mixed or unmixed) determines type of membership (residents or commuters). A triangular connection can be posited between internal structure, strategy, and immediate context. So an integrative strategy in which race is implicit could result in congregational structures in which little attention is paid to ethnicity. Playing down race could be a response by a congregation to a segregated neighbourhood that is hostile to its racial mix. A location in such a hostile neighbourhood would require that congregants not of the same racial group as local residents must commute, as happened under apartheid.

The potential for support or hostility in the immediate context is important for determining the policy and structure of a mixed congregation. An explicit church would find it difficult to operate in a segregated context, and would find it difficult to attract resident members. Commuting members pose no threat to the residents. Only where the neighbourhood is mixed would members tend to be residents; that is, when relocation is not part of the congregation's ideology. At Saint Francis there was an inverse relation between the upper class white commuters and the lower-middle class context of the church building. In such a situation there would be little attraction for commuters to move into the area, particularly as no impetus exists within the congregation's world view to justify relocation, as some congregations—like Lawndale Community Church in Chicago—required.

Table 2 serves as an opening statement which I hope will be surpassed or at least refined by other researchers. Additional types are no doubt needed to account for types of racial-ethnic congregations possibly not represented here. The proposed types need further verification against more examples for greater descriptive accuracy. The warnings mentioned elsewhere concerning reductionism apply here as well.

Mixed Congregations in Transitional Neighbourhoods

The direct correlation between congregations and their contexts that is so central to the transitional paradigm corresponds most closely to Saint Francis Xavier Catholic Church (a Type A) and Central Methodist Mission (a Type B). Yet the underlying implication of the paradigm—that such congregations will change in lockstep with demographic shifts in the surrounding neighbourhood—was weakly supported in both instances. The integration of these two congregations historically preceded the racial integration of their contexts. Saint Francis' parish area cycled from mixed (1930s) to white (1960s) to mixed again (1990s). Integration was aided by creation of coloured suburbs nearby, and by black parishioners who undertook financially-punishing pilgrimages from Soweto each Sunday. The leaders of the respective congregations employed quite different strategies of integration. Peter Storey of Central Methodist Mission initially opted for a racially-explicit integrative strategy. By contrast, leaders at Saint Francis did not so much pursue integration as such, but promoted a wider inclusive. The variations from the transitional paradigm indicates the need for a more open-ended alternative.

Examples that point beyond the scope of context as causal factor emerged during an older study that I conducted in the United States. Central (American) Baptist in Hartford, Connecticut, in 1993 was located in a stable unmixed neighbourhood, integrated around an implicit ideology. None of its commuter congregation came from its immediate context, but was drawn from across a wide urban area. The Jamaican and Anglo pastors of Central Baptist at the time described their congregation as "radically inclusive"—of economic differences, and of sexual preferences. They believed that there was no specific reason why their congregation was racially-mixed, except that the congregational culture emphasised inclusiveness and community. No explicit attempt was made to recruit specific ethnic groups.

Mixed Congregations in Non-Transitional Neighbourhoods

Mixed congregations in ethnically homogeneous neighbourhoods typically draw their members from beyond the borders of their immediate suburbs. Congregations from older denominations and newer independent types may experience such a situation. A congregation attended mostly by so-called commuter members will remain largely unaffected by localised demographic shifts, as demonstrated by South African mega-churches such as Rhema Bible Church in Randburg, or Hatfield Christian Church in Waterkloof Glen, Pretoria. Evidence from the Saint Francis and Central Methodist Mission case studies suggests that affiliates today feel less inclined to attend the nearest congregation in the parish within which they reside. Churches such as Central Methodist Mission in Cape Town drew the majority of their participants from beyond its denominationally-imposed boundaries.

Using the examples in Table 2, we can hypothesise about the characteristics of non-transitional and transitional types of racially-mixed congregation. As will become clear, non-transitional types of racially-mixed congregations (Types C and D) share differences and similarities with one another, as well as with transitional types (Types A and B). For purposes of our discussion, Type A transitional racially-mixed congregations will be represented by Saint Francis, Type Bs by Central Methodist Mission. Type C non-transitional mixed congregations will be illustrated by the example of Johweto. But for an example of a Type D non-transitional congregation, I have to reach beyond our three case studies, which did not include such a type. Rhema Bible Church, for which I had collected data for a different study, can be used to represent a Type D non-transitional racially-mixed congregation.

A Type C congregation like Johweto has an explicit focus on race, which it shares with Type B racially-mixed congregations such as Central. Unlike any other type uncovered by my research, Type C congregations engage in extensive social interaction beyond the Sunday meetings.

Type D congregations like Rhema share an implicit integration strategy with a Type A such as Saint Francis. Here, leaders and members advocated a welcoming attitude towards all people (in the case of Saint Francis, regardless of sexual preferences). But they do not actively seek to integrate their congregation in terms of any one of these categories. As a result, the Type D congregation—like the Type A—tends to have structures in which the racial ratios of the congregants are not represented. Formal processes in such congregations (e.g. ritual, worship, decision making) do not reflect the diversity of cultures of their congregants. Inevitably, this situation tends to favour assimilation into the ethnic culture that has been embedded in the language and style of that particular denomination, revealed in such elements as the liturgy, homiletics, and music. An alternative dynamic here is that a particular culture group within the congregation achieves dominance over the processes because the denomination's initial national origins supported its position. Here there is little social interaction between members. The ethnic groups are not represented in the leadership, and the individual attitudes of congregants towards racial groupings vary widely. Mainline or Catholic, these congregations pioneer denominational innovations, such as applying insights from Vatican II. In short, this type "looks different from those more homogeneous congregations...but it 'feels' similar" (Foster 1993b:5).

The possibility that even more types of non-transitional racially-mixed congregations could exist was confirmed in the early 1980s by evidence from the United States. A study of University Lutheran Church of the Incarnation in Philadelphia implied that a non-transitional congregation may be located in a stable racially-mixed neighbourhood (Leonard 1983). By contrast, Types C and D are associated with homogeneous contexts. University Lutheran was described in a study of the consolidation of 26 Lutheran congregations in transitional Philadelphia neighbourhoods (Leonard 1983:130). Yet University Lutheran was located in a non-transitional Philadelphia neighbourhood. Regrettably, the study was not formulated to highlight explicit or implicit causes of integration. Class seems to have played some role, as did the context. An explicit integration strategy seems to have been at work, as the study refers to many members who joined simply because the congregation *was* integrated (Leonard 1983:130). Additional evidence that places non-transitional congregations in mixed neighbourhoods is supplied by a 1984 survey which identified member-residence in a such a neighbourhood as a causal factor for mixed congregations (Hadaway et al 1984: 212,215).

INVERTING RACE RELATIONS WITHIN CONGREGATIONAL STRUCTURE

The integration strategies of congregational leaders can be incorporated into a typology of mixed congregations to highlight agency. Interventionist and *laissez faire* integrative strategies were observed in the data, differing from one another in the degree to which they were explicitly executed.

Congregational leaders that used an explicit, interventionist strategy deliberately devise and implemented steps to integrate congregations. Both Central Methodist Mission and Johweto provided examples, although differing in scale and extent of lay involvement. The interventionist, explicit strategy is unrelated to demographic trends, as shown by the general variation between Johannesburg's transitional versus Soweto's non-transitional neighbourhoods. Accordingly, it can be deployed in either demographic context. In the examples of explicit integration strategies that I observed, ethnic factors were more likely to be allowed to affect processes and structures.

Congregational leaders who apply an implicit, *laissez faire* strategy create broad, inclusive ideological parameters that integrate their congregations. Congregants are motivated to welcome people regardless of gender, sexual orientation, and racial or ethnic categories. Leaders do not exclusively recruit people of colour, as racially-defined groups constitute only one desired target category. Saint Francis provided a case in point, but I found three other implicitly integrated congregations located in the then-transitional Johannesburg suburbs of Martindale, Yeoville and Mayfair. This small sampling size precludes any conclusion about whether the implicit strategy could also be used by congregations located in non-transitional neighbourhoods. As implicit-type congregations do not focus directly on race, members are unlikely to engage in racial mixing outside formal church events. A variation of this type occurs where congregational leaders do not promote racial integration due to their own prejudice against incoming groups.

Both the explicit and implicit strategies of racial integration capture a sense of the voluntary nature of congregations, whose shape are determined by their congregants. Various distinct internal dynamics could also be observed, as I indicate below.

INVERTING RACIALISED NORMS OF SOCIAL INTERACTION

In several racially-mixed congregations I noted implicit and explicit attempts to transform the racialised norms of interaction that affected South African society. Leaders, buildings, and local theologies were used in efforts to transform the mutual expectations that affected the internal dynamics of congregations. The significance of such attempts in the context of oppression cannot be overstated. Yet their actual impact were obviously limited by the small percentage that racially-mixed congregations formed in all Christian denominations.

By the very act of integration, congregants overturned the legal demand of the apartheid state for racial separation and questioned its religious justification. The relative influences of individual participants as well as the prior socio-political history of each congregation were highlighted in the case studies. Ordained leaders played a particularly vital role in preparing and accompanying integration, especially in previously all-white congregations. Their actions, sermons and programme initiatives clearly expressed—as it contributed—to an ideology of racial unity that was also evident in other agencies who wanted to subvert the racial order. In the cases of Central and Johweto, ordained leaders benefited from prior exposure to black-white relations. So did lay congregants at Saint Francis, were some key parishioners had interacted across racialised social boundaries outside of the congregation. Congregants of colour who could speak English and were relatively at ease with interpreting the cultural cues of white English-speaking South Africans acted as dually-acculturate bridge-builders. Such congregants fulfilled integrative, transformative and mediative tasks in the formation of ethnically-diverse congregations (Porter 1992:8, 4). At Central, the earlier socio-political history of the congregation continued to draw blacks later on, as did the use of buildings as a space to display black concerns. Saint Francis' past as a mission church also continued to draw black African parishioners, as did its plaque commemorating the Sophiatown removals.

Some mixed congregations organised highly structured and formal settings to encourage social interaction between different racial groups. Congregants apparently equated unity between racial groupings with participation in formal events. Consequently, little informal interaction occurred outside organised church settings, nor was it commonly expected. Even rare instances of informal social interaction was mediated through organised church events, such as after-service tea sessions. This formal mode of interaction mirrored relations within early post-apartheid society, where integration was limited to formally structured settings (such as the workplace). Interaction between congregants occurred mainly through common tasks with limited, formal social interaction—such as reports at leadership meetings—between different status groups. Opportunities with a high potential for informal social interaction, such as integrated home meetings, were implicitly avoided, despite clear support for unified church services. Both Saint Francis and Central conformed to this strategy, despite Central's deliberate integration initiatives. Limited interaction was associated in these cases with little attention to the racial integration of all congregational structures.

A second strategy employed in mixed congregations for managing social interaction was to place a high premium on interaction inside and outside organised congregational gatherings. Congregants attempted to reflect the ethnic composition of the congregation in all structures and at least some of the liturgy. Social roles were extended to include all racial groupings. In some settings apartheid norms were reversed; for instance, where blacks counselled whites and led the liturgy. This strategy was evident at Johweto, where the congregation was initially integrated through interpersonal relations between founders and between members. As a result, Johweto's discourse continued to emphasise interaction as an ideological means of reinforcing identity and recruiting new participants. The stress on individual relationships tended to obscure the function of class. Here, as in the other two case studies, class continued to affect group relations (e.g. in decision-making) and to determine ideology (values, principles). At Johweto an overt ideology of care for the poor outside the congregation was matched by an obliviousness to discrepancies in class relations between low and high income groups inside the congregation. Consequently, differences between race groups (in terms of class, skills and economic resources) tended to maintain relations of white dominance and black dependency.

Congregations were more successful at overturning the social and legal expectations that dictated separate racial activities than at resolving the complexities of race and class. The dynamics of racialised relations, in South Africa always complicated by class and culture, continued to challenge the depth of integration in the cases studied. In racially-mixed congregations, as in society, class factors tended to negatively affect the constitution of leadership. This is due to the implicit influence of non-racialism, which was in some form a conscious ideology in South Africa's mixed congregations. Non-racialism prohibited the explicit use of race in allocating social roles, but had less effect on the functions of class. As a result, class tended to determine racial representation in the power structures of racially-mixed congregations. Class sometimes overlapped with racial categories to exclude black, coloured, and Asian individuals at leadership and other levels. Or, whites and blacks who shared higher statuses tended to be promoted to leadership to the exclusion of most working class black Africans. In all three detailed case studies, whites who participated in such congregations usually occupied higher income and education statuses. Recruits from other races generally (but not exclusively) belonged to lower status groups, although some were upwardly mobile. I only encountered two congregations that apparently contradicted this trend. In the one case, upwardly mobile blacks joined a lower status white church in Atlanta (Foster e.a. 1993). In the other, black academics joined a Fort Beaufort congregation consisting primarily of white farmers. No doubt these racially-mixed congregations represent the exceptions that prove the rule.

The case studies revealed that congregations had as much difficulty in dealing with cultural expressions than with class. Class and culture ameliorated racial interaction in a manner again reminiscent of the dominant political arrangements of early post-apartheid South Africa. Where coloureds, Indians, or black Africans were proficient in English, their particular cultural orientations tended to be ignored. In the end, congregations seemed to find non-racialism relatively easier to implement than multi-culturalism. This recalled the post-apartheid state's emphasis on black empowerment to redress racial imbalances in all sectors of society, and the state's gravitation towards English as language of choice. Assimilative cultural consequences seemed relatively less severe in congregations where integration was consciously worked through than in those that made no attempt to do so.

THEORISING RACIALLY-MIXED CONGREGATIONS UNDER APARTHEID

I now highlight some general and external social factors that affected the emergence of racially-mixed congregations under apartheid. I note how class and ethnicity played out in the interaction between groups in such congregations. By detailing the major external social influences I do not mean to explain all causes that contributed to the emergence and functioning of racially-mixed congregations under apartheid. Instead, I outline the social web of influences, extending from the global to the individual, that enabled some agents to take certain decisions and actions. My tentative explanations are not meant to devalue the vital initiatives taken by individual leaders, nor to deny the role of their theological motivations for integration. My focus is broader here simply because I emphasise normative change that affected social dynamics. In such a sociological perspective, theologically interpreted intentions may well motivate individual agency. My theoretical interpretations must necessarily be tentative, given the non-representative sample of congregations. Most congregations described in Chapter One were initiated by whites, as were two of the case studies in Chapters Two to Four, for example. Verification of my arguments awaits comparisons with racially-mixed congregations that were initiated by blacks, or that used to have only black congregants.

A General Interpretation in Terms of Norm Change

Any attempt to interpret change in normative terms must elaborate on the origin of the relevant norms, their subsequent historical trajectories, and their role in constraining and motivating individual and collective actors (Klotz 1995:121). In terms of origin, norms can be generated by hegemonic powers, and institutionalised through coercion. Or, norms can emerge from the interaction between less powerful actors in the form of incentives that are agreed upon through negotiation. A third possibility is that norms are constructed from "within previously existing social institutions" (Klotz 1995:122). Changes in norms may derive from alterations in the interests and powers of either a hegemon or of pre-existing institutions with independent functions. Decolonisation, for example, emerged from self-determination, itself premised on the institution of state sovereignty. Simultaneously, independent former colonies contributed to the institutionalisation of racial equality (Klotz 1995:124).

With regards the constraining function of norms, actors comply either involuntarily because of coercion, or voluntarily because of incentives. In the latter case, norms may fulfil legitimating functions that determine which means and goals are appropriate (Klotz 1995:125). Consequently, actors' interests change, which in turn motivates alternate patterns of behaviour. An emphasis on the influence of norms allows for attention to the interaction between domestic and external influences on state policies. With reference to our theme, "domestic strengthening of a norm of racial equality might thus result from broader transnational processes of norm strengthening" (Klotz 1995:126). Klotz's arguments about the imposition of norms by a hegemon finds a clear parallel in the implementation of segregation by South African regimes. Her comments about the variation of norms over time draws attention to shifts due to the interaction between settlers, natives, missionaries, and local and British administrators.

The case studies of racially-mixed congregations provide ways to link international institutions to South African actors. Klotz argues that racial equality was institutionalised in organisations outside of South Africa, which then effected increasing pressure on the apartheid regime. National actors like India and transnational movements formed by anti-apartheid groups played significant roles in institutionalising racial equality as a norm. But I would like to point out that so did those South Africans who worked with, in, and through those institutions. This perspective is obscured for Klotz, who focuses primarily on institutions and on synthesising opposing international relations theories. The racial integration of congregations demonstrates similarities with the compliance of transnational organisations and African states with sanctions against apartheid, as Klotz has argued. Just as the front-line states (Mozambique, Zimbabwe, Zambia) acted against their own economic and security concerns by engaging in sanctions, so too did individuals who participated in racially-mixed congregations. For individual congregants, the moral incentives that invited compliance with racially integrative norms were more compelling than the material incentives that drove segregation.

Participants in racially-mixed congregations in South Africa drew on both local and transnational norms in forming racially-mixed congregations. These individuals embodied norms of equality and integration in their neighbourhoods and, by doing so, contributed to their institutionalisation in society. As members of groups that extended beyond the boundaries of local congregations, a few even contributed to strengthening equality as norm in transnational institutions. Peter Storey, for example, at times fulfilled both local, national, and transnational roles as minister of Central, president of the Methodist Church of Southern Africa, and as part of the South African Council of Churches' delegation to the United Nations in 1984.

Racially-mixed congregations could be analysed as organisations in which several institutions intersect, including religion, gender, and leadership, as I argued in a different context.

Institutional change within a congregation, as within a denomination, can happen through extra-institutional mechanisms, such as values and norms that circulate within the institutional environment; for example, racial equality. Or, intra-institutional mechanisms such as antagonistic actors who oppose one another in the same institution could also prompt change (compare Koelbe, 1995:235). Internal conflict may indicate that the institutionalisation of a contested norm is under way. In such a case institutionalisation is only partial, as conflict diminishes to the extend that institutionalisation has been completed. Racial equality in a congregation has been institutionalised only to the extent that it has penetrated the consciousness of individual congregants (who come to believe that all races should be treated equally) and has been accommodated in the creation of formal roles (so that individuals from various racial groups are elected as leaders). Due to the partial institutionalisation of norms, some associated roles may change more than others. Blacks may be allowed to participate in leading worship, but may not be elected to chair financial committees. Or, when they are elected as leaders, blacks may be rendered ineffective by the attitudes of whites, for example.

Within a denomination, extra-institutional values (in the sense that they are apparently not shared by most members) are incorporated and unevenly distributed across denominational structures. Values that are institutionalised are expressed in denominational policies, but may not affect all congregations. While formerly segregated congregations may acknowledge the different value set contained in denominational and state policy regarding integration, this may not yet oust previous racial ideologies.

Conflict or continued racial prejudice in some racially-mixed congregations demonstrates how the existing social construction of race and its associated social relations hinder the replacement of one set of values, related norms, and roles.

External Contributing Factors to the Emergence of Racially-Mixed Congregations

The South African cases suggest how the usual sociological explanation for the formation of racially-mixed congregations can be extended. Such interpretations tend to assume that integration results in the first instance from ethnic change in the neighbourhood surrounding a congregation, which encourage people from other ethnic groups to join. We can extend this dominant interpretation by attending to deliberate attempts to integrate a congregation, and to the wider contributing dynamics that operate within a society (political ideology, assimilative forces, common culture).

Contrary to the standard explanation, the South African cases suggest that racial integration of congregations during apartheid depended on political and theological resistance rather than on urban demographic transition. Many white individuals in mixed congregations were implicitly bound together in an anti-apartheid alliance based on non-racialism. Preachers and laity in mixed churches articulated non-racialism in sermons and discussions, although not necessarily in so many words. Demographic transition did affect some congregations later in their life cycles, but was not the primary cause for the integration of, say, North End, nor of Central Methodist, Saint Francis, or Johweto. Massive neighbourhood transition did occur after the integration of Central, and —to a far lesser extent—at Saint Francis. Other apartheid-era congregations, such as Saint Antony's, depended on *mixed* (rather than transitional) neighbourhoods for integration.

Class differences also contributed to the racial integration of apartheid-era congregations. In isolated instances, informants told me that financial need drove some unemployed individuals to congregations attended by financially-advantaged whites. Such class differences depended upon relations of exploitation introduced in the colonial period when, ironically, it integrated masters and converted slaves into the same congregations.

Integration was also partly based on common cultural elements introduced by one ethnic group and absorbed by others. One or more ethnic groups needed to have assimilated a basic proficiency in the languages and associated cultural practices of the others. English remained the most commonly used language in almost all integrated congregations, as I discuss elsewhere. That meant that blacks, coloureds, and Indians had to assimilate cultural systems for the most part associated with white South Africans of British descent. Under apartheid the state attempted to enforce Afrikaans, which was also dominant in the rural areas of what is today the Northern Cape, Limpopo, and Free State provinces. In either case, the cultural assimilation of blacks and coloureds through educational institutions that were historically defined and dominated by whites aided integration into white-dominated congregations. The only alternative was to use direct translation in order to engineer bilingual understanding—a process which did not foster bilingual acculturation. An interpreter was so rarely used in multilingual congregations that I can only recall two examples from the 1990s, at Melodi Ya Tshwane in Pretoria, and at Stellenbosch Christian Fellowship.

Given the unequal relations of power that marked the era, racially-mixed congregations during apartheid involuntarily supported a wider assimilative process that involved institutions such as education, government, and entertainment. The formation of racially-mixed congregations was aided through the prior predominance of white European-derived cultures in South Africa, the absorption of indigenes into white-dominated institutions over three hundred years, and the loosening of cultural ties through urbanisation. Apartheid cities subjected all residents to assimilative forces that eroded their ethno-cultural heritage. In Johannesburg blacks tended to become culturally more like whites. Residents of Soweto are likely to gradually lose at least some of their ethno-cultural differences, despite past attempts by the apartheid state and the Inkatha Freedom Party to re-tribalise them. Christianisation among blacks, coloureds and Indians from the colonial to the apartheid periods was always accompanied by some transmission of European-based cultures. The European base of almost all denominations were embedded in their dominant organisational culture. For this reason, leaders at Central Methodist struggled to find a way around the 'Englishness' of its worship style. Some denominations, notably South African Catholics, attempted to reverse the direction of assimilative processes in the 1990s through the 'Africanisation' of ritual and liturgy.

Yet racially-mixed congregations also helped their congregants to resist ideological assimilation, as demonstrated by sermons, teachings, and activities in some of the congregations. In South Africa these worked against absorbing the dominant norms of apartheid. Central's stance against the government and police, like Johweto's position against conscription and white domination of church events, well illustrate the point. Compared to the racial segregation that the state enforced, and that most denominations adopted, racially-mixed congregations had a strong political counter-culture, and viewed themselves as representing an alternate, non-segregated society.

LIST OF WORKS CITED

Note regarding web citations: Where possible, URLs have been compressed and archived on WebCitation.org to provide persistent links. Should archived sites not display properly, readers can click on the original link at the top right corner of the displayed site on Webcitation (where it says "Showing WebCite for URL").

1892. *Cape Church Monthly and Pew Record*, August, Vol. 1 (1):3.

Agathangelus, Capuchin, ed. 1951. *The Catholic Church in Southern Africa. A Series of Essays*. Cape Town: The Catholic Archdiocese of Cape Town.

Akinwumi, Elijah Olu. 2002. "Dube, John Langalibalele. 1871 to 1946. Congregational, South Africa." Accessed February 23, 2005. webcitation.org/60Gu1gEUT.

Alves, Haynet. 1993. Interview Conducted by the Author on November 14, Johannesburg.

Anderson, Allan. 1992. *Bazalwane: African Pentecostals in South Africa*. Pretoria: Unisa.

Anderson, Allan. 2000. "Pentecostals and Apartheid in South Africa during Ninety Years 1908-1998." Accessed April 14, 2005. webcitation.org/60Gu1gEUm.

Association of Vineyard Churches South Africa. n.d. Accessed April 4, 2005. www.vineyard.org.za.

Atlantic Charter Committee. 1943. "Africans' Claims in South Africa." Accessed July 29, 2005. webcitation.org/60Gu1gEV5.

Balia, Daryl. 1994. "The Witness of the Methodist Church in South Africa." *International Review of Mission* lxxxiii,328:163-166.

Ball, Joanna. 1994. "The Ritual of the Necklace." Research Paper Written for the Centre for the Study of Violence and Reconciliation, March. Accessed April 15, 2005. webcitation.org/60Gu1gEVD.

Barron, Chris. 1998. "Edward King: a Priest Whose Presence Mattered." *Sunday Times*, August 16. Accessed April 14, 2005. webcitation.org/60Gu1gEVM.

Barrow, Simon. 2001. "Christian Unity—Is it a Waste of Time?" Accessed February 28, 2005. webcitation.org/60Gu1gEVV.

Bate, Stuart. 2001. "What Does It Mean that the Church is the Instrument of the Kingdom of God in the South African Context: a Catholic perspective. The Role of the Catholic Church in the Period of Struggle Against Apartheid and in the Post Apartheid Context." Paper presented at the International Roman Catholic - Reformed Dialogue, Cape Town, August 22-28, 2001. Accessed April 18, 2005. webcitation.org/60Gu1gEVd.

Beall, Jo, Owen Crankshaw, and Susan Parnell. 2001. "Towards Inclusive Urban Governance in Johannesburg." Report Prepared for the ESCOR Commissioned Research On Urban Development: Urban Governance, Partnership and Poverty. Accessed February 27, 2005. webcitation.org/60IZW2Pqi.

Beavon, K, 1992. "The Post-Apartheid City: Hopes, Possibilities, and Harsh Realities." In *The Apartheid City and Beyond: Urbanisation and Social Change in South Africa*, edited by David M. Smith, 231-42. Routledge, London, and Witwatersrand University Press, Johannesburg.

Beavon, Keith S. O. 1997. "Johannesburg: A City and Metropolitan Area in Transformation." In *The Urban Challenge in Africa: Growth and Management of its Large Cities*, edited by Carole Rakodi, 150-91. The United Nations University Press. Accessed February 27, 2005. webcitation.org/60LbZqvPB.

Beavon, Keith S. O. 2000. "Northern Johannesburg: Part of the 'Rainbow' or Neo-Apartheid City in the Making?" *Mots Pluriels* 13. Accessed March 25, 2005. webcitation.org/60Gu1gEW4.

Belydende Kring. 1999. "Testimony Before the Truth and Reconciliation Commission, East London, 18 November." Accessed February 18, 2005. webcitation.org/60Gu1gEWD.

Bickford-Smith, Vivian. 1989. "A 'Special Tradition of Multi-Racialism' ? Segregation in Cape Town in the Late Nineteenth and Early Twentieth Centuries." In *The Angry Divide*, edited by Wilmot G. James, and Mary Simons, 47-62. Cape Town: David Philip.

Bickford-Smith, Vivian. 1995. *Ethnic Pride and Racial Prejudice in Victorian Cape Town: Group Identity and Social Practice, 1875-1902*. Cambridge: Cambridge University Press.

Boston University School of Theology. 1999. "Rev. Dr. Peter Storey at STH." *Boston University School of Theology*. Accessed February 27, 2005. www.webcitation.org/60Q2aMgf3.

Brady, John E. 1951. "History of the Church in South Africa." In *The Catholic Church in Southern Africa. A series of essays*, edited by Rev. Fr. Capuchin Agathangelus, 114-122. Cape Town: The Catholic Archdiocese of Cape Town.

Brady, John E. 1960. "The Story of Johannesburg's Cathedral of Christ the King." In *Souvenir of the Solemn Dedication and Opening of the Cathedral of Christ the King*. Accessed April 1, 2005. webcitation.org/60Gu1gEWa.

Brain, Joy B. 1991. *The Catholic Church in the Transvaal*. Johannesburg: Missionary Oblates of Mary Immaculate.

Briston, Heather. 1998. "Reel T 160. PAC Programme: PAC for non-racialism, not multi-racialism (script included). Sound Recording. 26 November 1990." Audio Visual Collection. Recordings, 1978-1994 (Inclusive),

1981-1991 (Bulk). University of Fort Hare, National Heritage Cultural Studies Centre. Accessed July 19, 2005. webcitation.org/60LdOZSDi.

Brody, Donal 1998. "Dr. James Emmanuel Kwegyir Aggrey, 18 October 1875–30 July 1927, 'Let's Go! Eagles!' Part 2." *Great Epics Newsletter* 2,6. Accessed April 27, 2006. webcitation.org/60Gu1gEWr.

Brown, William Eric. 1960. *The Catholic Church in South Africa*. London: Burns & Oates. Edited by M. Derrick.

Burger, Delien, ed. 2003. *South Africa Yearbook 2003/04*. Houghton: STE Publishers. Accessed April 2, 2005. webcitation.org/60Gu1g EWz.

Byrnes, Rita M., ed. 1997. *A Country Study: South Africa*. Washington, D.C.: Library of Congress. Accessed July 17, 2006. webcitation.org/ 60Gu1gEX8.

Carruthers, Jane. 2000. "Urban Land Claims in South Africa: the Case of Lady Selborne Township, Pretoria, Gauteng." *Kleio* 32:23-41. Accessed January 4, 2005. webcitation.org/60Gu1gEXH.

Carte Blanche. 2000. "Crossing the Line." September 3. Accessed July 13, 2011. webcitation.org/60Gu1gEXQ

Catholic Archdiocese of Johannesburg. n.d. *History and Geography of the Diocese*. Accessed September 6, 2007. webcitation.org/60Gu1g EXY.

Cawood, Lesley. 1964. *The Churches and Race Relations in South Africa*. Johannesburg: S A Institute of Race Relations.

Central Methodist Church. 1967. *Commemorative brochure*. Unpublished document.

Central Methodist Church. 1969. *News & Views*. (Congregational Newsletter).

Central Methodist Church. 1971. *The Octagon*. (Congregational Newsletter). November.

Central Methodist Church. 1978. *What a Family*. (Congregational Newsletter). November.

Central Methodist Church. 1980a. *What a Family*. (Congregational Newsletter). June.

Central Methodist Church. 1980b. *What a Family*. (Congregational Newsletter). September.

Central Methodist Church. 1981. *What a Family*. (Congregational Newsletter). March.

Central Methodist Church. 1982. *What a Family*. (Congregational Newsletter). May.

Central Methodist Church. 1985. *Central Church News*. (Congregational Newsletter). July.

Central Methodist Hall. 1966a. *News & Views*. (Congregational Newsletter). August.

Central Methodist Hall. 1966b. *Central Methodist Church: Christian Stewardship Campaign*. Unpublished document.

Central Methodist Mission. 1987. *Central Methodist Mission: Visitation Evangel-*

ism. Unpublished report.
Central Methodist Mission. 1991. "The Central Methodist Mission, Johannesburg." Document compiled for use by incoming superintendent Mvume H. Dandala.
Charton, Nancy. 1994. "The Witness of the Church of the Province of Southern Africa." *International Review of Mission* lxxxiii,328:153-157.
Cheney, David M. 2005. "South Africa: Statistics by Diocese by Catholic Population." *Catholic Hierarchy*. Accessed July 27, 2006. webcitation.org/60Gu1gEXh.
Ching, David A. 1988. "Report From the Visitation Evangelism Cluster for Jan.-June." Unpublished document.
Ching, David A. 1989. "Report on Evangelism Cluster for 1989." Unpublished document.
Ching, David A. 1990. "Evangelism report 1990." Unpublished document.
Ching, David A. 1992a. Interview Conducted by the Author on February 2, Johannesburg.
Ching, David A. 1992b. "Evangelism report for 1991." Unpublished document.
Church World Service. 2003. "Church World Service Welcomes South African Methodist Bishop's Election as General Secretary of All Africa Conference of Churches." *Church World Service*, May 20. Accessed March 1, 2005. tinyurl.com/2q5h4w.
City of Johannesburg. n.d. a. "Chronology of Events in the Making of Soweto." City of Johannesburg Website. Accessed February 27, 2005. webcitation.org/60Gu1gEXy.
City of Johannesburg. n.d. b. "Jo'burg's Famous Pioneers." City of Johannesburg Website. Accessed February 27, 2005. webcitation.org/60Gu1gEY6.
Clegg, Arthur S. 1936. "Methodist Central Hall. Annual Report." Unpublished document.
Cochrane, James R. 1987. *Servants of Power. The Role of the English-Speaking Churches, 1903-1930*. Johannesburg: Ravan Press.
Colman, Andrew M. 1991. "Crowd Psychology in South African Murder Trials." *American Psychologist* 46, 10:1071–1079. Accessed February 27, 2005. webcitation.org/60Gu1gEYF.
Congress of South African Trade Unions. 1999. "Vlok Must Tell More." COSATU Communications Department, December 14. Accessed February 27, 2005. webcitation.org/60Gu1gEYN.
Contact. 1954. "Deeds as Well as Words. Muncipal Bye-Election Ward 9, Johannesburg, November 18, 1953." *Contact*, January. Accessed February 19, 2005. webcitation.org/60MxhoMvV.
Contact. 1959a. "Methodists Slate Unjust Laws." *Contact*, November 28, p. 7. Accessed March 3, 2005. webcitation.org/60My9ljKR.
Contact. 1959b. "Pipe Smoking Parson is Copperbelt's Huddleston." *Contact*,

March 7, p. 7. Accessed February 28, 2005. webcitation.org/60MyY-UscB.

Cracknell, Kenneth and Susan J. White, 2005. *An Introduction to World Methodism*. Cambridge: Cambridge University Press.

Daily Mail and Guardian. 2000. "Analysis of Chinese Immigration to South Africa." *Daily Mail and Guardian*, May 10. Accessed April 1, 2005. webcitation.org/60Gu1gEYv.

Dandala, H. Mvume. 1992. Interview Conducted by the Author in April, Johannesburg.

Dandala, H. Mvume. 1997. "Methodist Church of Southern Africa." Testimony before the Truth and Reconciliation Commission, East London, 17 November 1999. (Verbatim transcript.) Accessed January 24, 2005. webcitation.org/60Gu1gEZ4.

Dandala, H. Mvume. 1997. "The Methodist Church of Southern Africa." Submission to the Truth and Reconciliation Commission. Accessed February 27, 2005. webcitation.org/60Gu1gEZC.

Dandala, H. Mvume. 2005. E-mail to Author, April.

Davis, James Hill and Woodie W. White. 1980. *Racial Transition in the Church*. Nashville: Abingdon.

De Gruchy, John W. 1979. *The Church Struggle in South Africa*. Cape Town: David Philip.

De Kock, Leon. 1992. "Drinking at the English Fountains. Missionary Discourse and the Case of Lovedale." *Missionalia* 20,2:116-138.

De Villiers, Chief Justice Lord C. J., Justice J. Solomon and Justice J. Innes. 1913. "Judgment by Chief Justice Lord de Villiers, Justice J. Solomon and Justice J. Innes in the Supreme Court of South Africa (Appellate Division)." Published under the auspices of the Syrian Lebanon Christian Association, Johannesburg, South Africa. Accessed July 27, 2006. webcitation.org/66pSDD2Q8.

Denis, Philippe and Henry Mbaya. 1997. "Select Annotated Bibliography of the History of the Catholic Church in Southern Africa (1980-1996)." *Bulletin for Contextual Theology*, 4,1. Accessed April 18. 2005. webcitation.org/60Gu1gEZU.

Denis, Phillipe. 1995. "The Making of an Indigenous Clergy in Southern Africa: Agenda for Further Research." *Bulletin for Contextual Theology* 2,1. Accessed April 18, 2005. webcitation.org/60Gu1gEZc.

Dispatch Online. 1997. "Fighting Apartheid from Church." *Dispatch Online*, November 20. Accessed 28 December 2004. webcitation.org/66mA7Zf9g.

District Six Museum. Accessed Tuesday, 18 January 2005. www.districtsix.co.za.

Dixon, Norm. 1992. :Why Death Rides South Africa's Trains." *Green Left Weekly Home Page*. Accessed April 16, 2005. webcitation.org/60Gu1gEZt.

Dube, Pamela. 1993. "Man with a Mission: Peace in the Hostels." *The Weekly Mail*, October 15 to 21.
Dubow, Saul, 1989. *Racial Segregation and the Origins of Apartheid in South Africa, 1919-36.* Houndmills: Macmillan.
Edwards, Frederick and Stephen McCabe. 1987. "Getting Out 'God's' Vote: 'Pat' Robertson and the Evangelicals." The Humanist, May/June. Accessed June 14, 2006. webcitation.org/60Gu1gEa2.
Elbourne, Elizabeth. 2003. "The Sin of the Settler : The 1835-36 Select Committee on Aborigines and Debates Over Virtue and Conquest in the Early Nineteenth-Century British White Settler Empire." Journal of Colonialism and Colonial History 4,3. tinyurl.com/7rthmgs.
Encyclopædia Britannica Online. n.d. a. "Colonialism, Western." *Encyclopædia Britannica* Online. Accessed January 26, 2005. http://search.eb.com/eb/article?tocId=25892. (Outdated link).
Encyclopædia Britannica Online. n.d. b. "South Africa, History of—British Occupation of the Cape." *Encyclopædia Britannica Online*. Accessed February 4, 2005. http://search.eb.com/eb/article?tocId =44062. (Outdated link).
Encyclopædia Britannica Online. n.d. c. "Southern Africa—Changes in the Status of Africans." *Encyclopædia Britannica Online*. Accessed January 26, 2005. http://search.eb.com/eb/article?tocId =234065. (Outdated link).
Encyclopædia Britannica Online. n.d. d. "Southern Africa—Continuing Settler-Xhosa Wars." *Encyclopædia Britannica Online*. Accessed January 26, 2005. http://search.eb.com/eb/article?tocId= 234066. (Outdated link).
Encyclopædia Britannica Online. n.d. e. "Southern Africa—Growth of Missionary Activity." *Encyclopædia Britannica Online*. Accessed January 26, 2005. http://search.eb.com/eb/article?tocId=234067.
Encyclopædia Britannica Online. n.d. f. "Southern Africa—Growth of Racism." *Encyclopædia Britannica Online*. Accessed January 26, 2005. http://search.eb.com/eb/article?tocId=234001. (Outdated link).
Encyclopædia Britannica Online. n.d. g. "Southern Africa—The Expansion of White Settlement." *Encyclopædia Britannica Online*. Accessed January 26, 2005. http://search.eb.com/eb/ article?tocId=43800. (Outdated link).
England, Frank and Torquil Paterson. 1989. *Bounty in bondage. The Anglican Church in Southern Africa. Essays in honour of Edward King, Dean of Cape Town.* Johannesburg: Ravan Press.
F.L.O.C. 1991. "FLOC Annual Report." Unpublished document.
Fenn, Kevin. 1992. Interview Conducted by the Author on October 1, Johannesburg.
Fothergill, Gordon. 1992. Interviews Conducted by the Author on August 28 and September 25, Johannesburg.
Frederikse, Julie. 1990. *The Unbreakable Thread: Non-Racialism in South Africa.* Bloomington: Indiana University Press.
Fundneider, Thomas 1998. "Establishment of Sustainable Development Plan-

ning Principles for Marabastad, Pretoria." Dipl. Ing. thesis, University of Bodenkultur. Accessed February 23, 2005. webcitation.org/60Gu1gEaJ.

Giddens, Anthony. 1984. *The Constitution of Society: Outline of the Theory of Structuration*. Berkeley: University of California Press.

Gilliomee, Hermann n.d. "The Dutch Reformed Church and Chosen People: The Dynamics of the Rise and Decline of Apartheid." Accessed January 24, 2005. webcitation.org/66pRS5rh4.

Gilliomee, Hermann. 1989. "Aspects of the rise of Afrikaner capital and Afrikaner nationalism in the Western Cape, 1870-1915." In *The Angry Divide*, edited by Wilmot G. James and Mary Simons, 63-81. Cape Town: David Philip.

Goedhals, Mandy. 1989. "From Paternalism to Partnership? The Church of the Province of South Africa and Mission 1848-1988." In *Bounty in bondage. The Anglican Church in Southern Africa. Essays in honour of Edward King, Dean of Cape Town*, edited by Frank England and Torquil Paterson, 104-129. Johannesburg: Ravan Press.

Gray, Robert. 1849. *A Journal of the Bishop's Visitation Tour through the Cape Colony with an Account of His Visit to the Island of St. Helena, in 1849*. London: Society for the Propagation of the Gospel. Accessed February 15, 2005. webcitation.org/60N0AXux0.

Gray, Robert. 1853. *A Journal of the Bishop's Visitation Tour through the Cape Colony, in 1850*. London: Society for the Propagation of the Gospel. Accessed February 15, 2005. webcitation.org/60N03KbFX.

Hall, T.D. 1961. "The Methodist Central Hall, Pritchard and Kruis Streets, Johannesburg. The Church in the Heart of the City." 75th anniversary brochure of the commencement of Methodism in Johannesburg, and 42nd anniversary of the Methodist Central Hall.

Halsall, Paul. n.d. "Statute of Westminster 1931." *Modern History Sourcebook*. Accessed July 31, 2005. webcitation.org/60DzhcUTt.

Harper, Douglas. 2001. "Online Etymology Dictionary." Accessed August 10, 2006. webcitation.org/60Gu1gEar.

Hexham, Irving and Karla Poewe-Hexham. 1988. "Charismatics and Change in South Africa." *Christian Century* 17-24:739. Accessed April 13, 2005. webcitation.org/60Gu1gEaz.

Hinchliff, Peter B. 1968. *The Church in South Africa*. London: SPCK.

Hirson, Baruch n.d. "A Short History of the Non-European Unity Movement— An Insider's View." Accessed February 19, 2005. webcitation.org/60Gu1gEb8.

Homiak, Jake. n.d. "Dread History: The African Diaspora, Ethiopianism, and Rastafari." Accessed May 22, 2005. webcitation.org/60Gu 1gEbG.

Hope, Marjorie and James Young. 1981. *The South African Churches in a Revolutionary Situation*. Maryknoll, N.Y.: Orbis Books.

Horn, Nico. 1991. "Crossing Racial Borders in Southern Africa: a Lesson from History." *Cyberjournal for Pentecostal Charismatic Research*, June. Accessed April 14, 2005. webcitation.org/60Gu1gEbP.

Horn, Nico. 2005. "Power and Empowerment in the Political Context of South Africa." Paper presented at the joint EPTA/EPCRA Conference, Bueggen Castle, Rheinfelden, Germany, April 1, 2005.

Hourani, Guita G. 2000. "The Struggle Of The Christian Lebanese For Land Ownership In South Africa." *The Journal of Maronite Studies* 4,2. July-December. Accessed March 31, 2005. webcitation.org/60Gu1gEbX.

Hudson, Janet. 1992. Interview Conducted by the Author in April, Johannesburg.

Hunter, John. 1952. *A Short History of the Church of St. Mary, Stellenbosch, 1852-1952*. Stellenbosch: Pro-Ecclesia.

Human Rights Watch. 1991. "South Africa: Human Rights Developments." Accessed September 4, 2007. webcitation.org/60Gu1gEbm.

Hyam, Mike. 1992. Interview Conducted by the Author on September 9, Johannesburg.

Jeffrey, Anthea. n.d. "The Truth About the Truth Commission." *Human Rights* 27,2. Accessed April 16, 2005. webcitation.org/60Gu1gEbv.

John, Lizzie. 1992. Interview Conducted by the Author on February 8, Johannesburg.

Johnson, J. Albert. 1909. "Second Annual Report." In *A. M. E. Handbook*, edited by B. F. Lee, 134-135. Nashville, Tenn: A. M. E. Sunday School Union.

Johnson, Sandy. 1992. Interview Conducted by the Author on April 27, Johannesburg.

Johweto. 1987. "Observations Presented to Johweto Management Committee on the Structure and Running of Johweto on Wednesday 25th March." Unpublished document.

Johweto. 1988a. "Johweto Homegroup Fellowships at Kehillah. July." Unpublished document.

Johweto. 1988b. "Johweto Statement re Military Involvement. 18 September." Unpublished document.

Johweto. 1989a. "Minutes for [the Vineyard Leader's Day] Meetings Held at Johweto Kehillah, 24th June, 1-2." Unpublished document.

Johweto. 1989b. "Notes of the Discussion of the Johweto Congregation at the Vineyard leader's Day at the Kehillah on the 24th June." Unpublished document.

Johweto. ca. 1988c. "Johweto—a Proposal. May." Unpublished document.

Johweto. ca. 1988d. "Johweto Vineyard—Strategy for Growth. One Year Johweto Plans and Budget." Unpublished document.

Kelly, Brian. 1992. Interview Conducted by the Author on September 24, Johannesburg.

Kingdon, Geeta Gandhi and John Knight. 2001. "Unemployment in South

Africa: the Nature of the Beast." Working Paper, Centre for the Study of African Economies, University of Oxford. Accessed September 5, 2007. webcitation.org/60Gu1gEc3.

Kingdon, Geeta Gandhi and John Knight. 2005. "Unemployment in South Africa: a Microeconomic Approach." Accessed September 6, 2007. webcitation.org/60Gu1gEc3.

Kinghorn, Johann. 1986. *Die NG Kerk en Apartheid.* [The DRC and Apartheid.] Johannesburg: MacMillan.

Kinghorn, Johann. 1990. "The Theology of Separate Equality: a Critical Outline of the DRC's Position on Apartheid." In *Christianity Amidst Apartheid: Selected Perspectives on the Church in South Africa,* edited by Martin Prozesky, 57-80. New York: St Martin's Press.

Klotz, Audie. 1995. *Norms in International Relations: the Struggle Against Apartheid.* Ithaca, NY: Cornell University Press.

Kotze, Victor. 2005. E-mail to author, received May 7.

Krause, Bettina. 2002. "Church Calls for Unity in South Africa." *Adventist News Network,* April 18. Accessed April 4, 2005. webcitation.org/60Gu1gEcQ.

Krige, Skip and Ronnie Donalson. 1999. "Module 3. Dynamics and Inertia of the Post-Apartheid City." In *Spatial Transformation in Post-Apartheid South Africa: An Educational Project.* Accessed April 4, 2005. tinyurl.com/ytqblu.

Kubheka, Thema M. N. 2004. "Ancient Roots and a Blossoming Partnership." Accessed April 1, 2005. webcitation.org/60Gu1gEch.

Langham-Carter, R.R. 1977. *Old St George's. The Story of Cape Town's First Cathedral.* Cape Town: A.A. Balkema.

Laverty, Cathy. 1992. Interview Conducted by the Author on April 27, Johannesburg.

Lazerson, Joshua N. 1994. *Against the Tide : Whites in the Struggle Against Apartheid.* Boulder : Westview Press.

Lebos, Jimmy. [1997] 1998. "The Lebanese of South Africa—One People, One Origin, One Destiny." *The Journal of Maronite Studies.* Reprinted from *The Voice* 1, 2. Accessed March 31, 2005. webcitation.org/60Gu1gEcq.

Lewis, Cecil and G.E. Edwards. 1934. *Historical Records of the Church of the Province of South Africa.* London: SPCK.

Liebenberg, Helena. n.d. "Introduction to the Resolutions of the Council of Policy of Cape of Good Hope." Accessed July 2, 2005. www.webcitation.org/60Gu1gEcz.

Livas, Haris. n.d. "Bio-Communications." Accessed February 4, 2005. www.webcitation.org/60Gu1gEd7.

Loff, Chris. 1983. "The History of a Heresy." In *Apartheid is a Heresy,* edited by John W. De Gruchy and Charles Villa-Vicencio, 10—23. Cape Town: David Philip.

Lutheran World Federation. 1977a. *The Identity of the Church and its Service to the Whole Human Being*. Vol. I. Geneva: Lutheran World Federation.

Lutheran World Federation. 1977b. *The Identity of the Church and its Service to the Whole Human Being*. Vol. II. Geneva: Lutheran World Federation.

Lutuli, Albert. 1955. "Message to the people of the Western Areas." Accessed July 27, 2006. webcitation.org/60Q1fejI7.

Mabin, Alan. 1991. "The impact of apartheid on rural South Africa." *Antipode* 23 (1):33-46.

Maho, Jouni, comp. 2002. *Select Chronology of South African Legislation*. Department of Oriental and African Studies, Göteborg University. Accessed July 2, 2006. webcitation.org/60Gu1gEdO.

Man, Diane. 2005. E-mail to Author, received April 5.

Manoim, Irwin and Lucille Davie. n.d. "Three Georges Strike Paydirt." Johannesburg News Agency. Accessed February 27, 2005. webcitation.org/60Gu1gEdX.

Manoim, Irwin. 2003. "The City Without Water." Johannesburg News Agency. Accessed February 27, 2005. webcitation.org/60Gu1gEdg.

Marais, Johannes S. [1939] 1978. *The Cape Coloured People, 1652-1937*. New York: Longmans.

Masilela, Ntongela. n.d. "Isaac Wauchope." In *Xhosa Intellectuals of the 1880s*. Accessed May 5, 2006. webcitation.org/60Gu1gEdo.

Massie, R. K. 1993. "Local Churches in the New South Africa." *Journal of Theology for Southern Africa* 85:19-28.

Mathole, Ezekiel M.K.M. 2005. "The Christian Witness in the Context of Poverty, with Special Reference to the South African Charismatic Evangelicals." Ph.D. diss., Department of Science of Religion and Missiology, University of Pretoria, Pretoria.

Maylam, Paul. 1995. "Explaining the Apartheid City: 20 Years of South African Urban Historiography." *Journal of Southern African Studies* 21,1:19—29.

Mayson, Cedric. n.d. "Introductory Essay: *Pro Veritate*—Beyers Naudé." Accessed June 13, 2006. webcitation.org/60Gu1gEdx.

Mbeki, Govan n.d. *The Struggle for Liberation in South Africa*. Accessed February 11, 2005. webcitation.org/60Gu1gEe6.

Mbeki, Govan. 1964. *South Africa: The Peasants' Revolt*. Penguin African Library. Accessed March 5, 2005. webcitation.org/60Gu1gEeF.

McGavran, Donald and C. Peter Wagner. 1990. *Understanding Church Growth*. Grand Rapids: Eerdmans.

McGregor, Joan. 1992. Interview Conducted by the Author on October 28, Johannesburg.

Meara, William. 1931. *A Citizen of No Mean City. Methodist Central Hall and Circuit, Annual Report*. Unpublished document.

Millard, Joan 2003. "A Transatlantic Alliance: Two South Africans Changed their Country by Linking their Church with an African-American

Church." *Christianity History and Biography*. Christianity Today Library. Accessed January 25, 2005. http://tinyurl.com/3cxy6le.

Millard, Joan A. 1999. "Mogatla, David Modibane, c. 1814 to 1874 Methodist, South Africa." Accessed February 27, 2005. webcitation.org/60Gu1gEeZ.

Mills, T.F. n.d. "Cape Mounted Riflemen [1827-1870] and Cape Corps [1781-1991]." In *Land Forces of Britain, the Empire and Commonwealth*. Accessed July 7, 2006. webcitation.org/60Gu1gEei.

Missionary Oblates of Mary Immaculate. 2002. "Missionary Oblates of Mary Immaculate, Transvaal Province, South Africa." Accessed April 2, 2005. webcitation.org/60Gu1gEer.

Moroa, George. 1993. Interview Conducted by the Author on January 16, Johannesburg.

Morran, Elizabeth S. and Laurie Schlemmer. 1984. *Faith for the Fearful*. Durban: Centre for Applied Social Sciences, University of Natal.

Mothiane, John. 1993a. Interview Conducted by the Author on January 31, Johannesburg.

Mothiane, John. 1993b. Interview Conducted by the Author on January 3, Johannesburg.

Mukuka, George. 1997. "The Impact of Black Consciousness on Black Catholic Clergy and their Seminary Training." *Bulletin for Contextual Theology* 4,1. Accessed April 18. 2005. webcitation.org/60Gu1gEez.

Murray, Chris. 1992. Interview Conducted by the Author on January 24, Johannesburg.

Myeza, Lindy and Els Te Siepe. 1972. "WAAIC Steams Ahead." *Pro Veritate* 11,4:14–15. Accessed February 27, 2005. webcitation.org/60Gu1gEf8.

Naudé, C.F. Beyers. 1963. "Reconciliation: inaugural address as director of the Christian Institute, in the Methodist Central Hall, Johannesburg, Sunday 15 December." In *The Legacy of Beyers Naudé*, edited by Len D. Hansen (2005), 139-142. Stellenbosch: SUN Press.

Ndamase, Charmaine. 1993. Interview Conducted by the Author on February 11, Johannesburg.

Ntlha, Moss and Nick Mosupi. 1999. "Preface to the Submission of the Evangelical Alliance of South Africa to the TRC." Accessed April 15, 2005. webcitation.org/60Gu1gEfH.

Ntlha, Moss, Colin LaVoy and Derek Morphew. 1999. "Evangelical Alliance. Testimony before the Truth and Reconciliation Commission, East London, 18 November." Accessed April 15, 2005. webcitation.org/60Gu1gEfP.

Ntlha, Moss. 2004. Foreword to *Doing Reconciliation: Racism, Reconciliation and Transformation in the Church and World,* by Alexander F. Venter. Cape Town: Vineyard International Publishing.

Ntlhola, Trevor. 1994. Interview Conducted by the Author on September 13, Johannesburg.

Oosthuizen, G.C. 1968. *Post–Christianity in Africa. A Theological and Anthropological Study*. London: C. Hurst and Co.

Oosthuizen, G.C. 1990. "Christianity's Impact on Race Relations in South Africa." In *Christianity Amidst Apartheid: Selected Perspectives on the Church in South Africa*, edited by Martin Prozesky, 101-121. New York: St. Martin's Press.

Ortell, Claude. 1992. Interview Conducted by the Author in April, Johannesburg.

Paballo Ya Batho. n.d. "*Paballo Ya Batho*—Caring for the People." Accessed January 28, 2005. webcitation.org/60Gu1gEfY.

Parnell, Susan and Gordon Pirie 1990. "Johannesburg." In *Homes Apart—South Africa's Segregated Cities*, edited by Anthony Lemon, 129–146. London: Paul Chapman.

Pinnock, Don. 1989. "Ideology and Urban Planning: Blueprints of a Garrison City." In *The Angry Divide*, edited by Wilmot G. James and M. Simons, 150-168. Cape Town: David Philip.

Preyer, Mrs. 1993. Interview Conducted by the Author on February 20, Johannesburg.

Prinsloo, Riana. 1999. "Module 1. Historical, Social and Political Context." In *Spatial Transformation in Post-Apartheid South Africa: An Educational Project*. Accessed July 2, 2006. tinyurl.com/ynoolh.

Prior, Andrew, ed. 1982. *Catholics in Apartheid Society*. Cape Town: David Philip.

Reddy, Enuga Sreenivasulu. 1999. "AAM and the United Nations." Paper presented to the symposium on The Anti-Aparthied [sic] Movement: a 40-year Perspective, London, June 26. Accessed February 8, 2005. www. webcitation.org/60Gu1gEfp.

Retief, Frank. 1999. "Church of England in South Africa." Testimony before the Truth and Reconciliation Commission, East London, 17 November. Accessed February 18, 2005. webcitation.org/60Q5VTzP2.

Retief, Frank. 2005. E-mail to Author, received on February 22, 2005.

Rich, Paul B. 1996. *State Power and Black Politics in South Africa, 1912-51*. New York: St. Martin's Press.

Robbins, Thomas. 1988. *Cults, Converts and Charisma*. London: Sage Publications

Robertson, R.J.D. 1997. *The Small Beginning. The Story of North End Presbyterian Church East London 1962-1970*. Self-published.

Robertson, Robert J.D. 1963. "Multi-Racial Congregation in East London." *Pro Veritate*, 1, 9:9. Accessed June 13, 2006. tinyurl.com/7edvel6.

Robertson, Robert J.D. 1994. "Engaging the Powers: Some Presbyterian Non-Violence." *Non-Violence News* First Quarter:1-10.

Roca Report. 1989. "Church Leaders Support the Defiance Campaign." *Roca Report—A Confidential Assessment of Developments in Southern Africa*, August 16. Accessed February 27, 2005. http://www.ligstryders.org/main2.htm. (Outdated link).

Roozen, David A., William McKinney and Jack Carroll. 1984. *Varieties of Religious Presence.* New York: The Pilgrim Press.

Rosenberg, Greg. 1996. "Mandela Tells Farrakhan About Principles of Non-Racialism, Sexism." *The Militant* March 18, 60:11. Accessed February 8, 2005. webcitation.org/60Gu1gEgW.

Royston, Lauren. 1998. "South Africa: The Struggle for Access to the City in the Witwatersrand Region." In *Evictions and the Right to Housing: Experience from Canada, Chile, the Dominican Republic, South Africa, and South Korea,* edited by Antonio Azuela, Emilio Duhau, and Enrique Ortiz, 145-98. International Development Research Centre. Accessed April 19, 2005. webcitation.org/60Gu1gEge.

Rubin, Margot. 2004. "The Jewish Community of Johannesburg, 1886-1939." M.A. thesis, University of Pretoria. Accessed November 2, 2007. www.webcitation.org/60Gu1gEgn.

Rudolph, Joan 1992. Interview Conducted by the Author on May 29, Johannesburg.

Saayman, Willem. 1990. "Christian Missions in South Africa: Achievements, Failures and the Future." In *Christianity Amidst Apartheid: Selected Perspectives on the Church in South Africa,* edited by Martin Prozesky, 28-36. New York: St. Martin's Press.

Saayman, Willem. 1994. "Christian Mission in South Africa: a Historical Reflection." *International Review of Mission* 83,328:11-20.

Saayman, Willem. 1997. "Subversive Subservience: Z.K. Matthews and Missionary Education in South Africa." *Missionalia* 4,25:523-36. Accessed February 22, 2005. webcitation.org/60Gu1gEgw.

Saint Francis Xavier Catholic Church. n.d. *Liber Matrimoniorum, 1955-1993.* (Parish marriage registers).

Saunders, Christopher 2002. Review of *South Africa's Racial Past: The History and Historiography of Racism, Segregation and Apartheid,* by Paul Maylam. *H-Net Reviews,* January. Accessed April 4, 2005. http://tinyurl.com/2gmcbf.

Schoonakker, Bonny. 2004. "The Second Most Famous Mozambican." *Sunday Times,* August 1. Accessed February 27, 2005. webcitation.org/60Gu1gEhD.

Scott, J. 1981. "The People Centre—An Inner City Church-Sponsored Community Facility." Bachelor of Arts in Social Work dissertation, University of the Witwatersrand.

Sechaba. 1982. "John Langalibalele Dube—First ANC President-General." *Sechaba,* January. Accessed February 18, 2005. webcitation.org/60Gu1gEhM.

Sennelo, Gideon. 1992. Interview Conducted by the Author on February 8, Johannesburg.

Sheffield, Dan, with Kathleen Sheffield. 1998. "Ubunye Church and Community Ministries." In *Serving With the Urban Poor*, edited by Tetsunao Yamamori, Kenneth L. Luscombe, and Bryant L. Myers. Monrovia, CA: MARC Publications (World Vision). Accessed January 20, 2005. webcitation.org/60Q6HU9EE.

Silva, Penny n.d. "South African English: Oppressor or Liberator?" Accessed April 4, 2005. webcitation.org/60W7pbgQ2.

Simons, H. Jack and Ray Simons. 1968. *Class and Colour in South Africa, 1850-1950*. Baltimore: Penguin. Accessed May 17, 2005. webcitation.org/60Gu1gEhm.

Sisters of Notre Dame de Namur. n.d. "Sisters of Notre Dame de Namur—Places Served." Accessed April 5, 2005. webcitation.org/60Gu1g Ehu.

South African Catholic Bishops' Conference n.d. Accessed September 6, 2007. webcitation.org/60Gu1gEi8.

South African Church Magazine. 1850. *South African Church Magazine*. CPSA Diocese of Cape Town. Volume 1, Numbers 1-12. CPSA archives, Department of Historical Papers, University of the Witwatersrand.

South African History Online. n.d. a. " 'Locations' for Labour." In *Working Life, 1886–1940: Factories, Township and Popular Culture 1886–1940*. Adapted from Luli Callinicos. 1987. *Working Life, 1886–1940: Factories, Townships, and Popular Culture on the Rand (People's History of South Africa, Vol. 2.)* Johannesburg: Ravan Press. Accessed January 28, 2005. webcitation. org/66UTkKmfw.

South African History Online. n.d. b. "Indian Chronology." Accessed March 3, 2005. webcitation.org/60Gu1gEiI.

South African History Online. n.d. c. "Apartheid Legislation." Accessed February 10, 2005. webcitation.org/60Gu1gEiQ.

South African History Online. n.d. d. "Where Working People Lived." In *Working Life, 1886–1940: Factories, Township and Popular Culture 1886–1940*. Adapted from Luli Callinicos. 1987. *Working Life, 1886–1940: Factories, Townships, and Popular Culture on the Rand (People's History of South Africa, Vol. 2.)* Johannesburg: Ravan Press. Accessed September 4, 2007. www.webcitation.org/60Gu1gEiZ.

South African History Online. n.d. e. "1920s." Accessed July 22, 2005. webcitation.org/60UcTfAfH.

South African History Online. n.d. f. "Other Black Suburbs." In *Egoli, a History of Black Johannesburg*. n.a. Accessed February 03, 2005. webcitation.org/60Gu1gEiq.

South African History Online. n.d. g. "Fietas Pageview, Johannesburg." Accessed July 27, 2006. webcitation.org/60Gu1gEiz.

South African History Online. n.d. h. "Hendrik Frensch Verwoerd, 1901-1966." Accessed July 27, 2006. webcitation.org/60Gu1gEj8.

South African History Online. n.d. i. "Johannes Modise, 1929-2001." Accessed July 27, 2006. webcitation.org/60Gu1gEjG.
South African History Online. n.d. j. "Chronology-Walter M. Sisulu." Accessed July 27, 2006. webcitation.org/60Gu1gEjO.
South African History Online. n.d. k. "Non-racial Cooperation in the Unions." In *Working Life, 1886–1940: Factories, Township and Popular Culture 1886–1940*. Adapted from Luli Callinicos. 1987. *Working Life, 1886–1940: Factories, Townships, and Popular Culture on the Rand (People's History of South Africa, Vol. 2.)* Johannesburg: Ravan Press. Accessed September 4, 2007. webcitation. org/60Gu1gEjX.
South African History Online. n.d. l. "The Early Years." In *Working Life, 1886–1940: Factories, Township and Popular Culture 1886–1940*. Adapted from Luli Callinicos. 1987. *Working Life, 1886–1940: Factories, Townships, and Popular Culture on the Rand (People's History of South Africa, Vol. 2.)* Johannesburg: Ravan Press. Accessed September 4, 2007. www.webcitation. org/60Gu1gEjg.
South African History Online. n.d. m. "1700s." Accessed September 12, 2007. webcitation.org/60Gu1gEjo.
South African Institute of Race Relations. 1988/89. *Race Relations Survey*. Johannesburg: South African Institute of Race Relations.
South African Institute of Race Relations. 1989/90. *Race Relations Survey*. Braamfontein: The SA Institute of Race Relations.
South African Native Affairs Commission. 1904. "Testimony of Martin Lutuli of the Natal Native Congress, Before the South African Native Affairs Commission, May 28, 1904." *Minutes of Evidence, South African Native Affairs Commission, 1903-1905*. Accessed July 22, 2005. webcitation.org/60Gu1gEjx.
South African Native National Congress. 1914. "Petition to King George V, from the South African Native National Congress." *The Cape Argus*, 20 July. Accessed May 20, 2005. .
Statistics South Africa. 2001. "Census 2001 by Province, Gender, Religion Recode (derived) and Population Group." Accessed April 15, 2005. tinyurl.com/6nrh44p.
Stevens, Lucy and Stephen Rule. 1999. "Moving to an Informal Settlement: The Gauteng Experience." *The South African Geographical Journal* 8,3. Accessed April 15, 2005. webcitation.org/60Gu1gEk.
Storey, Peter J. 2002. *With God in the Crucible: Preaching Costly Discipleship*. Nashville: Abingdon Press.
Storey, Peter S. 1992. "Thank you CMM, Thank You God." *What a Family!* (Congregational Newsletter). Unpublished document.
Storey, Peter S. 1993. Personal Communication.
Storey, Peter S. 1994. Interview Conducted by the Author on May 25, 1994, Johannesburg.

Storey, Peter S. 2005a. E-mail to Author, March 17.
Storey, Peter S. 2005b. E-mail to Author, May.
Tankard, Keith. 2004. "Proto-Apartheid: Evolution of an Urban Society in the Eastern Cape From 1847 to 1923." Accessed April 4, 2005. webcitation.org/60Gu1gEkV.
Taylor, Vivien. 1992. Interview Conducted by the Author on October 5, Johannesburg.
Te Riele, Wolter. 1992. Interview Conducted by the Author on October 15, Johannesburg.
Thale, Thomas. 2003. "Soweto's Gravel Roads to Become History." City of Johannesburg website. Accessed June 7, 2006. webcitation.org/60Gu1gEke.
The Church for the Fellowship of All Peoples. n.d. "The Church for the Fellowship of All Peoples." Accessed May 19, 2006. webcitation.org/60XfRLM7D.
The Deaconess Order. n.d. Unpublished pamphlet.
The Rustenburg Declaration. 1990. Accessed April 18, 2005. http://tinyurl.com/6x75bnl
Theilen, Uta. 2003. "Gender, Race, Power and Religion: Women in the Methodist Church of Southern Africa in Post-Apartheid Society." Ph.D. diss., Philipps-Universität Marburg. Accessed October 11, 2006. webcitation.org/60Gu1gEl3.
Thompson, Leonard. 1990. *A History of South Africa.* New Haven: Yale University Press.
Tindall, B.A. And I. Grindley-Ferris. 1907. *Transvaal Law Reports.* Grahamstown: African Book Company.
Tirion, Isaac. ca. 1730. "Map of the Cape of Good Hope." Accessed November 16, 2005. webcitation.org/60Gu1gElC.
Truth and Reconciliation Commission, Amnesty Committee. 1995. "Application in Terms of Section 18 of the Promotion of National Unity and Reconciliation Act, No. 34 of 1995. Michael Bellingan Applicant (AM2880/96). Decision." Accessed February 6, 2005. webcitation.org/60Gu1gElK.
Truth and Reconciliation Commission. 1996. "Human Rights Violations. Submissions—Questions and Answers. Date: 23.07.1996. Name: Dale White. Case: Soweto. Day 2." Accessed February 6, 2005. webcitation.org/60Gu1gElT.
Truth and Reconciliation Commission. 1998a. "Special Hearing: Women." In *Truth and Reconciliation Commission. Final Report.* Volume 4, Chapter 10. Accessed February 5, 2005. webcitation.org/60Gu1gElb.
Truth and Reconciliation Commission. 1998b. "Truth and Reconciliation Commission. Amnesty Hearing. July 24. Name: Michael Bellinghan. Day 5. (Transcript.)" Accessed February 27, 2005. webcitation.org/60Gu1gElk.

Van den Berg, Lynne. 1993. Interview Conducted by the Author on February 18, Johannesburg.
Van der Merwe, Hugo. 1999. "The Truth and Reconciliation Commission and Community Reconciliation: An Analysis of Competing Strategies and Conceptualizations." Ph.D. Diss., George Mason University. Accessed April 16, 2005. webcitation.org/60Gu1gElt.
Venter, Alexander F. 1987. "The Johweto Vision." Unpublished document.
Venter, Alexander F. 1989a. Unpublished letter for benefit of Johweto's supporters locally and abroad.
Venter, Alexander F. 1989b. "Johweto Newsletter. January." Unpublished document.
Venter, Alexander F. 1991. "The Johwetan. Newsletter of the Johweto Vineyard." Unpublished document.
Venter, Alexander F. 1994a. Interview Conducted by the Author on July 15, Johannesburg.
Venter, Alexander F. 1994b. Interview Conducted by the Author on July 16, Johannesburg.
Venter, Alexander F. 1994c. Interview Conducted by the Author on July 17, Johannesburg.
Venter, Alexander F. 2004. *Doing Reconciliation: Racism, Reconciliation and Transformation in the Church and World*. Cape Town: Vineyard International Publishing.
Venter, Alexander F. and A. James Johnson. 1987. "Johweto Kehillah." Unpublished document, 1-18. [Revised version of the 1986 document].
Venter, Alexander F. and A. James Johnson. 1987. "The Johweto vision." Unpublished document.
Venter, Alexander F., Ron Gold and A. James Johnson. 1986. "Johweto Kehillah." Unpublished document.
Venter, Dawid. 1994. "The Formation and Functioning of Racially-Mixed Congregations." Ph.D. diss., University of Stellenbosch.
Venter, Dawid. 1995. "Mending the Multi-Coloured Coat of a Rainbow Nation: Cultural Accommodation in Ethnically–Mixed Urban Congregations." *Missionalia* 23:312–338.
Venter, Dawid. 1998. "The Inverted Norm: the Formation and Functioning of Racially–Mixed Congregations in South Africa." In *Religion in a Changing World*, edited by Madeleine Cousineau, 69–79. Westport: Greenwood.
Venter, Dawid. 1999. "Language, Nation, and Congregation: World-System and World-Polity Perspectives on Language Integration in South African Churches." Ph.D. diss., University of Stellenbosch.
Venter, Dawid. 2000. "Cultural Reproduction in the World System: Case Studies From a Semiperiphery, 1872-1997." *Society in Transition* 31 (2) : 184-95.

Vigne, Randolph. n.d. "*Contact*: 1954–1987. Historical Note." Accessed February 23, 2005. webcitation.org/60Gu1gEm1.
Villa-Vicencio, Charles. 1988. *Trapped in Apartheid: A Socio-Theological History of the English-Speaking Churches*. Cape Town: David Philip.
Visser, Wessel. n.d. "Strike Tendencies and Trends in South Africa in the 20th century." Accessed June 6, 2005. webcitation.org/60Gu1gEmA.
Von Veh, Bengt. 1992. Interview Conducted by the Author on January 24, Johannesburg.
Walls, Andrew F. 1998. "Aggrey, James Emman Kwegyir, 1875 to 1927. African Methodist Episcopal Zion Church, Gold Coast (Ghana)." In *Dictionary of African Christian Biography*. Accessed April 27, 2006. webcitation.org/ 60Gu1gEmI.
Webb, Joseph B. 1943. "The Methodist Central Hall. Annual Report." Unpublished document.
Webb, Joseph B. 1944. "The Methodist Central Hall. 25th Anniversary. Annual Report." Unpublished document.
Webb, Joseph B. 1946. "27th Anniversary Notes." Unpublished document.
Webb, Joseph B. 1949. "A Plea for Regular Giving. What Shall I Render to My God?" Unpublished document.
Webb, Joseph B. 1951. "The Vision Ahead, 1885-1951. Methodist Central Hall: 32nd Anniversary News Bulletin. 66th Anniversary of the Beginning of Methodist Work in Johannesburg." Unpublished document.
Webb, Joseph B. 1956. "70th anniversary brochure." Unpublished document.
The Weekly Mail. 1987. " 'Scrap Group Areas.' Advertisement in *The Weekly Mail*, 16—22 Oct 1987." In *Part III: Political Documents*. CAMP Guide - Karis-Gerhart Catalog, 36. Accessed February 27, 2005. webcitation.org/60Xg KXPIy.
Wessels, G. Francois. 1997. "Charismatic Christian Congregations and Social Justice—a South African Perspective." *Missionalia* 25,3:360–74. Accessed April 12, 2005. http://tinyurl.com/63vccgp.
Yap, Melanie and Diane Leong Man. 1996. *Colour, Confusion and Concessions: The History of the Chinese in South Africa*. Hong Kong: Hong Kong University Press.
Young, Wendy. 1992. Interview Conducted by the Author on May 5, Johannesburg.
Zaaiman, Johan. 1994. "Kerk en Geloofsaffiliasie in Suid-Afrika [Church and religious affiliation in South Africa]." *Nederduitse Gereformeerde Teologiese Tydskrif* 35,4: 565-74.

INDEX

African Enterprise, 60, n. 73, 138, 187
African National Congress
   and multi-racialism, 56
   and non-racialism, 55, 55 n. 31, 193
   and norms, contestation of, 190
   effect on racially-mixed churches, 130, 131, 132, 150, 153
   See also South African Native National Congress
African People's Organisation, segregation, opposition to, 180, 181
Allard, Marie J. F. (bishop of Natal), integration, supported, 29, 29 n. 4
amaXhosa, 8, 26, 39, 178, 196
   "locations", created for, 141, 184
   pass documents for, colonial, 37
anti-apartheid movement, 192, 194-95
   international, 198, 221
   racially integrated, 60
apartheid
   as national norm, 48-63
   as segregationism, 12
   church complicity with, 3, 19, 21-22, 75, 137-40
   church opposition to, ix-x, 14, 22, 51, 84-101, 121, 139, 202, 223
   effect on ecumenism, 22
   effect on urban organisation, 3, 20
      Apartheid City, 48, 49, 72, 93, 99, 169, 209
      Apartheid-City-in-Transition, 49
      Colonial City, 27, 31
      Homeland City, 49
      Post-Apartheid City, 1, 13, 20
      Segregation City, 21, 43
   first use of term, 47
   historical precursors of, 37, 184, 195
   periodisation of, 20-21
   theological defence of, 22
   theological rejection of, 51
apartheid legislation
   Bantu Authorities Act (1951), 49
   Bantu Education Act (1953), 48
   Black Local Authorities Act (1982), 147
   Industrial Conciliation Amendment Act (1956), 48
   Group Areas Act (1950), 14, 46, 48, 49, 57, 58, 85, 100, 111, 119, 120, 124 n. 83, 140, 181, 182, 184, 187
   Population Registration Act (1950), 48
   Prohibition of Improper Political Interference Act (1967), 60
   Prohibition of Mixed Marriages Act (1949), 48, 112, 187
   Separate Amenities Act (1953), 93
apartheid security legislation
   Public Safety Act (1953), 147
   Internal Security Act (1982), 96, 97
   Riotous Assemblies Amendment Act (1974), 97
   Unlawful Organisations Act (1960), 97

Beyers Naudè, C.F., 88, 149, 156
Black Consciousness, 53-54, 148, 156
    and segregationism, 193
    definition of, 53
    effects on Johweto, 148, 166, 168
Black Sash, 187
    effect on integration, 130
    multi-racial composition of, 60
Botha, Louis (prime minister)
    and segregationism, 22, 43
Botha, P.W. (president), 49, 141, 147
Bousfield, Henry (bishop of Pretoria)
    integration, support for, 40

Cape Colony, 25, 27, 69, 113, 178
    removal of black franchise, 36, 197
    Chinese, policy towards, 114
    education and black labour in, 33
    first use of "segregation" in, 10
    labour shortages and war in, 26
    "locations" and reserves in, 37, 183
    racial equality and segregation in, 179, 196
    racial views of colonists in, 69, 179
Cape Town, 85
    integration of, 25, 27, 31, 57 n. 32
    racial terms in census of, 178
    segregation of, 3, 32, 37, 179, 180, 184, 186
Church Women Concerned, 60
class, 95, 213, 215, 218-19
    and apartheid, 4
    and race, 18, 42 n. 16, 56, 75, 79, 128, 169, 191
    black working, 36, 75 n. 49
    divisions, 159, 168, 223
    effects, social and spatial, 27, 78, 178, 180
    formation, 23, 35, 174
    mercantile, white, 37
    middle, 60, 140, 141
    ruling, 35, 36, 47
congregations and parishes

Buitenkant Street Methodist, 53, 57, 59
Cathedral of the Sacred Heart, 59
Central Methodist Mission, Cape Town, 59, 66
Central Methodist Mission, Johannesburg, ix, 1, 2, 13, 58, 66, 71-109, 111, 135, 143, 203, 205, 211, 210, 213, 214, 216, 223, 224
Charisma, Lenasia, 66
Christ the King, Johannesburg, 66
Hatfield Christian Church, 138, 214
Johweto Family Vineyard, Soweto, 1, 2, 13, 54, 60, 61, 67, 105, 135-71, 201, 203, 209, 211, 214-17, 218
Melodi Ya Tshwane, Tshwane, 62, 62 n. 37, 66, 67, 68, 224
North End Presbyterian, 56-57, 91, 182, 185, 223
Parkview Vineyard, 143-144, 145, 152
Reformed Confessing Community, Tshwane, 61-62, 67
Rhema Bible Church, Randburg, 67, 209, 210, 214, 215
Saint Antony's United Congregational and Presbyterian Church, 58, 223
Saint Francis Xavier Catholic Church, 1, 13, 14, 66, 105, 110-33, 135, 136, 154, 169, 183, 201, 203, 206, 208, 209, 213-18, 223
Saint George (Cathedral Church of St. George the Martyr), 30-31, 41
Saint George's Presbyterian, 58
Saint James, Kenilworth, 46
Saint John the Evangelist, Parish of, Wynberg, 29. n. 6, 31
Saint Mary, Cathedral of, Kimberley, 34, 45, 59
Saint Mary's, Cape Town (Cathedral Church of Our Lady of the Flight into Egypt), 45, 51

INDEX   247

Saint Mary's, Johannesburg
  (Cathedral of Saint Mary the
  Virgin), 58, 99, 105
Saint Paul's, Rondebosch, 31, 51
Saint Paul's Mission Chapel, 30-31
Saint Peter's-by-the-Lake
  Evangelical Lutheran, 57
Saint Philip's Mission Chapel, 31
Saint Stephen's Dutch Reformed
  Church, 65 n. 39, 185, 191
Stellenbosch Christian Fellowship,
  Stellenbosch, 67, 224
Trinity Church, Cape Town, 29
Ubunye Free Methodist Church, 4
congregations, United States
  Church for the Fellowship of All
    Peoples, San Francisco, 211
  Church of the Savior, 148, 158
  Lawndale Community Church,
    Chicago, 211, 213
  Reba Place Church, Evanston, 148,
    158, 159, 160

Dandala, Mvume (bishop), 90, 102-3,
  106
denominations
  African Independent Churches, 4,
    11, 22, 42, 65, 92 n. 71, 138
  African Methodist Episcopal
    Church (est. 1896), 31, 64, 65, 74
    n. 46, 80, 181, 198
  Afrikaans-speaking, 3, 63
  Afrikaanse Protestantse Kerk (est.
    1986), 11, 64, 65
  Anglican Church of Southern
    Africa (est. 2006). See Church of
    the Province of Southern Africa
  Apostolic Faith Mission (est. 1910),
    22, 64, 65, 68, 137-38
  Assemblies of God (est. 1917), 4, 64,
    65, 137, 138, 142, 143, 144
  Association of Vineyard Churches
    in South Africa (est. 1997), 66 n.
    40, 139
  Baptist Convention of South Africa
    (est. 1927), 68, 138
  Baptist Union of South Africa (est.
    1877), 68, 138
  Catholic Church in South Africa,
    (est. 1834), 27-29, 31, 35, 47, 49,
    50, 51, 53, 64, 113, 116, 130, 131
  Church of the Province of Southern
    Africa (1870-2006), 3, 12, 28, 35,
    37, 41, 47, 54, 53, 64
    integrated services in, 29, 30, 51,
      59 n. 34, 67
    integration of, calls for, 52, 62
    leadership, indigenes excluded
      from, 34, 41 n. 13, 46, 50
    segregation within, 33, 41
    white Anglican prejudice, 31
  Dutch Reformed Church (est. 1665),
    3, 21-22, 24, 27, 31, 32, 33, 34, 37,
    38, 40, 47, 54, 59, 61 n. 36, 63, 64,
    65, 66, 68, 69, 136, 182, 185, 191
  Dutch Reformed Church in Africa
    (est. 1859), 40, 54, 62, 66, 67
  Dutch Reformed Mission Church
    (est. 1881), 38, 40, 54, 62, 66
  "English-speaking," ix, 3, 21, 22, 29,
    40, 41, 42, 63
  Ethiopian Church (est. 1892), 74,
    197-98
  Evangelical Lutheran Church in
    Southern Africa, (est. 1975), 50,
    57, 64, 65, 66
  Evangelical Presbyterian Church
    (est. 1875), 46, 64, 65
  Full Gospel Church of God in South
    Africa (est. 1951), 65, 68, 156
  Gereformeerde Kerke in Suid-
    Afrika (est. 1859), 22, 64, 65
  Hervormde Kerk in Suidelike
    Afrika (est. 1977), 65
  Indian Reformed Church in Africa,
    (est. 1947), 40, 61, 61 n. 36, 62, 66

International Federation of
   Christian Churches (est. 1996),
   67, 137
Methodist Church of Southern
   Africa (est. 1814), 11, 12, 27, 46,
   47, 51, 52, 53, 54, 55, 62, 64, 72-75
   76, 78 n. 55, 109, 221
Nederduitsch Hervormde Kerk of
   Africa (est. 1855), 64, 65, 179,
   182, 185, 191
Presbyterian Church of Africa (est.
   1898), 64, 65
Presbyterian Church of Southern
   Africa (est. 1897), 53, 56, 57, 64,
   65, 182
South African Baptist Alliance (est.
   2001), 68
Tembu National Church (est. 1884),
   42
United Congregational Church of
   Southern Africa (est. 1967), 64,
   67
Uniting Reformed Church (est.
   1994), 54, 62, 63, 64, 66, 68
Dlamini, Bonaventure (bishop of
   Umzimkulu), 51

East London, segregation at, 3, 32, 179,
   181, 184-85, 189

Fingo (Mfengu), 26, 31, 178
Freedom Charter, 55, 131, 140, 174, 193
freehold areas, 14, 59, 86, 111, 116-17

Gray, Robert (bishop of Cape Town),
   30, 32, 47, 29 n. 6, 75 n. 48
   integration, ambivalence about, 22,
      69, 189
Group Areas Act. *See* legislation

Hertzog, Barry (prime minister), 44,
   181, 183, 190, 198
Hoendervangers, Fr. Jacobus, 29
homelands, 49, 74, 85, 155, 195, 200

Huddleston, Fr. Trevor, 52 n. 29, 59, 86
Imbumba yamaNyama, 181, 198
institutionalisation, 14
   definition of, 7, 9
   informal, 179, 184
   of competing norms, 10, 18, 173-75,
      188-93, 222
   of global norms, 194, 200, 221
   of integration, 133, 186-88, 195
      complete, 63, 174, 175
   of racial equality, 195-97, 198, 221
   of segregation, 48, 177, 179-86, 195
      partial, 180, 185, 222
      complete, 9, 48-63, 174, 183
integration, racial, 2, 6, 10, 14, 100, 101
   and global norms, 195-96
   as national norm, 12, 194
   attitudes towards, 19
   calls for, 44, 52, 55
   formal, 11, 49
   in congregations, 6, 221-23
   in denominations, 63-68
   informal, 49, 58, 175, 186, 187-88
   limited racial, 18, 21, 24-42, 191
integrationism, 25, 45, 69, 132, 133
   and non-racialism, 10, 55
   as national norm, 12, 19, 68
   definition of, 10-12
   informal (incipient), 188-90, 193
   periodisation of, 9, 12, 174-77
   sources of, 25, 192
integrative strategies, 193, 203, 212,
   213-19

Johannes, Bentura, 32, 40
Johannesburg, 1, 75-79, 105-106
   "locations", historic, 2, 78, 118, 139
   spatial integration of racial groups
      in, 58, 79, 187, 189
   spatial segregation of racial groups
      in, 13, 14, 43, 79, 84-86, 100, 105,
      111, 117-120, 181

Kimberley, 32, 37, 181

Koinonia, 59, 60, 93 n. 73, 151

Lagden Commission, 43
Liberal Party (1953-68), 60, 119, 187
Lightfoot, Thomas F., (archdeacon), 30

Magoba, Stanley Mmutlanyane (presiding bishop, Methodist Church of Southern Africa), 54
Martindale suburb, 1, 14, 111, 115-20, 124, 126-27, 208, 216
Mdeleleni, Henry, 31
Merriman, Nathaniel (archdeacon and bishop of Grahamstown), 29, 41
methodology, 3-5
    analytical strategy, 20
    hypothesis, 12, 14, 212
    interviews, 5, 17, 83, 107, 123, 163
    participant observation, 5, 17
    qualitative focus, 1
    surveys, 1, 12, 128, 165
    units of analysis, 3-5
Mhalamhala, Josefa, 46 n. 21
Ministers United for Christian Co-Responsibility, 54, 156
Mnganga, Fr. Edward, 35
Mogatla, evangelist David M., 73
Mokitimi, Rev. Seth, 44, 44 n. 19, 46
Mokone, Rev. Mangena Maake, 74
Monyane, Mary Magdalen, 46
Mpete, Moekete Paul, 142-45, 148-68

Native Resettlement Board, 119
Ndabeni, Cape Town, 3, 180
Non-European Christian Conference on Race Relations (1948), 51
Non-European Unity Movement, 56, 193
non-racialism, 196, 197, 201, 202
    definition, 10, 55, 190
    emergence of, 45-46, 55-56, 176-77, 193
    in congregations, 50, 53, 133, 166, 193-94, 219, 223
    in liberation movements, 55-56, 193
norms, 6-9, 222
    alternating, model of, 176 fig. 4
    congregational norms, 17
    contested, 7, 11, 13, 69, 174, 177-92
    definition of, 7-8
    global, 7, 14, 174, 187, 192-200
    integrative, 18, 217, 221
    national, 8, 173-88, 192-94
    non-racialism as, 201-202
    origin of, 7, 220-21
    segregative, 173-88, 193
    transnational, 173, 221
Ntlhola, Trevor, 139, 156-59, 161, 163-164, 168

Orange Free State, 8, 27, 181, 183, 223
    constitutional inequality in, 36, 178, 179, 182

Pan Africanist Congress, 56, 181
paradigms of integration, 209-13
    transitional, 203-6, 213-14
    non-transitional, 206-09, 214-16
Phelps-Stokes Commission, 186
Philip, John, 38, 190, 196

race, definitions of, 5-6
racially-mixed congregations, calls for, 44, 52
Ricards, James D., (bishop, Cape of Good Hope Eastern District), 35
Robertson, Rev. R.J.D. (Rob), 56-58, 91, 106, 182

segregated seating, 18, 30, 32, 34, 45, 124, 132, 180, 182, 185
segregation, racial, 3, 6, 7, 8, 9, 13, 14
    as protective, 22
    basis of acceptance, 19, 189
    economic basis of, 33
    institutional, 32, 35, 43-48, 179-86
    origins, 10, 30, 40, 177, 179
    residential, 178, 180, 181, 182
segregation legislation, in Cape

Colony
(Cape) Native Reserve Location
Act (1902), 183
Ordinance 7 (1843), 40
Ordinance 50 (1828), 26, 32, 183, 191, 196
Parliamentary Voters Registration Act (1887), 36
Warden Line (1849), 8
segregation legislation, in Transvaal Colony (1902-07), 43, 78, 79, 105.
See also Lagden
Transvaal Asiatic Registration Act (1907), 115
Transvaal Ed. Act (1907), 105
segregation legislation, in Transvaal Republic (1852-57), 36, 183, 186
segregation legislation, in the Union of South Africa (1910-48), 182
Industrial Conciliation Act (1924), 45
Mines and Works Act (1911), 43
Native Laws Amendment Act (1937), 44
Natives Land Act (1913), 8, 33, 43, 44, 183, 196, 197
Natives Urban Areas Act (1923, 1930, 1945), 33, 43, 44, 49, 139, 182, 183
segregation legislation, in the Z.A.R. (1852-1900), 178, 181, 186
Act No. 3 (1897), 77
Gold Law (1885), 78
Regulations for Towns (1899), 78, 182
Transvaal Act (1885), 114, 115
segregationism, 22, 23, 36, 46, 68, 69, 183, 188, 189, 192
as national norm, 173, 175, 177, 191, 195, 202, 221
definition, 8-9, 10-12
Select Committee on Aborigines, House of Commons (1835-36), 22, 190, 196

Sisters of Notre Dame, 118, 120
slaves, 26, 37, 40, 57 n. 33, 196, 223
baptism of, 24, 25, 28
emancipation of (1834), 27, 189, 195
housed separately, 178, 179
provenance of, 24
seated separately, 18, 34, 180, 185
Smith, Rev. Nico, 59, 62, 67, 67 n. 41
Smuts, Jan (prime minister), 43, 80, 115, 139, 195, 198
South African Native National Congress, 196, 197, 198
segregationism, support for, 19
See also African National Congress
Sophiatown, 1, 14, 59, 76 n. 50, 86, 111, 112, 115, 116, 117, 118, 119, 120, 124 n. 83, 217
Soweto, 1, 11, 14, 58, 61, 67, 76, 79, 84, 90, 118, 120, 139-42, 145, 153, 155, 158 n. 91, 169, 206, 210, 216, 224
Stallard Commission (1922), 43, 183
Storey, Peter (bishop), 53, 57, 58, 59, 90-104, 106, 108, 109, 213, 221

Tile, Nehemiah, 42, 53
Tutu, Desmond (archbishop of Cape Town) 50, 138
trade unions, integrated, 45, 177. *See also* Industrial Conciliation Act

United States, church links with, 100, 101, 102, 136, 143, 145, 148, 151, 156, 158, 160, 161, 162, 186, 198

Venter, Alexander, 60, 139, 142-146, 148, 150, 152, 153 n. 90, 154-64

Verwoerd, Hendrik F. (prime minister), 49, 90, 119

Western Areas Native Township, 111, 116, 117, 118, 119

Zionist churches, segregated Zulu, 198

www.ingramcontent.com/pod-product-compliance
Lightning Source LLC
Chambersburg PA
CBHW032003220426
43664CB00005B/126